# Humanity at Risk

# About the Series

The **Political Theory and Contemporary Philosophy** series stages an ongoing dialogue between contemporary European philosophy and political theory. Following Hannah Arendt's and Leo Strauss's repeated insistence on the qualitative distinction between political *theory* and political *philosophy*, the series showcases the lessons each discipline can draw from the other. One of the most significant outcomes of this dialogue is an innovative integration of 1) the findings of twentieth- and twenty-first-century phenomenology, existentialism, hermeneutics, psychoanalysis, and deconstruction (to name but a few salient currents) and 2) classical as well as modern political concepts, such as sovereignty, polity, justice, constitution, statehood, self-determination, etc. In many instances, the volumes in the series both re-conceptualize age-old political categories in light of contemporary philosophical theses and find broader applications for the ostensibly non- or apolitical aspects of philosophical inquiry. In all cases, political thought and philosophy are featured as equal partners in an interdisciplinary conversation, the goal of which is to bring about a greater understanding of today's rapidly changing political realities.

The series is edited by Michael Marder, Ikerbasque Research Professor in the Department of Philosophy at the University of the Basque Country, Vitoria-Gasteiz.

Other volumes in the series include:

*Deconstructing Zionism* by Michael Marder and Santiago Zabala

*Heidegger on Hegel's Philosophy of Right* by Marcia Sa Cavalcante Schuback, Michael Marder and Peter Trawny

*The Metaphysics of Terror* by Rasmus Ugilt

*The Negative Revolution* by Artemy Magun

*The Voice of Conscience* by Mika Ojakangas

# Humanity at Risk

## The Need for Global Governance

Edited by
Daniel Innerarity and Javier Solana

Articles in Spanish and French translated by
Sandra Kingery and Stephen Williams

BLOOMSBURY

NEW YORK · LONDON · NEW DELHI · SYDNEY

**Bloomsbury Academic**
An imprint of Bloomsbury Publishing Inc

| | |
|---|---|
| 1385 Broadway | 50 Bedford Square |
| New York | London |
| NY 10018 | WC1B 3DP |
| USA | UK |

**www.bloomsbury.com**

**Bloomsbury is a registered trademark of Bloomsbury Publishing Plc.**

First published 2013

**Library of Congress Cataloging-in-Publication Data**
Humanity at risk : the need for global governance / [edited by]
Daniel Innerarity, Javier Solana.
pages cm
Includes bibliographical references and index.
ISBN 978-1-62356-702-6 (pbk.) – ISBN 978-1-62356-618-0 (hardcover)
1. Political science–Philosophy. 2. Risk–Sociological aspects.
3. Globalization–Social aspects. I. Innerarity, Daniel, 1959-
JA71.P63135 2013
320.01–dc23
2013015210

ISBN: HB: 978-1-6235-6618-0
PB: 978-1-6235-6702-6
ePub: 978-1-6235-6319-6
ePDF: 978-1-6235-6772-9

Typeset by Newgen Knowledge Works (P) Ltd., Chennai, India
Printed and bound in the United States of America

# Contents

# Contributors

**Ignacio Aymerich Ojea** Professor of Philosophy of Law at the Jaume I University (Castellón de la Palma, Spain). Director of the Human Rights Effectiveness Research Center. Director of the Human Rights Governance Programme at the Institute for Democratic Governance (San Sebastian, Spain). Former United Nations consultant on human rights indicators. Author of *Sociología de los derechos humanos* (Tirant lo Blanch, Valencia, 2001); *La libertad subjetiva en Hegel y Adorno* (Publicaciones de la Universidad de Sevilla, Sevilla, 2006); *Lecciones de derecho comparado* (Universidad Jaume I, Castellón, 2003) and other publications in the field of Legal Sociology and the Philosophy of Law.

**Ulrich Beck** Professor of Sociology at the University of Munich. Has been the British Journal of Sociology LSE Centennial Professor in the Department of Sociology since 1997. Honorary Doctorates from several European universities. Editor of *Soziale Welt* and of the *Edition Second Modernity* (Suhrkamp). Main publications: *Power in the Global Age* (Polity Press, Cambridge, 2005); *The Cosmopolitan Vision* (Polity Press, Cambridge, 2006); *The Cosmopolitan Europe* (with E. Grande, Polity Press, Cambridge, 2007); *World at Risk* (Polity Press, Cambridge, 2009).

**Christophe Bouton** Professor of Philosophy at the University Michel de Montaigne Bordeaux-3 (Bordeaux), Fellow at the Institut Universitaire de France. Visiting Professor at the University of Hamburg (2010), the University Laval in Québec (2011), visiting scholar at the University of Sydney (2012). His research area covers questions of time and history in contemporary philosophy. Main publications: *Temps et esprit dans la philosophie de Hegel. De Francfort à Iéna* (Paris, Vrin, 2000); *Le Procès de l'histoire. Fondements et postérité de l'idéalisme historique de Hegel* (Paris, Vrin, 2004); *Temps et liberté* (Presses Universitaires du Mirail, Toulouse, 2008); *Penser l'histoire. De Karl Marx aux siècles des catastrophes* (co-ed., Editions de l'Eclat, 2011); *Le temps de l'urgence* (forthcoming).

**Serge Champeau** Former Professor of Philosophy (Globernance, Bordeaux). Director of Knowledge and Technology Programme at the Institute for Democratic Governance (San Sebastián, Spain). Specialist in aesthetics and contemporary political philosophy. Author of *Borges et la métaphysique* (Vrin, 1990), *Ontologie et Poésie, trois études sur les limites du langage* (Vrin, 1995) and several articles of political philosophy, published in *Commentaire, Cités, Archives de Philosophie, Revue Philosophique de Louvain, Raison Publique*, etc. He has translated several political thinkers into French and English.

**Dimitri D'Andrea** Dimitri D'Andrea is Senior Researcher and Lecturer in Political Philosophy at the Department of Philosophy at the University of Florence. His publications include *Prometeo e Ulisse. Natura umana e ordine politico in Thomas Hobbes* (Nuova Italia Scientifica, Roma, 1997); *L'incubo degli ultimi uomini. Etica e* *politica in Max Weber* (Carocci, Roma, 2005); "Global Warming and European Political Identity" (in Cerutti F., Lucarelli S., (eds), *The Search for a European Identity. Values, Policies, and Legitimacy of the European Union*, Routledge, London and New York, 2008).

**Edgar Grande** Professor Grande holds the Chair in Comparative Policy Analysis (University of Munich, Germany) and is Board Member of the Munich Center on Governance (Munich). His research interests are focused on problems of governance, globalization, European integration and the future of the nation-state. Since 2010, he is the director of the Department of Political Science at the University of Munich. His recent publications include *Political Conflict in Western Europe* (co-author, Cambridge University Press, 2012); *Varieties of Second Modernity: Extra-European and European Experiences and Perspectives* (co-ed., British Journal of Sociology, Vol. 61, No. 3); *West European Politics in the Age of Globalization* (co-author, Cambridge University Press, 2008); *Cosmopolitan Europe* (co-author, Cambridge, Polity Press, 2007); and *Complex Sovereignty. Reconstituting Political Authority in the 21st Century* (co-ed., University of Toronto Press, 2005).

**Daniel Innerarity** Professor of Political and Social Philosophy and Ikerbasque Researcher at the University of the Basque Country (UPV/EHU). Director of the Institute of Democratic Governance (San Sebastián, Spain). Appointed Visiting Professor at the Robert Schuman Center for Advanced Studies of the European University Institute of Florence (2012). His latest books include: *The Transformation of Politics* (Peter Lang, 2010; first published in Spanish, 2002), *La sociedad invisible* (Espasa Calpe, 2004), *El nuevo espacio público* (Espasa, Madrid, 2006), *The Future and Its Enemies: In Defense of Political Hope* (Standford University Press, 2009; first published in Spanish, 2009) and *The Democracy of Knowledge* (Bloomsbury Academic, 2013; first published in Spanish, 2011), *Internet y el futuro de la democracia* (co-ed., Paidós, 2012), all of them translated into several languages. To be published: *A World of Everybody and None* (Columbia University Press).

**Gurutz Jáuregui** Professor Jáuregui is Professor of Constitutional Law at the University of the Basque Country, UPV/EHU. He has been a visiting professor at various universities in Europe, the United States, and Latin America. He has also served as scientific advisor to the UN (UNRISD). Author of numerous books and articles. Has supervised or participated in the publication of many collective books. Main publications: *Ideología y estrategia política de ETA. Análisis de su evolución entre 1959 y 1968* (Siglo XXI de España, Madrid, 1981, 1985); *Decline of the Nation-State* (University of Nevada Press, Reno, 1994); *La democracia en la encrucijada* (Editorial Anagrama, Barcelona, 1994, 1996); *La democracia planetaria* (Ediciones Nobel, Oviedo, 2001); *La democracia en el siglo XXI: un nuevo mundo, unos nuevos valores* (Instituto Vasco de Administración Publica, 2004).

**Zaki Laïdi** Professor and Research Director at the Institut d'Etudes Politiques (Paris). Director of Telos. Recent publications: *Limited Achievements: Obama's Foreign Policy* (Palgrave Macmillan, London, 2012); *Norms over Force. The Enigma of European*

*Power* (Palgrave Macmillan, London, 2008); *Sortir du pessimisme social. Essai sur l'identité de la gauche* (co-author, Hachette Litteratures/Presses de Sciences Po., Paris, 2007); *The great Disruption* (Polity, Cambridge, 2007); *La gauche à venir. Politique et mondialisation* (Editions de l'Aube, La Tour d'Aigues, 2001); *Le sacre du présent* (Flammarion, Paris, 2000).

**Elena Pulcini** Professor of Social Philosophy in the Department of Philosophy at the University of Florence. Her research revolves around the subjects of philosophical anthropology and social and political philosophy and, currently, around the transformation of identity and social bonds in the global age. Recent works: *Filosofie della globalizzazione* (co-ed., ETS, Pisa, 2001); *Umano post-umano. Potere, sapere, etica nell'età globale* (co-ed., Editori Riuniti, Roma: 2004); "The Responsible Subject in the Global Age" (in *Science and Engineering Ethics*, Springer, Dordrecht, 2010); "Le don à l'âge de la mondialisation" (Revue du Mauss, n° 36, Paris, 2010); *The Individual without Passions. Modern Individualism and the Loss of the Social Bond* (Lexington, Lanham, 2012); *Care of the World. Fear, Responsibility and Justice in the Global Age* (Springer, Dordrecht, 2012); "Community and Globalization" (in G. Parati, (ed.), *New Perspectives in Italian Cultural Studies, Volume 1: Definition, Theory, and Practices*, Rowman & Littlefield, Lanham, 2012).

**Javier Solana** Former Minister in the Spanish government. Former Secretary General of NATO. Former High Representative for Common Foreign and Security Policy. Currently, President of the ESADE Center for Global Economy and Geopolitics (Barcelona) and Distinguished Senior Fellow at the Brookings Institution.

**Daniel M. Weinstock** Professor at the McGill University Faculty of Law (Montréal, Québec). Chairman of the Canadian Research Chair on Ethics and Political Philosophy. Former director of the Research Centre on Ethics at the University of Montreal. His research interests include, among others, the governance of certain types of liberal democracies, especially the exploration of the effects of religious and cultural diversity on the political and ethical philosophy of public policy. Recent publications: *Pluralism: Contemporary Political Philosophy: An Introduction* (Blackwell Publishing, 2012): "Can Thinking about Justice in Health Help Us in Thinking about Justice in Education?" (*Theory and Research in Education, 2010*); "Berlin's Methodological Parsimony" (*San Diego Law Review, 2009*); "Motivating the Global Demos" (*Metaphilosophy, 2009*); "Pour une philosophie politique de la ville" (*Rue Descartes, 2009*).

**Michel Wieviorka** Currently President of the Fondation Maison des sciences de l'homme (Paris), and Professor at the École des Hautes Etudes en Sciences Sociales (Paris). He has been president of the International Sociological Association from 2006 to 2010. His main publications include, in English, *The Making of Terrorism* (University of Chicago Press, 2003); *The Arena of Racism* (Sage, London, 1995), *The Lure of Anti-Semitism* (Brill, Leiden and Boston, 2007); *Violence: A New Approach* (Sage, London, 1995); *Evil* (Polity Press, Cambridge, 2012).

**Michael Zürn** Director of the Research unit "Transnational Conflicts and International Institutions" of the Social Science Research Center Berlin (WZB); founding Dean of the Hertie School of Governance in Berlin. Member of the Berlin-Brandenburg Academy of Science. Has published articles in numerous international journals. Among most recent publications are *Handbook on Multi-Level Governance* (co-ed., Edward Elgars Publishers, Cheltenham, 2010); *Rule of Law Dynamics in an Era of International and Transnational Governance* (co-ed., Cambridge University Press, 2012); "Can the Politicization of European Integration Be Reversed?" (co-author, Journal of Common Market Studies, 2012); "The View of Old and New Powers on the Legitimacy of International Institutions" (co-author, Journal of the British Political Studies Association, 2010).

# Preface

This book derives from an international conference held in November 2010 in San Sebastián (Spain) at the initiative of the *Instituto de Gobernanza Democrática* (www. globernance.org) and the *Instituto Vasco de Competitividad*, a conference funded by the Spanish *Ministerio de Ciencia e Innovación*. At the time of this conference, there were many reasons to believe that global risks were a central issue for our societies. Various terrorist attacks (New York, Madrid, etc.) created an acute awareness of our societies' vulnerability. Many ecological catastrophes, particularly global warming, had taken place, and others were appearing on the horizon of our day-to-day lives. The social repercussions resulting from the collective catastrophe known as "the economic crisis" were already well represented. But we could not have guessed that this problem would become even more topical. Since then, several events have increased our concern for the future of humanity including, with a singular violence, the tsunami in Japan and the associated nuclear disaster. Instability in the southern Mediterranean region is another factor contributing to the feeling that we are now caught in an avalanche of risk that is difficult to control.

When it comes to dangers that the future has in store, it is hardly comforting to have been right all along. It would have been better to be contradicted by reality. But what interested us then was how to avoid these evils, producing at least a few concepts that would allow us to understand the risks we face today and, if possible, provide us with clues on how to deal with them. If only for this reason, the themes and issues presented in this book are essential.

A long chain of events has highlighted the fragility and instability of the world in which we now live. To those who predicted the end of history, it is becoming increasingly clear that history goes on, if by that we understand conflict, instability, and the multiplication of threats. We are not entering into a simpler world, quite the contrary: this new cycle which will likely unfold before us is characterized by generalized uncertainty, which is not necessarily a bad thing if we learn how to manage this new logic.

As those who are responsible for this publication, we hope that reading it will provoke thought about our way of life and that it will make the reader better understand the nature of global risks. Furthermore, since the road of hope is not one of ignorance but of comprehending reality, we intend to help the reader identify practical recommendations on how to handle these risks. We need new insights into the principles of prevention, precaution, responsibility, and anticipation. We must also develop the collective aspect of these provisions such as prudence and serenity, giving up techniques with undesirable side effects. We must deepen the debate surrounding global governance as a goal to which humanity must strive with all its might. This might seem like a tough program, but there is no pessimism in it: governing global risks is the major imperative of humanity if we do not want the thesis of the end of history to be confirmed, not as the climax of the quiet victory of liberal democracy, but as that of the most terrible of collective failures.

Javier Solana and Daniel Innerarity

# Foreword to the English Edition

In the Introduction, Daniel Innerarity identifies the range of problems posed by global risks, that is risks (1) originating from humans; (2) that affect all humans; (3) that are usually unpredictable because they result from long and complex chains of causality; (4) that are irreversible, beyond a certain point; (5) that represent a major, sometimes fatal threat to humanity; (6) that are, however, not beyond all understanding by human beings; and (7) that can be managed at a global level, thanks to this understanding, even if it is illusory to believe that we can manage to completely control them. Such risks include, for example, ecological risks, those linked with nuclear terrorism, or even the collapse of financial institutions.

Even if these risks cause excessive anxiety, even if the illusion of radically eliminating them exists and must be condemned, even if the perception of such risks is subjective and cultural, and even if it gives rise to numerous debates and varied sentiments, global risk is indeed a major factor in our societies, as reflected by political discourses and practices which are now entirely oriented toward the prevention of risk. From this, several fundamental questions arise: How should we define and evaluate these global risks? How can we predict them rather than merely correcting them? What role can politics play in predicting them? From the answers given to the first two questions, Innerarity focuses specifically on answering the last question. Technocratic politics, based on the idea of the absolute power of science and technology, seems to be inappropriate today, but the same goes for the thinking of those who have doubted the achievements of technology. Dismissing both the technocratic Right and the neo-Marxist Left, Innerarity argues that technical failures, rather than successes, solicit, and encourage a renovation of politics: "It now turns out that politics is being called upon to resolve the problems caused by technology's weakness." Risk management can be seen as a new source of political legitimacy. We are witnessing a return of politics, regarding global risks, in three basic forms: the return of the state (which does not mean a return to Keynesian politics), the recovery of political logic, and finally, the requirement of a democratic management of risk. On this last point, Innerarity delivers a message of hope against those who fear that the political management of global risks will lead to authoritarian regimes. He believes that the conflicts of risk societies are an opportunity to democratize society: "we must find a new culture of insecurity, a sort of 'third way' between aversion to risk and recklessness, a way which explores the possibility of regaining a functional equivalent of the complete security of the past, in the form of building confidence, regulation, and cooperation." In other words, "a more uncertain world has no reason to be less democratic than the lost world of certainty."

The 12 essays that follow address these three issues: the characteristics of global risks, the best way of predicting them, and the role of politics (what type of politics?) in this prediction. But they each approach these questions in their own way. On the one hand, this is because of the decisively interdisciplinary approach of this conference, bringing together sociologists, philosophers, and legal experts, and on the other hand, because of the choice of similar, yet sometimes divergent theoretical perspectives. In retrospect, this is why we have classified these themes into three sections. Even if each essay addresses the entirety of the three issues outlined by Innerarity, one group focuses particularly on defining global risks from a sociological and legal perspective, exploring different ways of dealing with them, while questioning whether they are sufficiently novel to validate the claim that we have entered into a "risk society" (Part I: Global Risks and Risk Society). A second group of essays includes a more philosophical than sociological approach to the representation that citizens make of risks and of the future. They not only identify concepts, but also the affects by which risks are understood, as well as the various motivations they generate, those that lead to confronting them as well as those that lead to ignoring them (Part II: Representation of Risks: Categories, Affects, Motivations). Finally, the third group of essays, from the perspective of political science and political philosophy, focuses on giving a precise meaning to the notion of the "governance" of global risks (Part III: The Governance of Global Risks).

In "Living in and Coping with a World Risk Society," the first chapter of Part I: Global Risks and Risk Society, Ulrich Beck seeks first to identify three characteristics of new global risks produced by human activity: they are delocalized, incalculable, and non-compensable. On the basis of this analysis, three reactions seem possible: denial, apathy, and transformation. The author seeks to explain the last reaction by highlighting the logic of communication, that of worldwide risks: they compel "communication between those who do not wish to have anything to do with one another," "cut through the self-absorption of cultures, languages, religions, and systems as well as the national and international agenda of politics, they overturn their priorities and create contexts for action between camps, parties, and quarrelling nations, which ignore and oppose one another." Global risks bring together states and societies which can no longer address risks in isolation; they force us to strive for cosmopolitism, which is no longer only a philosophical ideal, like in Kant's time, but rather "actual cosmopolitism." They lead us to reinterpret science and politics in a very different way than dominant neoliberalism does. Risks lead us to devise radically democratic politics and globalization: "Such risk conflicts do indeed have an enlightenment function. They destabilize the existing order, but the same events can also look like a vital step toward the building of new institutions. Global risk has the power to tear away the facades of organized irresponsibility." Risk is thus *not only* an ally to the nation-state and to globalized capital, as the theoretical traditions of Mary Douglas and Michel Foucault may assert.

In "Global Risks and Preventive Governance," Edgar Grande, continuing Beck's work, seeks particularly to link the theory of "risk society" and the analyses of world politics conducted within the framework of the theory of international relations: "The transition from a 'Cold War' into a 'global risk society' fundamentally challenges institutions, principles, procedures, and basic programs of world politics." On the basis of a very detailed analysis of the notion of global risk, which reveals the essential characteristics of new risks, the author addresses international relations by distinguishing the "state of prevention" of the past (particularly the "welfare state") from what he calls "preventive governance," characterizing the "state of prevention" in the era of risk societies. In a constant dialog with the work of Michel Foucault, Grande identifies the essential features of the modern "state of prevention." It is not based, as Foucault thought, on scientific knowledge, but rather on non-knowledge: "The state of prevention of 'risk societies' depends on a totally different logic of power, on knowing the *power(lessness) of not being able to know.*" It is also characterized by *the absence of the functional limits of preventive action* (not so much a totalitarian state as an omnipresent state). Its new features also imply a new practice and concept of law, the state being required to take appropriate measures in particular situations, given the risks (which can encourage a state of prevention to become a state of exception). Finally, it is a state which undertakes a "preventive governance" that goes far beyond politics confined to the framework of a nation-state, to the extent that it assembles a broad constellation of public and private agents, uses a very wide range of instruments to act, and can take many forms. Toward the end of the chapter, Grande focuses particularly on identifying in detail the specificity of this "transnational" governance, which would not follow in the footsteps of great international institutions nor eliminate the nation-state, but would considerably change the context in which it carries out its functions. Grande insists on an important point: that this transnational preventive governance, far from being consensual, gives rise to new types of conflict (*epistemological, normative, distributive,* and *moral*): "The worldwide risk society is subject to a powerful process of centrifugal diversification: the coexistence, and probably even competition between different types of risk society, different cultures of risk." The author identifies three challenges to the politics of preventive risk management today, those related to institutional complexity and the fragmentation of transnational governance, those having to do with media representation of the overall perception of risk and the communication of risks, and finally, those related to democratic legitimacy and new forms of transnational governance. The stakes of this last challenge are immense: "Is a 'worldwide state of exception' established by the permanent danger of global risks in any way compatible with democratic norms, institutions, and procedures?"

In "World Risk Society and National Democracy," Michael Zürn extends the analyses by Beck and Grande by arguing that "the simultaneous demand for and resistance to forms of preventive governance lead to a politicization of international institutions" and that this transforms "not only the basic rules of world politics, but also the functioning of national democracies in the western part of the world." Since they have actual power, transnational institutions that have arisen to deal with global risks are in fact contested. This is because they have particular properties—they are not directed only toward nation-states, but toward the entirety of social agents; they infringe on national legislation, etc. What follows is a politicization of these institutions, in the form of opposition or collaboration or a request to strengthen these institutions by various agents (anti-globalization groups, governments of developing countries, organizations pushing for national sovereignty, etc.). This politicization, which is strongly selective and uneven, depends on factors which are sociocultural, institutional (the existence or not of specialized forums), and technological (access or not to media and to the internet). Toward the end of the chapter, the author focuses particularly on analyzing one of the aspects of this politicization: tension with the nation-state. There is indeed an obvious discrepancy between the people—who are more favorable than generally believed toward transnational institutions—and politicians and the media. Politics is not an endangered species; it is just in the process of migrating. But the fact remains that these institutions give rise to resistance, a strong, communitarian "anti-cosmopolitan politicization," focused on the borders and values of the national community. The author insists that such anti-cosmopolitanism does not come down to extreme-right populism—which is a simplistic version of it, just as simplistic versions of cosmopolitanism exist. Zürn views this opposition between cosmopolitanism and communitarianism as the most fundamental ideological divide of the century. If we manage to escape it, it will only be by reforming international and transnational institutions, which all too often reproduce inequalities (e.g. between rich and poor countries).

In the chapter "(How) Do We Need to Modify Political Philosophy to Take Risk into Account?" Daniel M. Weinstock questions the core of the "risk society," which is the framework of the previous chapters. In his view, philosophers and sociologists have classified excessively heterogeneous factors under the notion of risk, preventing a unique response to these questions: "Is there something radically new about the kinds of risks that modern societies face today? If so, do these differences require that we rethink the tasks of the modern state? And how should political philosophy respond to these changes? Are the conceptual resources and arguments that have occupied the state in the modern era inadequate to address the new imperatives it faces?" Neither the transnational scope of risks, nor their significance nor their complexity nor the fact that they come from human activity nor their irreversibility seem to be sufficient criteria to talk about a "new age of risk." Several risks that humanity has experienced in the past possessed one or more of these characteristics (e.g. pandemics) and the modern state is designed to deal with these risks. According to Weinstock, we tend to exaggerate the novelty of risks, partly because we have science and technology that allow us to better understand the causes and damages of modern risks (paradoxically, our increased ability to master risks has allowed us to better perceive our inability to master them completely), and partly because we, as rich nations, are no longer sheltered from risk. The fact remains that certain contemporary risks have a scope, a complexity, and an irreversibility allowing us to distinguish them from past risks. These new risks call for a reorientation of nation-states which are ill-equipped to address transnational risks. The author focuses particularly on the political and philosophical consequences of irreversibility—from now on, politics must account for potential persons, with all the theoretical problems that come with them: for example, how do we compare different current political options relative to their future incidence? Regarding complexity, he highlights the serious political problems it generates—as proven by conflicts between those who, like Cass R. Sunstein, have more confidence in experts and those who feel that public opinion should not be considered epistemically inferior.

In the chapter "Global Risks and Popular Sovereignties," Ignacio Aymerich Ojea focuses on the sociolegal dimension of governance, particularly in the ability of a globalized society's legal system to reduce uncertainties by ensuring predictability of the sequence of individual actions. The author defends the thesis that the increased rational predictability afforded by modern legal systems, derived from the rationalist theories of natural law, has led to a new type of risk. Modern legal systems have actually experienced a double evolution: they have rationalized social interaction—in societies with a high division of labor, laws have made everyone's actions more predictable and more controllable in the economic and administrative domain—and at the same time, in order to streamline interaction, the legal system has increased individual autonomy by recognizing public liberty and fundamental rights. The result was a set of behaviors not legally subjected to an obligation of justification (free choice). This autonomy is the basis for new risks: "The lack of obligation to justify signifies that there is no legal obligation to respond rationally or to predict the way one's own action intersects with the actions of others and the extent to which one must be able to vouch for possible chain reactions." In such a system, uncertainty can only grow: "While the interdependence of individual actions increases and extends over the entire planet, all *gaps* and courses of actions that are beyond the need of rational justification and thus, the type of predictability that the legal system can make, are also increasing." Potentially, these indeterminacies contradict the traditional concept of the sovereignty of democratic states, that "we all simultaneously decide (in a single act of decision) on the whole." We are thus faced with the task of having to "govern from uncertainty," in a system where individuals do not develop the habit of thinking about the series of effects of their preferences. The chapter's conclusion examines what such a government might be, excluding any backwardness—governments that reduce individual freedoms are no better able, far from it, as Amartya Sen has shown, to address global risks: "Given these risks, the possibilities of the traditional normative response are already scarce, and in the era of the knowledge society, will require reconsidering legal security in a globalized society, starting from other bases."

Part II: Representation of Risk: Categories, Affects, Motivations opens with a chapter by Christophe Bouton, "The Dark Horizon of the Future: Opacity, Disaster, and Responsibility." The author focuses on identifying more or less explicit categories with which our societies imagine the future. He begins by recalling Koselleck's four categories which have until recently dominated our vision of the future: novelty, progress, acceleration, and action (of human beings making history). The development of our societies has led us to abandon this vision and to replace these categories with categories of "indeterminacy" (innovation now taking the form of several imaginable future scenarios), "disaster" (the future is no long thought of within the category of progress, but within a series of threats), "opacity" (predictable acceleration has become an enigmatic and incalculable future), and "responsibility" (replacing the category of action). The author identifies many reasons for this change in categories—the empowerment of technical processes, the interdependence of even more agents, etc. The end of the chapter is dedicated to highlighting the fundamental role of the category of responsibility. In response to Jonas, Bouton considers that the core ethic of our era is responsibility, that is the limitation of our power: "Acceleration has become synonymous with opacity, novelty has been taken over by indetermination, progress has been eclipsed by disaster, and feasibility has been transformed into responsibility. People do not design and produce history like they could a product for sale, but they are responsible for it in an especially prospective manner insofar as these decisions may affect the future course of events. This forward-looking responsibility is collective and political, even if political decisions then translate into individual and private actions. It is an answer to the increasing gloominess of the future."

In the chapter "Re-Learning to Fear: The Perception of Risks in the Global Age," Elena Pulcini moves from the transformation of *homo faber* into *homo creator*, whose action "projected toward new unlimited goals and conquests, has ended up producing unforeseen and undesired consequences, which are increasingly resistant to all human capacities of control." The author provides a detailed analysis of the feeling of *fear* generated by global risks, "a dizzy feeling of impotence and disorientation" that differs both from premodern types of fear (confronting nature and not human action) and from the modern type of fear (generated by the certainty of danger and not by its inherent uncertainty). Contemporary fear is more like the "anxiety" addressed by Freud and Heidegger, even if it can be distinguished from that concept in that this fear indeed has an object, but it is an object which is invisible, incalculable, and elusive. Pulcini then sets out what she considers this fear's fundamental characteristic: the fact that it has lost any productive nature, that it is devoid of positive effects, making it paralyzing. Through the study of the psychological defense mechanisms at the root of this fear—the "denial of reality" (Freud) and "self-deception" (Davidson)—Pulcini accounts for this unproductive fear. Such mechanisms actually alter the perception of risks, making a schism between knowledge and feeling—we know the risks of nuclear arms, yet this knowledge, in order to protect us from overpowering emotions, does not reach the seat of emotions. Such anesthesia toward fear explains the paradoxical combination of power and powerlessness faced by the risks characterizing our society. The author concludes that we must learn how to fear again, a fear *for* mankind's fate. This will only be possible if we can reconcile our reason and our emotions: in order to bring about an "ethics of responsibility," we need to rediscover the "emotional foundations of ethics."

In the chapter "Certainty, Risk, and Uncertainty," Serge Champeau argues that, on the one hand, citizens in our societies are confronted not only with calculable risk, but also with certainty (e.g. the need to control the state budget) and uncertainty (brought about by new global risks), and on the other hand, they develop individual "affects" when faced with risk, certainty, and uncertainty. These reactions are, of course, not new. Humanity has developed various affects when faced with the certainties of existence (life, death) and its uncertainties (famine, war): wonder, gratitude, resignation, revolt, hope, despair, doubt, etc., as Heidegger and Wittgenstein have clearly shown. But the age we live in reminds us that certainties and uncertainties generated by less universal and more contingent situations and events also generate a whole range of feelings, as Keynes keenly observed in his theory of animal spirits. Building on Keynes, the author argues that these affects need not be opposed to reason; they can be adaptive (inciting action) or non-adaptive (inhibiting action). This is why they must be the object of particular attention and work by everyone in our societies who bears political or social responsibility. Carrying out politics also means handling affects in order to deflect them, modify them, sometimes upset them, depending on what is considered the common good. The chapter calls for affect management which is not technocratic, but democratic and collective, allowing us to learn, for example, to borrow the phrase from Roosevelt, to "fear fear itself."

In the chapter "Global Warming as a Globalized Risk and Global Threat for Future Generations," Dimitri D'Andrea intends to conduct "an analysis of some of the emotive and cognitive processes that make it so difficult to deal with *global* challenges." After distinguishing *globalized* phenomena (leading to a situation of interdependence among people) from *global* phenomena (giving rise to community since they concern everyone, in the same way, and cannot be fought by only one action) on one hand, and on the other, the concept of "risk" (an event which will happen if another event occurs) from the concept of "threat" (an event which will happen if we do not urgently intervene), D'Andrea shows that global warming is currently changing from a globalized risk to a global threat. This threat makes us responsible *for* others, because it is our everyday behavior—compounded by everyone else's—that is producing this threat: radical evil is the result of ordinary actions (actions over which the isolated individual has very little control). This discrepancy makes it quite difficult for an individual to truly realize this threat. For the author, it follows that there is no selfish motivation—in Hobbes's sense (e.g. individual fear leading to a calculation of long-term interest)—capable of being generalized so as to encourage the current generation to fight global warming: "When selfish fear constitutes a suitable rationale for the size of the commitment because the harmful events have drawn near and become radical and generalized, in all likelihood it will be too late to avoid worst case scenarios." Responsibility is then necessarily collective and moral. The current generation must act politically for "the interests of future generations." Comparing various motivations implemented in the fight against various global risks (nuclear arms, the degradation of the ozone layer, etc.), D'Andrea concludes with the idea that "moral responsibility is not necessarily an ineffective motivation." Even if, for many reasons, it is much more difficult to implement in the case of global warming than it has been in the case of the depletion of the ozone layer. If humanity wants to effectively fight against global warming, it will have to pay the price.

Part III: The Governance of Global Risks opens with a chapter by Gurutz Jáuregui, "A New Political Order for the Twenty-First Century: From State *Governments* to Global *Governance*." The author examines "some of the 'spatial' or territorial consequences that globalization has on the present political world order, particularly on democratic systems." He begins by precisely defining the concept of global "governance," which he distinguishes from "government." Globalization and the emergence of its intrinsic global risks require democratic state systems to transform into a system of supra-state democracies and even global democracy, a system composed of multiple levels—transnational institutions, international agencies, national governments, NGOs, etc.—designed to achieve specific goals (including the prediction of global risks), in a way that will be considered legitimate by citizens. This last point is essential, to the extent that the development of these supranational agencies may give all power to experts and might end up making national democracies regress (as we can see with the democratic deficit suffered by the European Union). The fundamental political question is: "How, within this new complexity of institutions and bodies, can it be made possible to apply the two golden rules of democracy, maintaining control by the ruled over the rulers, and maintaining mutual control among rulers?" In order to offer a reply to this question, the author first imagines three models of global governance—the "Westphalian model," the "UN model," and the "Cosmopolitan model"—and he identifies their structure as well as their merits and limitations. The end of the chapter suggests a fourth model, the "Complex model," better able to integrate different levels of global governance (intergovernmental and non-governmental supranational organizations, nation-states, civilian organizations, etc.) in a non-hierarchical relationship, based on sharing, coordination, and subsidiarity—a model Jáuregui calls, following Roseneau, "Governance without Government." The author examines the legal problems generated by such a model and calls attention to the size of the task: "This requires, of course, an intense coordination and cooperation among the various regional, national, transnational, and international entities that are involved. Realistic coordination has nothing to do with the idea of a formal cosmopolitan government that is supposed to miraculously be able to solve every problem." The European Union, as it exists today, is far from being a good model of complex governance, but it is after all the closest thing we have to it. In particular, it is outlining what may become the concept of sovereignty in years to come: "The EU is the basis for a new way to structure a complex, multilateral world order."

In the chapter "Mediations between Personal and 'Global' Topics," Michel Wieviorka finds that our age is characterized by two powerful trends: individualism and globalization. Having characterized these two ambivalent, multifaceted, and sometimes contradictory trends, the author shows that they feed on each other, with the effect of weakening the mediations that are traditional nation-states. This is why it is important to study the major implication of these trends for democracy. Wieviorka seeks to give precise content to what is commonly called "the crisis of representative democracy." One of its facets is the difficulty of applying national democracy to issues of a global, planetary nature, for example environmental issues, which call for political answers beyond the framework of the nation-state. The conclusion of the chapter considers different responses to the crisis: enriching democracy by complementing it with forms of participation or deliberation or replacing it with a "post-democracy," whether in an authoritarian or technocratic form or even an opaque set of pressure groups. The author's conclusion is that the future is open. A future more in tune with the democratic ideal is emerging, with the appearance of a global civil society and of international institutions with renewed legitimacy.

In the chapter "Europe as a Risk Averse Power" Zaki Laïdi supports the thesis that "the European Union is a political actor whose identity and strategy in the international field are based on a strong aversion toward risk." The author begins by defining what a risk averse political power is: it avoids the use of force or of unilateral responses, preferring cooperation in cases of conflict or systemic risks, striving to apply global standards already legitimized by international institutions, constantly seeking the support of strong public opinion. He then proposes criteria to measure this aversion—the attitude toward the five risks of job loss, biotechnological risks, global warming, financial risks, and the risks of war. It should be noted that the attitude toward these risks varies culturally: "The United States relies on risk evaluation that can be scientifically measured (sound science), whereas Europeans insist on risks resulting from the *uncertainty* of scientific results." On the basis of these criteria, Laïdi arrives at a nuanced conclusion: at least in certain domains, Europe is characterized by a strong aversion to risk. The reasons are many: cultural (social preferences resulting from a long history of wars, for example), contingent (in the case of attitudes toward food risks, for example), and institutional. This last type of reason is the object of a particularly accurate analysis by the author who relates the European Union's aversion to risk first to the non-state nature of the Union: "The European Union is not a state. Therefore, it cannot independently fulfill the traditional security functions generally assigned to states. At the same time, European citizens cannot think themselves out of Europe, despite their political disaffection for it. On the one hand, they cannot address all their demands to their respective states (as the Americans, Chinese, Indians, and Brazilians are tempted to do), nor can they redirect them toward Europe. European risk aversion results primarily from this ambivalence." But the European Union's aversion to risk is also due to the existence of a deliberative European space for the preferences of citizens to manifest themselves, the legacy of a social model to mitigate market risk, and finally, to the fact that Europeans no longer need Empires. The conclusion of the chapter focuses on identifying the political consequences of European aversion to risk. According to Laïdi, we must beware of two trends: idealizing the cultural identity of the European Union—we must not forget, for example, that "if Europe's Copenhagen commitments seem ambitious—more ambitious, it is true, than those of the United States—it is also because it is less expensive to reduce greenhouse gas emissions in Europe than in other world regions"—and contempt for this identity, in the manner of some Americans. The author's conclusion is that aversion to risk is in itself neither a quality nor a weakness: "It is, rather, a manner of being in the world. Europe's question is not to find out whether or not it should repudiate this identity, but to find out *how* it might put it to use and how it might accord value to it in the context of the current international system." A possible answer to this last question is one that emphasizes the need for harmonization of European positions toward risk (so that, for example, the underperformance of Copenhagen would not happen again). It is unfortunate that the normative power of the European Union "tends to stop precisely where it should begin." It follows from this study of the European Union faced with risk that "the question is not risk aversion in itself, but the possibility of shared strategic action. What is at stake then is less risk aversion as such than the inhibition to make choices as if making choices in Europe is becoming a risk in and of itself."

Javier Solana, whose responsibilities at international, European and national levels are well known, is tasked with concluding the works of this conference, in pages that are so clear and so deep that it seems futile to summarize them. His lecture, "How to Manage a Changing World," which ought to be read in all our schools, ends with these words:

"To sum up, today's world is very different from the world of yesterday. I believe we are not yet aware of the extent to which this is true or the changes the world will face or the speed at which changes are occurring. It would be best if we started thinking quickly and seriously about all of this and found both solutions and the leadership needed to implement them. We have not yet secured long-term leadership or ways of thinking about these issues. There are others who are already at work on them. If we do not begin to tackle them ourselves, we will surely lose out."

Serge Champeau

# Introduction: Governing Global Risks

Daniel Innerarity

*University of the Basque Country and*
*Instituto de Gobernanza Democrática*

The British magazine *The Economist* defines itself in this way: "This magazine has been published since 1843 to take part in a severe contest between intelligence, which presses forward, and an unworthy, timid ignorance obstructing our progress." This liberal declaration, with its epic touch, now carries an anachronistic tone. Apart from a few heroic exceptions, we can say today that precaution has replaced planning itself, and that we are faced with a rather preventive relationship with the future.

For those who grew up with the fears of the 1970s and 1980s (growth and its limitations, the nuclear threat, the ecological crisis, resource shortages, etc.), the word "progress" seems frivolous. Now, in the midst of the crisis, using the language of "management," which exalts the culture of risk and the predisposition for failure, seems provocative. In general, being progressive today has nothing to do with progress, but rather with precaution toward science and technology. Therefore, it has become very common to quote Benjamin's quip against Marx, saying that what is revolutionary is resorting to history's emergency brake. And today, after the financial crises and the problems of climate change, this provocative idea of progress has only intensified.

The presumption of the danger inherent to technological and scientific breakthroughs has progressively filled the ideological void that appeared after the collapse of the idea of the ingenuity of progress. Newness and progress are presented under the rubric of risk. What began as skepticism of the avant-garde is now assumed. At best, we expect from politics the possibility of warding off threats that may arise in the future. It comes as no surprise then that the idea of sustainable development achieved such resonance that the principle of precaution was formulated and applied with such intensity.

Considering the gravity of the risks with which we are faced, fear is not totally ungrounded. There are those who disapprove of the excess of alerts and the aversion to risk, seen as a sort of paranoid delusion suffered in wealthy countries. Obviously, hysteria is hardly a reasonable means of confronting risks, but this does not preclude their existence; risks continue to be a source of anxiety even when our way of confronting them may turn out to be excessive or ridiculous. What we need is in fact a detailed study of the limits of the precautions that are helpful.

Let us take a recent example. The winter of 2009–10 will probably go down in history as the Era of Alerts, among which especially was the "swine flu" (H1N1 virus) and the prevention of certain potentially catastrophic weather phenomena. I do not know whether this was due to the guilty conscience of not having anticipated the economic crisis, but the fact remains that governments multiplied alerts for possible infections or tornados, whose mere names ("explosive cyclogenesis," "the perfect storm") were themselves tainted by a notion of warning. Governments prefer to warn rather than eventually face the accusation of not having foreseen the worst. This attitude appears commendable but also has some disadvantages, even when things do not turn out as we had been made to fear. It is clear that we cannot devote ourselves entirely to every risk; all preventive actions carry a certain price, either because they cost money or because precaution is inevitably selective and dealing with one particular risk may lead to neglecting another. Nobody claims responsibility for inducing panic, for the costs of fear, for money badly spent, or for the attention diverted from other important matters. An excess of alerts is less serious than a lack of them, but it is not optimal either.

The lessons we should draw from excessive alerts is that programs meant to exclude risks entirely generate counter-productive effects. The attempt to use total prevention to completely eliminate fear is absurd since fears are part of the human condition, of its open nature, and of the resulting indetermination of liberal democracies (Sunstein 2005). Prevention generally leads to certain prohibitions, which, in an open society, must be established . . . with the greatest possible prevention. A general ban on innovation would be extremely risky. Where would society then get the innovations necessary to fight hunger, disease, poverty, or disasters? The irresponsibility related to science is the foundation of its success, and nobody currently holds a monopoly on the ability to distinguish between bad risks and good innovations.

So prevention has its price, and it is not rare to provoke a new fear wherever another fear is removed. The change in the definition of "pandemic" by the WHO is a recent example of this: the redefinition allowed medicines and vaccinations to be introduced in an emergency, that is with less guarantees and larger risks. We could also mention the danger of spreading fear and its bad effects or the perverse consequences of excessive or incidental legislation. Prevention also carries risks, especially when it is redundant (Wildavsky 1988). Moreover, this must all be considered with a perspective that is time-conscious: numerous models and methods that were once recognized and welcomed in good conscience, seen as reliable plans, now have the effect of being simple exercises in irresponsible frivolity.

I do not think it is going too far to assert that our main discussions in the future will be focused on this topic: how do we evaluate risks and which actions do we then recommend? Political confrontation is currently focused on the probabilities of danger or on anticipating risks. Political actors are similar in that they all devote themselves in the same way to foreseeing the imminence of determined dangers, offering to save us from disaster; they are distinguished only by the risks they consider most dangerous, whether it be a loss of identity or a lack of social protection, risks related to a lack of safety or those stemming from the potential abuse of the authorities. Yet they hardly make any effort to imagine what would be *desirable* for fear of *possible* harm. Rivalries among threats appear to have taken precedence over rivalries among projects. Political agents have fewer ideologies than resources to sound the alarm.

These so-called controversies are fueled by the fact that the perception of risk contains a strong degree of subjective perception. Ulrich Beck ventures to say that this opposition could spread to a worldwide scale and lead to a "war of risk religions" (2006). The fact that certain cultures fear what, to other cultures, is considered normal takes on a new geopolitical dimension: this is due to the emergence of countries such as China or India onto the world stage, which also involves the arrival of very different risk cultures from those to which we are accustomed. Different risk cultures tend to find an opportunity in every danger, whose appearance they estimate in terms of likelihood. Risk taking, which we used to consider normal, will become less and less "normal."

This debate has intensified after the appearance of the problem of global risk onto the political time frame. Climate change, new security threats, health and food risks, and financial crises immediately challenge our conception of these uncertain futures. How can we know possible risks? How do we take action upon risks, which are not verifiable facts but rather latent possibilities whose very identification is open to controversy? How do we account for the improbable? Every uncertain future confronts us with dilemmas of a very particular difficulty: which precaution is reasonable? How can we preempt the causal chains of catastrophes? How do we deal with our inevitable ignorance of future events?

First off, we must fully understand the nature of these risks if we want to adequately manage the uncertainty they contain. Risks, particularly global risks, resist calculation in terms of scientific criteria, and for that reason faith, whether a reality or not, becomes a decisive factor. What makes no sense is to confront the rational vision held by experts of real risks with the "poorly informed opinions" of people on so-called risks. All too often, expert rationalism with its calculation of likelihood makes as many mistakes as when alarmists exalt fear to the rank of the ultimate system of knowledge. Populist alarmism is just as dubious as technocratic frivolity.

We must agree then as to acceptable risks. Regarding the numerous decisions dealing with risks, we should not choose between safe or risky alternatives, but rather between alternatives which are always risky. As I just noted, all preventive measures entail risks, both in regards to what we are doing and what we refrain from doing. Fear is a sign, and signs should be neither dismissed nor exaggerated. Up to now, we have not managed to articulate a concept or a strategy to deal with what ought to be a reasonable balance between risk and security, of which we have an outdated opinion. All this gives the impression that we have understood neither the extent to which risk is embedded in our societies nor the uselessness of a concept of security formulated in another area. This is why our premonitions of fear become particularly vulnerable. Dealing with a future that entails unknown dangers is one of the most difficult courses of action: all too often, we are fearful without sufficient reason, and in other cases, we are reckless beyond what is reasonable.

For classical authors on sociology such as Parsons or Durkheim, uncertainty had a negative aspect, like irregularities that should be reoriented toward security. Today, another way of thinking is beginning to make inroads: it includes uncertainty as the element that causes this flexibility and this capability of learning that is so fundamental for an innovation society. It would be wrong to think that uncertainties or insecurities could be completely known and calculated. Given the complexity of social systems, we have a rather hard time identifying and reducing insecurities. This is why we must find a new culture of insecurity, a sort of "third way" between aversion to risk and recklessness, a way which explores the possibility of regaining a functional equivalent of the complete security of the past, in the form of building confidence, regulation, and cooperation.

In complex societies, where everything is closely linked, the main problem consists of knowing how we can protect ourselves from our own irrationality. Catastrophic chains of events from which we should protect ourselves stem from our irresponsible tendency of fearing too much or not enough. For example, in the economic crisis, those who handle financial innovations were less fearful than they should have been; and now, the mistrust for economic agents can be explained because they are perhaps too fearful. Generally speaking, we should surely generalize an ex ante regulation allowing us to predict what is not possible to remedy, to anticipate rather than to react, to prevent rather than correct. And, given that fears cannot be completely eliminated, we need new strategies to govern them. This is why institutions exist; one of the functions of a good government is to generate confidence and predictability, to keep fear from turning to panic, or to keep audacity from promoting irresponsibility.

Contemporary societies are faced with the crucial problem of how to re-determine the relationship between risk and security. The search for socially acceptable methods for managing risks effectively has become a task of particular interest both for political reflection and for the *praxis* of governance.

What role does politics play in this context? More concretely, what political innovations are needed in a society that is enormously dependent on technological innovations yet that also understands their undesirable effects, in ecological, economic, and social terms or regarding their compatibility with the values of liberty and justice?

In our collective imagination, technology appears as a potential threat. This presumption stems from the fact that not so long ago, both the Right and the Left conceived of technology as a strong, successful, and incontestable reality. Some hoped that political matters could be addressed (or even resolved) thanks to the vision of experts and to the accuracy of their procedures. Others deplored this process of technocratic "depoliticization," which would only mean control, manipulation, destruction, and homogenization. Whatever the case, these considerations appeared after agreeing on the fact that this "technification" of the world would eventually prevail. To cite but one exemplary case of pessimistic premonition, we can all recall the warning made by Lane (1966) that we were at the beginning of a new era where scientific knowledge would reduce the significance of politics.

Today, the reality is quite different: in addition to techniques which are beneficial, we are surrounded by others that have failed. Certain current cases are making us more and more aware of the existence of risks produced by human beings that are constantly increasing and growing out of control. Toxic waste in the Gulf of Mexico, the economic crisis produced largely by the failure of sophisticated technological financial mechanisms, climate change brought about by our model of development are not only disasters with serious social repercussions but are also, and from the outset, resounding technological failures. In the light of such fiascos, we might conclude that the technocrats were wrong, but so were those who feared the failures of technology less than its successes.

What is interesting in this historical turmoil is that it radically changed our way of understanding the articulation between politics and technology. Neither the technocratic Right nor the neo-Marxist Left of the 1960s and 1970s thought that the renewal of politics could one day arise from the failure of technology. On the contrary, they imagined its triumphant ascent, whatever might happen, whether it was celebrated or feared. The criticism of technocracy is currently being suppressed by the fact that we are in the presence of clumsy technology and a type of politics whose intervention is claimed everywhere. We were expecting politics to protect us from the power of technology, and it now turns out that politics is being called upon to resolve the problems caused by technology's weakness.

Far from transforming politics into an anachronism, technology (or rather its resounding failures or its potential risks) has reinforced the prestige of politics, which we now hope will provide what other authorities have not. This is why it is no exaggeration to assert that managing these risks may be a new source of the legitimacy of political action (Czada 2000). Whether politics knows how to successfully exercise this responsibility or has the instruments necessary to do so is another question.

Therefore, politics is making a comeback in three fundamental areas: as the return of the state, as a recovery of political logic, and finally as the demand for a democratic management of risks. Let us briefly look at each of these three points.

From the outset, disasters like financial or environmental crises indicate the outline of a new form of regulatory statehood. While the neoliberal reversal of the situation assumed a withdrawal of the state, the gradual awareness of the dangers of technological civilizations is encouraging the state to take on new tasks, albeit in very different contexts from the contexts where the state was accustomed to acting sovereignly. At this point, we should not let ourselves be pulled in by what could be called a neo-Keynesian optical illusion: the state which is returning is not a wealthy sovereign state but rather an indebted state that is in need of cooperation. The sooner we understand this new reality and explore its possibilities, the less time we will waste celebrating the fact that history has once again proven us right.

We can experience a moment of "re-politicization" precisely because of the discrediting of the so-called experts. Those who had monopolized accuracy and efficiency have failed; resorting to science and technology to put an end to controversies has become ideologically suspect; the world of the experts has turned out to be as rarely unanimous as our pluralistic societies. What this means is that we are giving the political system the power to redefine the situation; we have a new opportunity to recover politics. In other words, we can employ the art of transforming our lack of clarity into decisions.

Handling risks, dangers, and disasters may also contain an element of democratization. A more uncertain world has no reason to be less democratic than the lost world of certainty. Quite the opposite. The evolution of the ecologist movement is a striking example of this. Ecological discourse, which in the 1960s was characterized by anti-state rhetoric, has since been transformed into a demand for a regulatory state. The very fact of introducing environmental protection into the duties of the state has opened a source of legitimacy for regulatory politics whereas the so-called legitimacy of the welfare state, focused on the politics of redistribution, seems to be coming to an end. Submitting technological risks to formal political procedures has made the conflict between ecology and the economy infiltrate the governmental system. There is nothing subversive or destabilizing about it. The rise of the Greens, especially in Germany, is an eloquent example of this. After a long struggle, the faction that preferred to enter into government coalitions prevailed over the faction that advocated external opposition. What some have called the "ecological civil war" surrounding nuclear energy has failed to overwhelm the political authorities of the Federal Republic of Germany, as many had feared or hoped. Ecologists, who were discussing an abolition of the state monopoly on violence at the beginning of the 1980s, came to recognize in 2000 that their goals could only be achieved through politics and law.

Therefore, we could fully assert that while older disasters gave way to undemocratic states of exception, the conflicts of the "risk society" have taken on a democratizing function and have launched a political culture of dialogue and conflict resolution. Our way of conceiving how to confront dangers in a democratic society can be clearly distinguished from the authoritarian license granted to a sovereign state in order to resolve exceptional situations. The dangers of a "risk society" do not require a state of exception in the traditional meaning of the term. Instead, they require putting into place as much normality as possible when managing threats. Exceptional situations occasionally exist in a democracy, and we would prefer they be dealt with so as to return to a state of normality. However, for the reactionary jurist Carl Schmitt, the state of exception does not accompany disasters, but appears when fighting against one. For Schmitt, the supreme power is making the sovereign decision as to whether or not there is a state of exception. What is at play here is more than a simple theoretical nuance: the distinction between the democratic management of current catastrophes and sovereign authority is precisely the concern for normality.

As a result, we find ourselves faced with a strange paradox: politics has not been strengthened through technological perfection, but through its failure. Technology needs political regulation now more than ever. Scientific breakthroughs have expanded political territory since they have produced new normative requirements and regulation. Whenever technological failures are perceived as a serious threat to citizen rights, we demand that politics assumes the responsibility of creating the conditions that will allow us to meet these consequences as a society. Without the resources of democratic legitimation and functioning states (now also in the form of global governance), there is no way to confront insecurities, dangers and accidents posed by modern technologies.

Where we used to believe that there would be a technological solution for every problem in the future, our response has now been reversed (even if with more modesty): we can now be reasonably certain that problems brought about by technology will be solved politically or not at all.

# Bibliography

Beck, U. 2006. "Living in the World Risk Society." *Economy and Society* 35(3): 329–45.

Czada, R. 2000. "Legitimation durch Risiko. Gefahrenvorsorge und Katastrophenschutz als Staatsaufgabe." *Politische Vierteljahresschift* 31: 319–45.

Lane, R. E. 1966. "The Decline of Politics and Ideology in a Knowledgeable Society." *American Sociological Review* 31: 649–62.

Sunstein, C. R. 2005. *Laws of Fear. Beyond the Precautionary Principle.* Cambridge: Cambridge University Press.

Wildavsky, A. 1988. *Searching for Safety.* New Brunswick/Oxford: Transaction Books.

# Part I

# Global Risks and Risk Society

# 1

# Living in and Coping with a World Risk Society

Ulrich Beck
*University of Munich*

The narrative of global risk is a narrative of irony. This narrative deals with the involuntary satire, the optimistic futility, with which the highly developed institutions of modern society—science, state, business and military—attempt to anticipate what cannot be anticipated. Socrates has left us to make sense of the puzzling sentence: I know that I know nothing. The fatal irony, into which scientific-technical society plunges us, is, as a consequence of its perfection, much more radical: We do not know what it is we do not know—but dangers arise from these things that threaten mankind! The perfect example here is provided by the debate about chlorofluorocarbons (CFCs) as a cooling agent. In 1974, about 45 years after the discovery of CFC, the chemists Rowland and Molina put forward the hypothesis that CFCs destroy the ozone layer of the stratosphere and that increased ultraviolet radiation would reach the earth as a result. The chain of unforeseen side effects would lead to a significant increase in cancer all over the world. When coolants were invented, no one could know or even suspect that they would create such a danger.

The irony of risk is that rationality, that is, the experience of the past, encourages anticipation of the wrong kind of risk, the one we believe we can calculate and control, whereas disasters arise from that which we do not know and cannot calculate. The bitter varieties of this risk irony are virtually endless: mad cow disease, the 9/11 terrorist attacks, global financial crises, swine flu, and the latest but not the last, volcanic ash clouds disrupting air traffic in Europe and elsewhere.

To the extent that risk is experienced as omnipresent, there are only three possible reactions: denial, apathy, or transformation. The first is largely inscribed in modern culture, the second resembles post-modern nihilism, and the third is the "cosmopolitan moment" of the global risk society (Beck 1992, 2007). First, I would like to demonstrate this in three steps, drawing on empirical research findings from the Munich Research Center "Reflexive Modernization":

- Old Dangers—New Risks: What is new about the global risk society?
- Historical Tricks: To what extent are global risks an uncontrollable global force in present and future world history, which also open up new opportunities of action for states, civil society actors, etc.?
- Consequences and Perspectives: In order to understand the manufactured uncertainty, lack of safety, and insecurity of the world risk society, is there a need for a paradigm shift in the social sciences?

## Old dangers—new risks: What is new about the global risk society?

Modern society has become a risk society in the sense that it is increasingly occupied with debating, preventing, and managing risks that it itself has produced. That may well be, many will object, but it is indicative rather of a hysteria and politics of fear instigated and aggravated by the mass media. On the contrary, would not someone who is looking at European societies from the outside have to acknowledge that the risks which get us worked up are luxury risks, more than anything else? After all, our world appears a lot safer than that, say, of the war-torn regions of Africa, Afghanistan, or the Middle East. Are modern societies not distinguished precisely by the fact that to a large extent they have succeeded in bringing under control contingencies and uncertainties, with respect to accidents, violence, and sickness, for example?

As true as all such observations may be, they miss the most obvious point about risk: that is, the key distinction between risk and catastrophe. Risk does not mean catastrophe. Risk means the anticipation of catastrophe. Risks exist in a permanent state of virtuality and only become "topical" to the extent that they are anticipated. Without techniques of visualization, without symbolic forms, without mass media, etc., risks are nothing at all. In other words, it is irrelevant whether we live in a world which is in fact or in some sense "objectively" safer than all other worlds; if destruction and disasters are anticipated, then that produces a compulsion to act.

The theory of the world risk society maintains that modern societies are shaped by new kinds of risks, that their foundations are shaken by the global anticipation of global catastrophes. Such perceptions of global risk are characterized by three features:

Delocalization: Its causes and consequences are not limited to one geographical location or space. They are in principle omnipresent.

Incalculableness: Its consequences are in principle incalculable. It is fundamentally a matter of "hypothetical" risks, which are based on science-induced not-knowing and normative dissent.

Non-compensability: Early modernity's dream of security was based on the scientific utopia of making uncertain consequences and the dangers of decision-making ever more controllable; accidents could occur, as long and because they were considered compensable. If the climate has changed irreversibly, if progress in human genetics makes irreversible interventions in human existence possible, if terrorist groups already have weapons of mass destruction available to them, then it is too late. François Ewald (2002) argues that, given this new quality of "threats to humanity," the logic of compensation breaks down and is replaced by the principle of precaution through prevention. Not only is prevention taking precedence over compensation, we are also trying to anticipate and prevent risks whose existence has not been proven. Let me explain these points—delocalization, incalculableness, non-compensability—in greater detail.

The delocalization of incalculable interdependency risks takes place at three levels:

- Spatial: The new risks (e.g. climate change) do not respect nation-state or any other borders.
- Temporal: The new risks have a long latency period (e.g. nuclear waste), so their effect over time cannot be reliably determined and limited.
- Social: Thanks to the complexity of the problems and long chains of consequences, it is no longer possible to assign causes and effects with any degree of reliability (for the financial crises, for example).

The discovery of the incalculability of risks is closely connected to the discovery of the importance that not-knowing holds for risk calculation, and it is part of another kind of irony, that surprisingly this discovery of not-knowing occurred in a scholarly discipline, which today no longer wants to have anything to do with it: economics. It was Knight and Keynes who insisted on a distinction between predictable and non-predictable or calculable and non-calculable forms of contingency early on. In a famous article, Keynes wrote: "By 'uncertain' knowledge, let me explain, I do not mean merely to distinguish what is known for certain from what is only probable (. . .). The sense in which I am using the term is that in which the prospect of a European war is uncertain, or the price of copper and the rate of interest 20 years hence, or the obsolescence of a new invention, or the position of private wealthowners in the social system in 1970. About these matters there is no scientific basis on which to form any calculable probability whatever (. . .). We simply do not know" (Keynes 1937). However, Keynes' admonition to open up the field of economic decision-making to unknown unknowns was entirely neglected in the subsequent development of mainstream economics (including mainstream Keynesian economics), and this denial of non-knowing became a causal condition for the emergence of the global financial crisis in 2009.

The crucial point, however, is not only the discovery of the importance of non-knowing, but that the knowledge, control, and security claim of state and society was, indeed had to be, simultaneously renewed, deepened, and expanded. The irony lies in the institutionalized demand for security, for controlling something, even if one does not know whether it exists. It is precisely the existence of unknown unknowns which provoke far-reaching conflicts about the definition and construction of political rules and responsibilities with the aim of preventing worst case scenarios. For the time being, the last and most striking example of that are the volcanic ash clouds in spring 2010: the flights are back, but so is the ash.

If we anticipate catastrophes whose potential for destruction ultimately threatens everyone, then a risk calculation based on experience and rationality breaks down. Every possible scenario, no matter whether it is more or less improbable, must be taken into consideration. For this reason, we must add imagination, suspicion, fiction, fear to the knowledge drawn from experience and science. The boundary between rationality and hysteria becomes blurred. Given the rights conferred upon them to avert dangers, politicians, in particular, may find themselves forced to proclaim a security that they cannot uphold. This is so because the political costs of omission are much higher than the political costs of overreaction. In future, therefore, it is not going to be easy, in the context of state promises of security and a mass media hungry for catastrophes, to actively limit and prevent a diabolical power game with the hysteria of not-knowing. I do not even dare think about deliberate attempts to instrumentalize this situation.

## Historical tricks: Global risk is an unpredictable and impersonal force in the contemporary world

It is best to begin with an example: in 2004, Hurricane Katrina destroyed New Orleans. This was a horrifying act of nature, but one which, as a global media event, involuntarily and unexpectedly took on a simultaneous illuminating role which broke down all resistance. Within a few days, it achieved something no social movement, no political party, and certainly no sociological analysis (no matter how well grounded and brilliantly written) would have been able to achieve: America and the world were confronted by global media pictures of the repressed *other* America, the largely racialized face of poverty. How can this relationship between risk and the creation of a global public be understood? In his 1927 book, *The Public and Its Problems*, John Dewey explained that consequences, not actions, lie at the heart of politics. Although Dewey was certainly not thinking about global warming, mad cow disease, or terrorist attacks, his idea is perfectly applicable to a world risk society. A global public discourse does not grow out of a consensus on decisions, but out of dissent over the consequences of decisions. Modern risk crises are constituted by just such controversies over consequences. Where some may see an overreaction to risk, it is also possible to see grounds for hope. Because such risk conflicts do indeed have an enlightenment function. They destabilize the existing order, but the same events can also look like a vital step toward the building of new institutions. Global risk has the power to tear away the facades of organized irresponsibility.

Egoism, autonomy, autopoiesis, self-isolation, the improbability of translation— these are key terms which, not only in sociological theory, but also in public and political debates, distinguish modern society. The communicative logic of global risk can be understood as the exact opposite principle. Risk is the involuntary, unintended compulsory medium of communication in a world of irreconcilable differences, in which everyone focuses on themselves. Hence a publicly perceived risk compels communication between those who do not wish to have anything to do with one another. It assigns obligations and costs to those who refuse them—and who often even have current law on their side. In other words, risks cut through the self-absorption of cultures, languages, religions and systems as well as the national and international agenda of politics, they overturn their priorities and create contexts for action between camps, parties and quarrelling nations, which ignore and oppose one another.

I propose that a clear distinction be made between the philosophical and normative ideas of cosmopolitanism on the one hand and "impure," actual cosmopolitanization in the sociological sense on the other. The crucial point about this distinction is that cosmopolitanism cannot, for example, only become real deductively in a translation of the sublime principles of philosophy, but also and above all through the back doors of global risks, unseen, unintended, enforced. Throughout history, cosmopolitanism bore the taint of being elitist, idealistic, imperialist, and capitalist; today, however, we see that reality itself has become cosmopolitan. Cosmopolitanism does not mean—as it did for Immanuel Kant—an asset, a task; it does not mean to order the world. Cosmopolitanism in world risk societies opens our eyes to uncontrollable liabilities, to something that happens to us, befalls us, but at the same time stimulates us to make border-transcending new beginnings. The insight that, in the dynamic of world risk societies, we are dealing with a cosmopolitanization under duress robs "impure" cosmopolitanism of much of its ethical attractiveness. If the cosmopolitan moment of the world risk society is both deformed and inevitable, then it is seemingly not an appropriate object for sociological and political reflections. But that would be a serious mistake.

As important as all these arguments are, the decisive question is a different one: to what extent do the threat and shock of world risk societies open the horizon to historic alternatives of political action? I answer this question more fully in my book, *Power in the Global Age* (Beck 2007). I only have enough space here to outline the broad idea.

There are two premises we must keep in mind: (1) The world risk society brings a new, historic key logic to the fore: no nation can cope with its problems alone. (2) In the global age, it is possible to find a realistic political alternative that counterbalances the loss of power of state politics to globalized capital. The condition is that globalization must be decoded not as economic fate, but as a strategic game for world power. A new global domestic politics that is already at work here and now, beyond the national–international distinction, has become a meta-power game, whose outcome is completely open-ended. It is a game in which boundaries, basic rules, and basic distinctions are renegotiated—not only between national and international spheres, but also between global business and the state, transnational civil society movements, supra-national organizations, and national governments and societies.

Action strategies, which global risks open up, overthrow the order of power, which has formed in the neoliberal capital-state coalition: global risks empower states and civil society movements because they reveal new sources of legitimation and possibilities for action for these groups of actors; on the other hand, they disempower globalized capital because the consequences of investment decisions and externalizing risks in financial markets contribute to creating global risks, destabilizing markets, globally operating banks, and activating the power of both the state and the sleeping giant that is the consumer. Conversely, the goal of global civil society and its actors is to achieve a connection between civil society and the state, that is, to bring about a cosmopolitan form of statehood. The alliances entered into by the neoliberal state instrumentalize the state (and state-theory) in order to optimize and legitimize the interests of capital worldwide. Conversely the idea of a cosmopolitan state in the form of civil society aims at imagining and realizing a robust diversity and a post-national order. The neoliberal agenda surrounds itself with an aura of self-regulation and self-legitimation. Civil society's agenda, on the other hand, surrounds itself with the aura of human rights, global justice, and struggles for a new grand narrative of radical-democratic globalization.

Why is this not wishful thinking, why is it an expression of a cosmopolitan realpolitik? The cosmopolitan perspective suggests that there is a hidden link between global risk and Immanuel Kant. It is precisely the stark realism of the cosmopolitan imperative: *either Kant or catastrophe, either cooperate or fail*, which is also cause for hope.

## Consequences and perspectives

It is evident, that what I call "methodological nationalism," the nation-state frame of reference that has been taken for granted, prevents the social and political sciences from understanding and analyzing the dynamics and conflicts, ambivalences and ironies of the world risk society. This is also true—at least in part—of the two major theoretical approaches and empirical schools of research that deal with risk, in the tradition of Mary Douglas on the one hand and of Michel Foucault on the other. These traditions of thought and research have undoubtedly raised key questions and produced extremely interesting detailed results as far as understanding definitions of risk and risk policies. This is work that we cannot do without, and it will always remain an essential component of the social science research on risk. Its achievement and evidence opens risk as a battleground for the redefinition of state and scientific power.

An initial defect lies in regarding risk more or less or even exclusively as an ally, failing to perceive it as an unreliable ally or as a potential adversary, as a force hostile both to the power of the nation-state and to global capital. Surprisingly, the research traditions of Douglas and Foucault define their problem in such a way that the battle over risk always comes down to the reproduction of the social and the state order of power. Because the nation-state, which attempts to deal with global risks in isolation, resembles a drunk man, who is trying to find his lost wallet on a dark night by the light of a streetlamp. When asked whether he actually lost his wallet there, he said, no, but at least I can see to look for it in the light of the streetlight.

In other words, global risks are producing "failed or bankrupt states"—even in the West (the last example was Greece, but in the near future it may also be Italy or Great Britain or even the United States). The state-structure evolving under the conditions of the world risk society could be characterized in terms of both inefficiency and post-democratic authority. A clear distinction, therefore, has to be made between rule and inefficiency. It is quite possible that the end-result could be the gloomy perspective that we have totally ineffective and authoritarian state regimes (even in the context of the Western democracies). The irony here is this: manufactured uncertainty (knowledge), insecurity (welfare state), and lack of safety (violence) undermine and reaffirm state power beyond democratic legitimacy. Given the maddening conditions of the world risk society, Foucault's classic critical theory is in danger of becoming simultaneously affirmative and antiquated, along with large areas of sociology, which have concentrated on class dynamics in the welfare state. It underestimates and weakens the communicative cosmopolitan logic and irony of global risks; consequently, the historic question about where politics has lost its wallet, that is, the question of an alternative modernity, is analytically excluded by the vain search near the light of the nation-state streetlight.

Cosmopolitan social sciences, which confront the challenges of global risks, must also, however, shed their political quietism: society and its institutions are incapable of adequately conceptualizing risks, because they are caught up in early modern conceptions of the nation-state, believing in scientific certainty and linear progress, which have now become unsuitable. It has to face the question: how can non-Western risk societies be understood by a sociology that has until now taken for granted the belief that its object—Western modernity—is at once both historically unique and universally valid? (Beck and Grande 2010). How is it possible to decipher the internal link between risk and race, risk and enemy image, risk and exclusion?

# Bibliography

Beck, U. 1992. *Risk Society*. London: Sage Publications Ltd.
— 2007. *World at Risk*. Oxford: Polity Press.
Beck, U. and E. Grande. 2010. "Varieties of Second Modernities: European and Extra-European Experiences and Perspectives." *British Journal of Sociology* 6: 3.
Ewald, F. 2002. "The Return of Descartes's Malicious Demon: An Outline of a Philosophy of Precaution." Translated by Stephen Utz. In *Embracing Risk*. Edited by T. Baker and J. Simon, Chicago: University of Chicago Press. 273–301.
Keynes, J. M. 1937. "The General Theory of Employment." *Quarterly Journal of Economics* 51(2): 209–23.

2

# Global Risks and Preventive Governance

Edgar Grande
*University of Munich*

## New risks as a worldwide political problem

This article[1] rests on the assumption that world politics is increasingly confronted with a new type of self-generated risks; for instance, high-risk modern technologies such as nuclear energy and genetic engineering, new types of environmental and health problems ("global warming," worldwide pandemics), new forms of transnational terrorism, as well as new systemic risks of the global economy and finances. On a first glance, these phenomena do not seem to have practically anything in common—beside the fact that they have taken on an increasingly important role in national government work programs, international organizations, global summits, and public debates over the last three decades. However, if we take a closer look, it is possible to identify essential common characteristics that will make it possible to include them under the category of "new global risks."

The fact that modern societies are increasingly shaped by the existence of a new type of risk, clearly differentiated from the dangers, threats, and risks of the industrial society, was already recognized by sociologists in the 1980s. In studies by Ulrich Beck, Anthony Giddens, Scott Lash, and other authors, new risks to civilization, individualism, and globalization, in their own way, have undermined the foundations of industrial society (Beck 1992, 1994, 1997; Giddens 1990, 1994; Beck, Giddens, and Lash 1994; Adam, Beck, and van Loon 2000; van Loon 2002). Ulrich Beck's theory of "risk societies" is the most prominent in this respect. "Risk society" means "that the exponential growth of productive forces in the process of modernization gave rise to potential risks

[1] Article written for the workshop "The Governance of Global Risks" organized by the Munich Center on Governance at Spitzingsee, on April 23 and 24, 2010. This article has taken full advantage of the seminars held at the Universities of Munich and Toronto in 2009 and of the common work on cosmopolitanism, globalization, and preventive governance by Ulrich Beck, Louis W. Pauly, and Bernard Zangl. The author is thankful to the Deutsche Forschungsgemeinschaft (DFG) for financing his research within the framework of its Special Project on Reflexive Modernization.

and threats of an unprecedented magnitude" (Beck 1992, 19). Scientific-technical "progress" threatens the very existence of modern societies and, more generally, the process of social modernization turns against its own foundations. In recent years, Beck especially has developed the theory of a "late" or "second" modernity into a global sociological theory of the "global risk society" (Beck 1999, 2005, 2009). He upholds that the border-crossing nature of economic transactions and risks to civilization (such as climate change) devalues the tools of nation-states and fundamental institutions of industrial societies. The "risk society" is necessarily becoming a "global risk society" (Beck 2009).

From this perspective, sociological theories of the risk society can and should be associated with research in international relations. Moreover, as this chapter will show, they have become an indispensable source of inspiration for studies on the post-Cold War in terms of world politics. Climate change, international terrorism, and the international financial crisis, to name only a few of the most obvious examples, present international relations with a new type of global problem (Daase 2002; Beck 2005; Kessler 2008; Pauly 2009). Political responses considered necessary to deal with these problems not only go beyond the capabilities of normal nation-states but also overextend the capabilities of the great powers and established international organizations. The transition from a "Cold War" into a "global risk society" fundamentally challenges institutions, principles, procedures, and basic programs of world politics.

In this chapter, I assert that global risks require new forms of preventive governance which go beyond the functional limits and territorial boundaries of the nation-state. These new forms of preventive governance must not be compared or confused with existing forms of "state of prevention" or with the concepts of "world governance." This argument will be developed in four steps. First, I will present several conceptual distinctions allowing us to identify global risks and to distinguish them from other forms of risk, disasters, and uncertainties. Second, I will analyze the political implications of a risk society more generally. I will show that the concept of "risk society" corresponds to a new type of *preventive governance* which is clearly different from the well-known concepts of the prevention and regulation of risk. Third, I will apply the concept of preventive governance to global politics, and I will examine the similarities and differences between current concepts of world and transnational governance. Finally, I will identify certain themes that future research on world governance should consider.

## Conceptualizing new global risks

Using the term "risk" in the context of recent global political problems seems inappropriate since risk has been a characteristic defining modern societies from the beginning. In addition, modern societies have developed sophisticated instruments to identify and calculate risks and a vast array of strategies to deal with them—from the creation of private insurance to modern welfare states and all types of international organizations. So it is important to highlight that it is not risk itself, but rather a *new dimension of risk* which is responsible for the transition of world politics into a "global risk society." In order to understand this new dimension of risk, we must use several distinctions introduced particularly by Ulrich Beck in his theory of the "global risk society" (Beck 1999, 2005, 2007; Beck and Grande 2007, ch. 7).

The *first* distinction we must make is the *distinction between new risks and natural disasters and catastrophes.* The new risks of the "risk society" are self-generated risks; they are produced by human beings, whereas the origin of natural disasters such as earthquakes, volcanic eruptions, or floods does not depend on humans. Ulrich Beck (1994) and Anthony Giddens (1994) invented the term "fabricated uncertainties" to define this new aspect of technological risks, environmental disasters, financial crises, etc. This does not mean that these risks are the deliberate product of human activity. They are rather the result of the "involuntary side effects" of the technological, economic, cultural, and political innovations of global capitalism, which has also "progressively revolutionized its own social foundations" (Beck et al. 2003, 2). The consequences of climate change, which is itself an involuntary product of modern industrial society, may obscure the distinction between "natural" and "social" risks since they are supposed to increase the probability and intensity of natural disasters. This, however, does not negate the fundamental distinction.

*Secondly,* we must *make the distinction between "real" and "expected" disasters.* New social risks could result in real disaster but this does not necessarily have to be the case. They are, above all, social constructs, "potential dangers" (Arnoldi 2009b, 1), that is "hypothetical risks" (Häfele 1974). The dangers of nuclear energy were foreseen and formulated well before and independently from any real catastrophe. Accidents within nuclear power plants, particularly at Chernobyl, have surely reinforced and amplified fears and consolidated social movements and political parties that are against nuclear energy; however, they did not bring about these fears or their political articulation. Moreover, risks to civilization such as nuclear energy or genetic engineering are characterized by the fact that the predicted damage can only be evaluated in abstract terms and cannot be observed empirically. Any attempt to apply the optimism of the natural sciences to these problems would turn all of society into a laboratory (Krohn/Weyer 1989).

*Thirdly,* they *go beyond the distinction between "calculable risks" and "incalculable uncertainty"* established by Frank Knight (1964) for the economy. Two questions are particularly pertinent here. The first question is *causal complexity.* The security of nuclear plants or the reliability of new financial products can undoubtedly be calculated using complex models (Arnoldi 2009a). However, the sociologist Charles Perrow (1984), in his studies on great technological systems, has shown that these systems, with their implicit complexity and the interconnection of their components, tend to take on highly risky and unpredictable behaviors. Moreover, as we have seen with the latest financial crisis, scientific models whose aim is to calculate risks can increase risks rather than reducing them because they evoke, erroneously, the idea of predictability and control. The second question, which I will return to in greater detail, is actually *incalculable uncertainty* in the way described by Knight. Here, the lack of sufficient knowledge causes an uncertainty as to the existence of problems, their causality, or possible remedies. Even though "unknown unknowns" are a relatively recent phenomenon in international relations and the politics of security (Daase 2002; Daase and Kessler 2007), they are well known in the sociology of knowledge (Wehling 2006). Health risks for genetically modified foods, cell phones, and nanotechnology are concrete examples of this.

*Fourthly,* new risks are different because of the *magnitude of potential damage.* Compared with the limited damage of former risks, new social risks are characterized by their potentially unlimited damages. This does not mean that in the past there were no natural disasters, wars, and pandemics which caused enormous damage. Nevertheless, it is important to highlight that new risks represent a very precise arrangement of factors characterized by a "weak probability" and "heightened damage." In the worst case, the very existence of humanity is threatened by climate change, nuclear war, etc. In these cases, the classical definition of risk, which calculates risk as a product of the probability of its occurrence and the scale of damage, becomes useless. As the scope of (hypothetical or feared) damage is potentially incalculable, the risk is not acceptable for society, no matter how weak the probability of it occurring may be.

*Finally,* new risks tend to be *global in scope.* They can originate locally, as in the case of pandemics, terrorist attacks, or the recent financial crisis, but they go beyond territorial boundaries. Nuclear fallout from the accident at Chernobyl was not limited to its place of origin, but was dispersed over a large part of the European continent. Fatal viruses can travel easily across continents, as we saw in the case of SARS; and global warming will affect all regions of the planet, although differently and to varying degrees.

Table 1.1 summarizes the five aspects of risks introduced above. In order to avoid erroneous interpretations, I must make two clarifications. First of all, we must not take the terms used to label risks too literally. They do not imply that "old" risks no longer exist or that they are no longer important. The recent earthquake in Haiti, hurricane Katrina in 2005, and the tsunami in the Indian Ocean in 2004 all demonstrate that advanced modern societies are inevitably confronted with the threat of natural disasters and catastrophes. Moreover, I should highlight that the two types represent Weberian ideal types. In reality, we can definitely observe several combinations of these aspects. However, the explosive nature of new global risks results in the *coexistence and interaction of these five aspects.* If the magnitude and scope of dangers were limited and

**Table 1.1** Typology of risks

| Type of risk<br>Aspects of risks | "Old" risks | "New" risks |
|---|---|---|
| Cause | Natural | Human |
| Empirical basis | Observation | Prediction |
| Epistemological basis | Calculable | Incalculable |
| Scope | Local | Global |
| Magnitude | Limited | Unlimited |

local, incalculable risks would surely be less menacing; and the fact that there are social constructions of expected disasters opens a whole panorama of different attitudes and approaches, from scientific modeling to mass hysteria.

This typology is particularly useful in the context of international relations to make the distinction between "global risks" and what are called "global problems." Clearly, these two concepts are not identical. World politics is confronted with a multitude of old and new global problems, for example military conflicts, human rights issues, conflicts about rare resources (such as water and mineral resources), which are transnational but do not share the characteristics of global risks as defined here. These problems are mostly the observable consequence of deliberate human intervention and admit different strategies to confront their consequences. International terrorism, and particularly the possibility of terrorists using weapons of mass destruction, is a borderline example here. It shares all the characteristics of global risks, but it follows a different logic because it depends on intentional human action. In Beck's theory of a global risk society, it is nonetheless classified with new global risks because of its incalculable threat (Beck 2005, 2009).

## Risk society, state of prevention, and preventive governance

The new risks identified in the preceding chapter entail a significant transformation of the function of the state. They are the object of the needs and requirements for detailed preventive regulation which are handled particularly by public authorities. The magnitude of these risks means that we cannot totally ignore them, nor can they be treated by institutions already in place to compensate for damages or cases of need, that is private charities, commercial insurance, and the welfare-state. Consequently, "global risks" are considered one of the most pressing problems—if not *the* most pressing—of governance in contemporary societies. As opposed to natural disasters and catastrophes, the fact that they are the product, albeit involuntary, of human intervention suggests that they can also be avoided thanks to human intervention; and the potentially unlimited magnitude of harm implies that they *must* be avoided (at almost any cost).

The concept of "global risks" presents a completely new perspective on the state and both domestic and international governance, revealing that the state is not only being reduced and reconstructed, but also that the scope of the functions of the state is *expanding* in contemporary societies. In addition, the underlying logic of state activity is undergoing radical changes. We can summarize this evolution in the following hypothesis: *In the (global) risk society, the state is transformed into a preventive state designed to eliminate risk. Functionally, a state of prevention is the form corresponding to a "risk society."* To realize the explosive nature of this argument, we must more closely examine four aspects of the state of prevention.

1. A state of prevention is primarily characterized by the fact that the causes and motives of state actions are transferred from the past and present toward the future. Its

attention is not concentrated on claims founded on historical bases or on contemporary needs, but on the risk of menacing catastrophes. The state of prevention is guided by the imperative of preventing catastrophes, whether they are potential accidents in nuclear plants, global pandemics such as SARS, terrorist acts with "weapons of mass destruction," or the climate disaster that is presumed to be imminent. These cases represent new types of risks on civilization, and they all follow the same logic. The state can only intervene when the disaster has actually taken place. It must—at least according to society's expectations—foresee these threats, and it must be activated by the responsibility of dealing with these socially produced risks in a preventive fashion.

It is true that preventive action by the state is nothing new, and does not necessarily need to be associated with a new form of "risk society." As Michel Foucault showed in his historical analysis of "governmentality," it was inherent to the modern state from very early on. The paradigmatic case for the modern preventive state and for a corresponding new form of governmentality was the introduction of the vaccine for smallpox as well as other diseases in the eighteenth century. Consequently, a new type of security technology appeared within the state (Foucault 2004a, 12, 57). In addition, measures to inspect factories introduced in the nineteenth century for safety and health concerns focused on preventing danger and accidents resulting from new industrial plants (for Germany, see Ellwein 1993, 378). The fundamental logic of Keynesian economic policy was also preventive. Fluctuations of the economic cycle and the resulting economic crises had to be avoided by preventive ("anticyclical") management of the economy. Thanks to the intervention by the state and macroeconomic coordination, a "modern" capitalism, that is a capitalism without crisis, was supposed to have been established (Shonfield 1965).

From this point of view, the risk society's state of prevention only appears to be a new variety of Foucault's governmentality. Richard Ericson and Kevin Hagerty (1997) make a more explicit argument. They assert that the "knowledge of risk," achieved through new surveillance technologies, leads to complete "police control" within risk societies. However, if we examine it more closely, we can observe that it is not the preventive nature of the state's action in itself but rather the epistemological basis of the state's action, knowledge available to public authorities, which differentiates the state of prevention of a risk society from previous forms of state. In a risk society, the state must confront a new type of risk, whose manifestations and consequences are insufficiently, or even not at all, revealed by empirical knowledge (established scientifically). The risk in "risk societies" and the actions that respond to it result from new dimensions of risk that cannot be sufficiently comprehended by differentiating between risk (calculable) and uncertainty (incalculable). "Fabricated uncertainties" (Giddens 1994, 4; Beck 1994) produced by modern society are characterized by a particular form of "non-knowledge," which cannot be converted into calculable knowledge: what can be called "unknown unknowns" (Beck 1994; Wehling, 2006). Since we do not know what we do not know, we cannot study these "unknown unknowns" using the usual procedures of scientific analysis. This problem acquires particular force due to the principle that these "unknown unknowns" cannot simply be ignored. On the contrary, "risk societies" are flooded by the fear that these very "unknown unknowns" could have catastrophic consequences.

In risk societies, the instrumental understanding of science and technology characteristic of a modern industrial society is in a state of crisis—and consequently, the epistemological basis of the state's action becomes just as delicate (Preuss 1994). Whereas industrial societies assumed that problems could be (better) solved with (more) knowledge, this relationship crumbles and is perhaps even reversed with the appearance of new risks for civilization. This is the main difference with the logic of Foucault's governmentality: governmentality depends on positive knowledge and the capacity for knowing, that is the power of knowledge. The history of security technologies, used by the new governmentality, is tightly linked to the development of scientific knowledge (statistics and calculations of probabilities, for example). However, the state of prevention of "risk societies" depends on a totally different logic of power, on knowing the *power(lessness) of not being able to know*. As Preuss correctly warned, the boundary between "risk" and the "residual risk" calculated through a scientific calculation of risk is "not epistemological but rather normative" (Preuss 1994, 530)—and the same is true when it is a question of "non-knowledge." At the end of the day, the state of prevention of "risk societies" must determine how acceptable "residual risk" is for society and how serious are the unknown risks of modern technologies or global financial markets. The decision concerning these problems cannot be made scientifically, only politically; and decisions must be based on "moral" certainty rather than scientific certainty. Ericsson and Haggerty (1997, 6) highlighted this point perfectly. Analyses of risk and classification of risk are necessarily imprecise and incomplete, but they "infuse a moral certainty and legitimacy to the facts they produce, thus allowing people to accept them as normative obligations and consequently, as scripts of action."

2. The need for preventing risks shifts responsibility from the private sector to public authorities, whatever its exact organizational structure may be. In order to understand the transforming power of "new risks" completely, it is important to take into consideration another characteristic of the state of prevention of "risk societies": the *absence of functional limits of (state) preventive action*. This does not imply that all state functions are subject to the same logic of prevention or that the state is held responsible for the entirety of society's problems. Both the welfare state of industrial societies and the prevention state of "risk societies" are exposed to the dangers of unlimited activity and growth. However, each case follows a different logic. The expansion of the welfare state is the result of unlimited expectations and demands (Bell 1976). Potentially, all problems with social regulation and all regulatory sectors belong to the state. Industrial society's welfare state tends to be *universally responsible*. The reasons for the unlimited development of "prevention states" are varied. Their responsibility can be limited to a few specific regulatory problems that have particular urgency and importance (such as climate change and the fight against transnational terrorism). However, in order to confront these problems successfully, no area of life, no matter how insignificant, can escape state intervention. "The objective of preventive action by the state is [. . .] any possible form of behavior, and everyone is a potential suspect" (May 2007, 92). In short, the state of prevention of risk societies has come to be *omnipresent*.

Foucault also highlights the absence of functional limits for the state's preventive action. He asserts that governmentality in modern states cannot be limited by an external force but only through the functional rationality of areas of society, in particular the economy (Foucault 2004b, ch. 1). The explosive force of the current transformation of political authority stems from the fact that economic limitations of state activities do not equally affect the two forms of public activity under consideration here—the welfare state and the prevention state. Economic constraints primarily limit welfare states working with and dependent on financial resources. However, the calculation of the risks of a prevention state does not follow economic parameters. This seems to be the case even during the current worldwide financial crisis, when national governments have had to move vast sums of money in order to save banks and insurance companies that have "systemic importance." The critical limits of the fight against the risks of terrorism and transnational crime, to give another example, are not defined in economic terms but by the tensions between "individual liberty" and "public safety": "The nature of the prevention state means that citizens must be deprived of even more freedoms in order to ensure safety in return; this inevitably implies a tendency toward excess because security can never be sufficient" (Prantl 2007, 15; see Huster and Rudolph 2008).

Owing to the lack of functional limits on the prevention state, modern "risk societies" are confronted with the problem of controlling and limiting political authority in a new form. In this case, the root of the problem is not citizens' excessiveness, as a neo-conservative critic of the welfare state would suppose, but rather the excessiveness of public authority. However, the consequences would be the same in both cases, namely an over-extension of state structures (Denninger 1988, 2). Problems cannot be resolved with criteria of scientific rationality or economic constraints. The citizens of a "risk society" are faced with the challenge of finding *political* solutions to this problem.

3. The prevention state is characterized by a significant transformation of the function of law. On the national level, we have seen two changes that are not mutually exclusive. Both were reflected in an exemplary fashion in German legal discourse in the twentieth century. In the first case, according to the logic of legal positivism, the goal is to regulate new risks by means of legal instruments. Consequently, the law loses its universal nature and is transformed into what Ernst Forsthoff described in the 1950s, in German, as *Maßnahmengesetz*, a law of planning measures (Forsthoff 1964): "The characteristic of this law is that it moves logically from the goal and the objective to the means. It is only an action which can create nothing and only intend to make decisions which serve and are subordinate to the realization of a goal. The *Maßnahmengesetz* then stems from a particular situation and maintains a comprehensible and logically coherent relationship with it" (Forsthoff 1964, 85). Forsthoff himself located this change within the context of increasing state functions, and more precisely, within the expansion of the twentieth-century welfare state. With the responsibility of precaution toward new types of risks to civilization, this problem has intensified even further: "Each technologically complex project that interacts with the social environment is

a 'prototype' for which there is no sequence, for which there are no past experiences and for which the legal duty of determining the boundary between the protected area of the fundamental right to life and the respect for physical integrity and the residual risk accepted by all citizens must be redrawn every time" (Preuss 1994, 542). This is why, in "risk societies'" state of prevention, the law tends to be transformed into a *Maßnahmengesetz*.

The other case, foretold by Carl Schmitt (2006), is even less attractive. In this case, the law as an instrument of political authority is replaced by sovereign political decisions. In a state of political emergency, according to Schmitt, legal order must be subordinate to the necessary measures to restore order and stability. In this case, the state works in an "uncertain territory between public law and politics, between legal order and life" (Agamben 2004, 8). In recent years, this "no-man's land" has been central to Giorgio Agamben's analysis of the "state of exception." His main argument is that "given the inexorable intensification of what has been defined as a 'worldwide civil war,' the state of exception in contemporary politics (turns out to be) more and more the dominant paradigm of government" (Agamben 2004, 9). The "state of exception" assumes its archetypal form in the "war" against transnational terrorism, where the constitutional state is transformed into a state of prevention: "The state is now developing its security system essentially beyond penal law because the strict principles of the protection of possibly innocent individuals are no longer in force there" (Prantl 2007, 15). We could generalize this example and apply it to the state in a "risk society." Pushed to the edge, the prevention state in a "risk society" takes the form of a *Maßnahmenstaat*, a state of planning measures. Ulrich Beck has defined in this way: "The risk society is a society of disaster. The *state of exception threatens to become a normal state*" (Beck 1992, 24: emphasis added).

Even though both evolutions (the transformation of the constitutional state into a *Maßnahmenstaat* on one hand, and on the other, the replacement of universal law by a *Maßnahmengessetz*) are based on different conceptions of the state and the law, they carry the same consequence: in a risk society, the importance of decisions (on a single case) increases. "Reflexive modernization" may end up as "reflexive decisionism" (Beck and Lau 2005, 548–9). As long as these decisions are made by the political system, modern society becomes, strictly speaking, a "political society" (Greven 1999).

4. Predicting the catastrophic consequences of the new risks produced in the processes of reflexive modernization means much more than a quantitative increase in the functions of the state and public activities and the transformation of the state into a state of prevention. In its greatest expression, it requires *shifting from a preventive state to preventive governance*. In a "worldwide state of exception" (Beck 2009 [2007, 146]), a preventive state must be transformed into preventive governance. Here, we can at least partly follow Foucault's historical analysis on power and the distinction he makes between a government centered on the state and based on sovereignty and "governmentality" which goes far beyond the state and its usual instruments of control (Foucault 2004a, 2004b). In the same way, we can differentiate preventive governance

from the well-known forms of prevention states (the regulating state, welfare state, and monitoring state) on two levels: regarding (1) involved agents and organizations and (2) instruments of governance.

First of all, preventive governance goes far beyond the state and its instruments. This is true both for the object of preventive activity as well as its subject. In order to "save the world," everyone and every possible form of behavior becomes useful. In his theory of a "worldwide risk society," Beck maintains that global risks lead to a "social delimitation of the state of exception" (*"soziale Entgrenzung des Ausnahmezustands"*) (Beck 2009 [2007, 147f]). Politics relating to climate change do not stop at the door of global summits. They also influence our way of cleaning up and taking out the garbage. Moreover, the decision relating to the "worldwide state of exception" will not be made by governments, but rather by anonymous private agents and organizations. Consequently, preventive governance necessarily leads to complex arrangements of actors and institutional frameworks, from global regime complexities to local initiatives by citizens, and from governments and public organizations to all sorts of private activities and organizations.

In addition, preventive governance implies a considerable expansion of the instruments of governance. Preventive governance of new global risks potentially affects everyone and every possible form of behavior. For this reason, it is not enough to round up the usual suspects—whether through legal or illegal means. Preventive governance is based on the combination of "hard" and "soft" instruments and the complex interaction between them. This does not mean replacing the law with arbitrariness or even despotism, but rather with new approaches of control and of self-control.

It is clear that there exist significant differences between the various types of new global risks. Whereas terrorist attacks and worldwide financial risks have unexpectedly put the state back in "the center" (resulting in a very controversial debate), health risks and climate change have actually streamlined private organizations, foundations, and charitable works. And in certain cases, such as when there are technological and environmental risks, scientific knowledge—although incomplete and uncertain—has become essential, whereas in other cases, such as transnational terrorism, "hard" forms of control and monitoring seem to prevail. This shows that shifting from a preventive state to preventive governance can produce a variety of different arrangements, different *regimes of preventive governance*, characterized by different arrangements of national, international, public, and private agents and by different sets of instruments. Identifying these regimes of governance in different areas of global risk and analyzing their operation calls for empirical research.

## "Worldwide Risk Society": Preventive governance beyond the nation-state

However, new global risks not only transform the functions of the modern state. This would mean focusing too strongly on the state, a perspective whose scope would be much too restricted. Global risks require a major reconstruction of political authority, its institutional architecture, and the territorial extent of its activities. For this reason, by analyzing "global risks," the attention of research on governance must be expanded and include a *transnational* level. In academic and public debates, there exists a growing awareness of the impossibility of conveniently treating the problems of regulating global risks within the framework of the nation-state. New risks for civilization (climate change, transnational terrorism, worldwide health problems, and international financial markets) are supposed to create a "cosmopolitan moment" (Beck 2009, 47) for political action: "Global risks are the main detonators of an explosive transformation revealing the contours of society in the twenty-first century" (Beck 2009, 55).

Global risks are not the only field for international cooperation and for building transnational politics, but they have substantially contributed to the current trend of political transnationalization. In recent decades, the scope of international organizations has consistently grown and gotten stronger, and new territorial levels of political decision-making have been established (Meyer et al. 1997; Held 2004; Katzenstein 2005); new forms of transnational governance involving a variety of arrangements of public and private agents have been developed (Rosenau and Czempiel 1992; Grande and Pauly 2005; Grande et al. 2007). The importance of private agents in the production of public goods, especially worldwide public goods, has increased.

Comparable to the concept of preventive governance in relation to the prevention state, the concept of "transnational governance" introduces a *new conceptual vision* of politics beyond the nation-state. The conventional perception of "international politics" as a "state-centered" institution whose system of power and decision-making is determined exclusively by nation-states has been seriously challenged by the concept of "transnational governance." There are at least three challengers: (1) the growing importance and independence of international institutions and organizations, which have gained, at least partially, skills as autonomous agents in recent decades (see especially Barnett and Finnemore 2004); (2) the private agents who play a more and more decisive role in governance beyond the nation-state, either as lobbyists or in determining or applying norms (Cutler et al. 1999; Hall/Biersteker 2002; Cutler 2003; Porter 2005); and (3) an intense interconnectedness and integration of several levels of political decision-making within multilevel systems of governance (for the exemplary case of Europe, see Hooghe and Marks 2001). As a result, the distinctions established between "public" and "private," between "interior" and "exterior," and between "national" and "international" have become vague (Grande 2006).

The result of these developments is a vast *spatial reconfiguration of political authority*. However, the nation-state is not dissolved in this process; it becomes part of the new institutional architecture of political authority. These new transnational authorities are distinct from premodern concepts of politics because the fundamental principles of modern political authority, especially principles of state sovereignty and democratic legitimacy, maintain validity. At the same time, they mark a historic rupture in the development of modern societies, given that political authority goes beyond the territorial boundaries of the nation-state and transforms its sovereignty (see Grande and Pauly 2005a). But above all, they transcend the duality of "national" and "international," which is constitutive of the modern nation-state (Sassen 2006). The nation-state becomes part of new *cosmopolitan spheres of action* and new transnational forms of governance. Analyzing the governance of global risks then requires a multi-scalar and multi-agent approach (Jessop 2008), which incorporates concepts of international relations and comparative politics (Grande and Risse 2000). As for methodology, we move from "methodological nationalism," which has until now been dominant in social sciences to "methodological cosmopolitanism" (Beck 2006; Beck and Grande 2010; Zürn 2001).

It is true that these empirical developments have been on the global governance research agenda since the field was developed in the 1990s. In this context, a substantial number of analyses has been presented; they convincingly demonstrate that in the age of globalization, national institutions and politics tend to become insufficient, inefficient and illegitimate. From this point of view, new global risks seem to represent only one particular case that strengthens the general argument in favor of new political institutions beyond the nation-state.

In fact, the theory of a "worldwide risk society" shows a strong normative preference for new agreements of cooperation established in order to deal with global risks. In this context, it emphasizes three arguments. First of all, it presumes that new global risks produce what are called "*cosmopolitan imperatives*": ecological and technological risks, risks associated with worldwide pandemics, the financial crisis and terrorists armed with nuclear, biological, or chemical weapons create a tangle of consequences and sequenced political decisions between states and their citizens, which change the nature and the dynamic of systems of government defined territorially. Global risks of this sort bring all parts of the world, both rich and poor, together in an unexpected way. What we are seeing in response to global interconnections is not a normative cosmopolitanism in a world without borders. There exists instead a cosmopolitan imperative from which nobody can escape. This is where the generalized possibility of "communities of risk" appears, and they come forward, are established, and take note of their cosmopolitan composition. In this way, "cosmopolitan communities" are the opposite of established geopolitical notions that summarize territorial forms of social order (such as the nation-state) because "cosmopolitan communities" appear with the awareness that we can no longer socially define dangers and uncertainties in space or time.

Secondly, the theory affirms that cosmopolitan imperatives intensify the pressure for cooperation, inciting new institutional forms of transnational governance. It presumes that these plural domains, overlapping with political authority, are new forms of *governance*, in the sense that they adopt collectively restrictive decisions on collective problems on an economic, social, and political scale; and it maintains that *these* forms of governance, these new transnational networks of distributed power, represent the distinctive trait of political authority in a "worldwide risk society." They are comprised of states (but not only of states), but they are not states themselves. The level of institutional complexity and the means of integrating such regimes are converted into key variables for the analysis of transnational forms of governance.

Thirdly, the theory affirms that, in the process of globalization, the modern nation-state is transformed into a "state of transnational cooperation" (Beck 2005). According to this concept, the nation-state does not become obsolete. Instead, there is a transformation of the scope of public authority (transnational instead of national) and of the structure of power relations (cooperative instead of hierarchical) in the modern state. The term, however, does not claim to describe the whole of new transnational authority. Even if states play an important or essential role in the current institutional architectures, "*as a whole* and with good reason, they lack the character of a state" (Habermas 2004, 134; emphasis in the original).

Empirically, we can observe a great variety of new institutional architectures of political authority beyond the nation-state. From a conceptual point of view, we can differentiate them according to the horizontal and vertical integration of individual levels, institutions, fields and agents involved in the process of elaborating political programs, and the difference between decision-making and putting politics into action. Until now, research has mainly concentrated on new forms of symmetrical and cooperative transnational governance. In this context, the term "transnational political regime" describes the entirety of institutions, organizations, agents, relations, norms and rules (both formal and informal) involved in the production and application of collectively restrictive decisions beyond the nation-state (Grande 2004; Grande and Pauly 2005b). In particular, the term takes into account *three problematic aspects* which are pertinent here: first, the strengthening of institutions; second, their territorial scope; and third, the arrangement of involved agents and organizations (see Grande and Pauly 2005b, 286; Grande et al. 2007). Transnational political regimes are thus distinct from nation-states, on the one hand, and international regimes and organizations on the other.

In the dominant perspective of research on international relations, these new forms of governance are not only very interesting from an empirical point of view, but also, normatively speaking, they are the most desirable type of political authority. However, this does not mean that symmetrical forms of the elaboration of transnational politics are the only way of dealing with new global risks. The theory of a "worldwide risk society" fully accepts the possibility that another new type of political power may appear, namely *postcolonial empires*. We must not interpret these empires as a resurgence of the colonial imperialism of the nineteenth century. These new asymmetrical structures of political power must indeed be classified as empires since they are tightly integrated with and subject to a logical expansion of power. However, these new empires are different from the old empires and previous forms of imperialism in two respects. First, they are made up of sovereign states and secondly, their formation and internal integration are not based on conquest, violence, and coercion but on voluntary membership, law, and consensus. Currently, the model that best exemplifies this postcolonial cosmopolitan empire is Europe (Beck and Grande 2007; Zielonka 2006).

The asymmetrical power between agents, represented by new forms of empire, are but one of the many possible variations on the standard model of transnational governance. A second source of variation can be related to the *informalization* of global politics (Daase 2009). The standard model of transnational governance assumes that cooperative pressure gives rise to new types of formal institutions, established by formal treaties, and recognized by national governments. Institutional agreements on global environmental policies, such as rules on the climate or the Kyoto Protocol, are instructive examples. Progress in strengthening transnational institutions is measured by the strength of formal institutions in relation to their member states and the objects of their politics. However, strengthening transnational institutions may take another route. In recent years, we have seen an astonishing increase in *informal agreements and the strengthening of informal institutions* (Greven 2005; Daase 2009). In various domains—from the regulation of public infrastructures to security policy—the forms of cooperation that are institutionalized with less restrictive agreements and less implicit rules are gaining importance. I believe that these informal agreements are not insignificant, and we are not dealing with a simple transitory phenomenon toward formal institutional reinforcement. Empirical proof coming from the EU (Christiansen 2003; Eberlein and Grande 2005) indicates that they must be interpreted as a response to the structural weakness of formal institutions, particularly institutional obstacles and gaps in formal regulation. In addition, informal agreements seem to be one of the ways of dealing with the growing institutional complexity of transnational politics.

Another source of variation could be the *intensity of conflicts in the governance of risk*. It is not realistic to presume that the cosmopolitan imperatives produced by new global risks can be easily transformed into an overall consensus of fundamental norms, institutions and policies, as suggested by normative positions of cosmopolitanism (see Held 2004). On the contrary, given that global risks are social constructs shaped by cultural norms and means of organization, we must expect significant variations between various societies and from one country to the next, concerning their perception, comprehension, and definition of risks (Douglas and Wildavsky 1983; Douglas 1986). The existence of different perceptions of risk and of diverse cultures of risk may represent a source of new, more intense conflicts. In this context, we can distinguish at least *four types of "risk conflicts"*:

1. *Epistemological* conflicts on the existence of risks: Does climate change really exist? Are new technologies safe?
2. *Normative* conflict on the perception of risk and the acceptability of risk: How much risk are we prepared to accept?
3. *Distributive* conflicts on the cost of preventive governance: How should we distribute the costs of policies on climate protection (among countries, within societies, between generations)?
4. *Moral* conflicts and dilemmas created by preventive policies: How much individual freedom are we willing to sacrifice in exchange for safety?

Apparently, the "worldwide risk society" is characterized by two contradictory processes. On one hand, there is a process of centripetal unification, the creation of new "cosmopolitan imperatives." At the same time, the worldwide risk society is subject to a powerful process of centrifugal diversification: the coexistence, and probably even competition between different types of risk society, different cultures of risk. These conflicts can be translated into new forms of "systemic conflicts and competition" which cross current economic and cultural boundaries (Kriesi et al. 2008). In the

**Table 1.2** Features of preventive governance of risks

| Features | Possible characteristics |
|---|---|
| Type of agents | Public or private |
| Agent arrangement | Symmetrical or asymmetrical |
| Degree of institutionalization | Formal or informal |
| Institutional complexity | Low or high |
| Means of problem solving | Cooperative or non-cooperative |
| Intensity of conflicts of risk | Low or high |
| Instruments of governance | Hard or soft instruments |

worst case, these "risk conflicts" could result in new wars against terrorism or scarce resources (Welzer 2008).

## Empirical challenges for research on the global governance of risks

If we combine the developments in both dimensions of preventive governance, that is the functions of the state and the territorial scope of governance, the emergence of new global risks seem to produce a single arrangement: a "worldwide state of exception" (Beck 2009 [2007, 146]), which can be characterized by three elements: first, with the shift toward preventive governance, society's demands regarding public responsibility and state action experience an overall increase; secondly, on the other hand, the importance of the state as a (more or less exclusive) supplier of public goods decreases; and thirdly, the institutionalized responsibility of risk prevention shifts from the national to the international realm. Still, preventive governance can take many different forms. We can observe variations in several aspects which reflect different types and arrangements of agents, different institutional architectures, different means and instruments of problem solving. Table 1.2 summarizes the main features and the range of possible characteristics.

In reality, it must be expected that the possible characteristics of these features will combine in different ways. The normative ideal of transnational governance integrating public and private agents in symmetrical forms of cooperation is only one possibility among many. Empirical research on the governance of global risks should then focus on two key questions. First, it should focus on the *empirical* types of preventive governance in the various fields of global risks. It should identify the distinctive traits for each case and the differences and similarities between cases. Despite certain basic similarities between various types of global risks, we cannot expect the same form of preventive governance in each one of these domains. Moreover, we cannot only attribute observable differences to the characteristics of certain individual risks. It is true that political responses to climate change may call for specific institutions and political instruments which are considerably different from those necessary to prevent financial crises or terrorist attacks. However, variations between domains may also stem from cultural and political perceptions, risk cultures, political strategies and different arrangements of power. The second task of empirical research is then to identify the causes of political and institutional variations and their consequences.

Furthermore, current studies on the institutionalization of new forms of governance beyond the nation-state have revealed that "transnational risk governance" is faced with great challenges in governance. Three problem areas seem to be of particular interest: (1) the institutional complexity and fragmentation of transnational governance; (2) media coverage of the global perception and communication of risks; and (3) the democratic legitimacy of new forms of transnational governance.

1.  *Institutional complexity and fragmentation:* From an institutional point of view, the current main problem of transnational risk governance is the deep *institutional fragmentation* of transnational politics. The institutional reality of "transnational governance" is made up of a multitude of considerably fragmented regulatory structures, which partially overlap and partially compete with each other in their territorial and functional scope, without melding into a coherent overall structure. This institutional fragmentation has caused a certain number of problems for the transnational governance of risk. First, the weak specialization of transnational institutions often leads to a restricted perspective that is out of proportion with existing regulatory problems. In the case of climate protection, for example, a great number of political domains such as energy, transportation and trade, play an important role beyond environmental politics. However, the current regime of climate protection, despite its great complexity, does not let us take them into sufficient account. Competing responsibilities and conflicts of norms are another problem caused by institutional fragmentation. This is evidenced by frequent conflicts between economic, environmental, and social objectives in global politics.

2.  *Media coverage of the construction and communication of risks*: The second main challenge of preventive risk governance concerns the *perception and communication of risks*. Sociological and socio-psychological research has made it clear that new "risks to civilization" are essentially social constructs. Their construction is part of a communicative process in which public articulation and intermediation through (electronic) media play a central role. As a result, the intensity of the public consciousness of risks is only weakly related to their importance for society. Media coverage in contemporary societies also implies that the communication of risks, the perception of risk, and the construction of political legitimacy are subject to the specific logic of the media and its necessity to produce and dramatize news. Following recent changes in media, the publicized construction of social reality is characterized by shorter attention spans, growing self-referentiality, and a vast economization of information production. This has various consequences for research on the governance of risk. One cannot assume that the perception of the problem by social agents and political institutions is oriented toward the "objective" priorities and necessities of society's problems; on the contrary, the media's construction of regulatory problems, its own criteria and mechanisms of selectivity, and the prerequisites

of communication and sustained public attention must be the primary object of research. Namely the following issues must be addressed in transnational comparative research: (1) How are global risks, their urgency, alternative regulatory options (or rather the lack thereof!), relevant agents in governance, and the legitimacy of their decisions constructed by the media? (2) How are the rules of attention and selectivity in the media different from the description and perception of risk in politics, science, and public opinion? (3) How does media representation of global risk affect the intensity of political activity and the choice of political options by agents of governance? (4) Does transnational risk governance encourage the establishment of transnational public areas or are agents always focused on national propaganda?

3.  *Democratic legitimacy of transnational governance*: The third focus of research is centered on the prerequisites, possibilities, and institutional options for the democratic legitimacy of transnational risk governance. Because of the growing importance of transnational institutions and the fact that their autonomy from member states continues to increase, we can observe an ever-growing vacuum of political control and democratic legitimacy. In short, if nation-states give up their exclusive decision-making competence, if they are forced to share it with international organizations and regimes as well as with several sorts of nongovernmental organizations (NGOs), new emerging forms of transnational governance will require a proper democratic legitimacy, independent from the member states and organizations that founded them. In recent years, specialists on "cosmopolitan democracy" have made a considerable effort to analyze these questions (see, for example, Archibugi 2008). However, these efforts concentrate more or less exclusively on symmetrical types of formal cooperative institutions. But what about asymmetrical and informal transnational arrangements? Can they somehow be democratized? And how can we reconcile democratic normative requirements for equality with the asymmetrical structure of postcolonial empires? Is a "worldwide state of exception" established by the permanent danger of global risks in any way compatible with democratic norms, institutions, and procedures?

This short list of questions for future research is far from complete. The three problems of transnational risk governance outlined here, that is the fragmentation and complexity of preventive risk governance, media coverage of the perception and communication of risk, and deficits in the democratic legitimacy of transnational risk governance, should illustrate the potential that global risks may have on empirical research into international relations. In all likelihood, there are many other factors that should be added to this research program.

# Bibliography

Adam, B., U. Beck, and J. v. Loon (eds) 2000. *The Risk Society and Beyond: Critical Issues for Social Theory*. London: Sage.

Agamben, G. 2004. *Ausnahmezustand.* Frankfurt: Suhrkamp.

Archibugi, D. 2008. *A Global Commonwealth of Citizens. Toward Cosmopolitan Democracy.* Princeton: Princeton University Press.

Arnoldi, J. 2009a. *Risk.* Cambridge: Polity Press.

— 2009b. *Alles Geld verdampft. Finanzkrise in der Weltrisikogesellschaft.* Frankfurt:Suhrkamp.

Barnett, M. and M. Finnemore. 2004. *Rules for the World. International Organizations in Global Politics.* Ithaca: Cornell University Press.

Beck, U. 1992. *Risk Society. Towards a New Modernity.* London: Sage.

— 1994. "The Reinvention of Politics: Toward a Theory of Reflexive Modernization." In *Reflexive Modernization. Politics, Tradition and Aesthetics in the Modern Social Order.* Edited by U. Beck, A. Giddens, and S. Lash (eds). Cambridge: Polity Press. 1–55.

— 1997. *The Reinvention of Politics. Rethinking Modernity in the Global Social Order.* Cambridge: Polity Press.

— 2000. *What is Globalization?* Cambridge: Polity Press.

— 2005. "World Risk Society and the Changing Foundations of Transnational Politics." In *Complex Sovereignty: Reconstituting Political Authority in the 21st Century.* Edited by E. Grande and L. W. Pauly. Toronto: University of Toronto Press. 22–47.

— 2006. *Power in the Global Age. A New Global Political Economy.* Oxford: Blackwell.

— 2009. *World at Risk.* Cambridge: Polity Press.

Beck, U. and E. Grande. 2007. *Cosmopolitan Europe.* Cambridge: Polity Press.

— 2010. "Varieties of Second Modernities: European and Extra-European Experiences and Perspectives." *British Journal of Sociology* 61(3): 409–43.

Beck, U. and C. Lau. 2005. "Second Modernity as a Research Agenda: Theoretical and Empirical Explorations in the 'Meta-change' of Modern Society." *British Journal of Sociology* 56(4): 525–57.

Beck, U., W. Bonß, and C. Lau. 2003. "The Theory of Reflexive Modernization: Problematic, Hypotheses and Research Programme." *Theory, Culture & Society* 20(2): 1–33.

Beck, U, A. Giddens, and S. Lash. 1994. *Reflexive Modernization. Politics, Tradition and Aesthetics in the Modern Social Order.* Cambridge: Polity Press.

Bell, D. 1976. *The Cultural Contradictions of Capitalism.* New York: Basic Books.

Christiansen, T. (ed.) 2003. *Informal Governance in the European Union.* Cheltenham: Elgar.

Cutler, C. 2003. *Private Power and Global Authority.* Cambridge: Cambridge University Press.

Cutler, C., V. Haufler, and T. Porter. 1999. *Private Authority and International Affairs.* Albany: Suny Press.

Daase, C. (ed.) 2002. *Internationale Risikopolitik.* Baden-Baden: Nomos.

— 2009. "Informalisierung internationaler Organisationen." In *Die organisierte Welt.* Edited by K. Dingwerth, D. Kerwer and A. Nölke. Baden-Baden: Nomos. 290–308.

Daase, C. and O. Kessler. 2007. "Knowns and Unknowns in the 'War on Terror': Uncertainty and the Political Construction of Danger." *Security Dialogue* 38(4): 411–36.

Denninger, E. 1988. "Der Präventions-Staat." *Kritische Justiz* 1: 1–15.

Douglas, M. 1986. *Risk Acceptability According to the Social Sciences.* London: Routledge & Kegan Paul.

Douglas, M. and A. Wildavsky. 1983. *Risk and Culture.* Berkeley: University of California Press.

Eberlein, B. and E. Grande. 2005. "Reconstituting Political Authority in Europe: Transnational Regulatory Networks and the Informalization of Governance in the European Union." In *Complex Sovereignty. Reconstituting Political Authority in the 21st Century.* Edited by E. Grande and L. W. Pauly. Toronto: Toronto University Press. 146–67.

Ellwein, T. 1993. *Der Staat als Zufall und als Notwendigkeit. Die jüngere Verwaltungsentwicklung in Deutschland am Beispiel Ostwestfalen-Lippe* (Band 1). Opladen: Westdeutscher Verlag.

Ericson, R. V. 2007. *Crime in an Insecure World*. Oxford: Blackwell.

Ericson, R. V. and A. Doyle. 2004. *Uncertain Business: Risk, Insurance, and the Limits of Knowledge*. Toronto: University of Toronto Press.

Ericson, R. V. and K. D. Haggerty. 1997. *Policing the Risk Society*. Toronto: University of Toronto Press.

Forsthoff, E. 1964 [1955]. "Über Maßnahme-Gesetze." In *Rechtsstaat im Wandel. Verfassungsrechtliche Abhandlungen 1950–1964*. By E. Forsthoff. Stuttgart, Kohlhammer.

Foucault, M. 2004a. *Sécurité, Territoire, Population: Cours aux Collège de France, 1977–78*. Paris: Gallimard/Seuil.

— 2004b. *Naissance de la biopolitique: Cours aux Collège de France, 1978–79*. Paris: Gallimard/Seuil.

Giddens, A. 1990. *The Consequences of Modernity*. Cambridge: Polity Press.

— 1994. *Beyond Left and Right. The Future of Radical Politics*. Stanford: Stanford University Press.

Grande, E. 2004. "Vom Nationalstaat zum transnationalen Politikregime—Staatliche Steuerungsfähigkeit im Zeitalter der Globalisierung." In *Entgrenzung und Entscheidung*. Edited by U. Beck and C. Lau. Frankfurt: Suhrkamp. 283–97.

— 2006. "Cosmopolitan Political Science." *British Journal of Political Science* 57(1): 87–111.

Grande, E. and L. W. Pauly (eds) 2005a. *Complex Sovereignty. Reconstituting Political Authority in the 21st Century*. Toronto: Toronto University Press.

— 2005b. "Complex Sovereignty and the Emergence of Transnational Authority." In *Complex Sovereignty. Reconstituting Political Authority in the 21st Century*. Edited by E. Grande and L. W. Pauly. Toronto: Toronto University Press. 285–99.

Grande, E. and T. Risse. 2000. "Bridging the Gap: Konzeptionelle Anforderungen an die politikwissenschaftliche Analyse von Globalisierungsprozessen." *Zeitschrift für Internationale Beziehungen* 7(2): 235–66.

Grande, E., M. König, P. Pfister, and P. Sterzel. 2007. "Political Transnationalization: The Future of the Nation-state—A Comparison of Transnational Policy Regimes." In *Globalization. State of the Art and Perspectives*. Edited by S. A. Schirm. London: Routledge. 98–121.

Greven, M. T. 1999. *Die politische Gesellschaft. Kontingenz und Dezision als Probleme des Regierens und der Demokratie*. Opladen: Leske & Budrich.

— 2005. "The Informalization of Transnational Governance: A Threat to Democratic Government." In *Complex Sovereignty. Reconstituting Political Authority in the 21st Century*. Edited by E. Grande and L. W. Pauly. Toronto: Toronto University Press. 261–84.

Habermas, J. 2004. "Hat die Konstitutionalisierung des Völkerrechts noch eine Chance?" In *Der gespaltene Westen*. J. Habermas. Frankfurt: Suhrkamp.

Häfele, W. 1974. "Hypotheticality and the Pathfinder Role of Nuclear Energy." *Minerva* 12: 303–22.

Hall, R. B. and T. J. Biersteker (eds) 2002. *The Emergence of Private Authority in Global Governance*. Cambridge: Cambridge University Press.

Held, D. 2004. *Global Covenant. The Social Democratic Alternative to the Washington Consensus*. Cambridge: Polity Press.

Held, D. A. McGrew, D. Goldblatt, and J. Perraton. 1999. *Global Transformations. Politics, Economics and Culture*. Cambridge: Polity Press.

Hooghe, L. and Marks, G., 2001. *Multi-level Governance and European Integration.* Oxford: Rowman & Littlefield Publishers.

Huster, S. and K. Rudolph (eds) 2008. *Vom Rechtsstaat zum Präventionsstaat.* Frankfurt: Suhrkamp.

Jessop, B. 2008. *State Power. A Strategic-Relational Approach.* Cambridge: Polity Press.

Katzenstein, P. J. 2005. *A World of Regions. Asia and Europe in the American Imperium.* Ithaca: Cornell University Press.

Kessler, O. 2008. *Die internationale Politische Ökonomie des Risikos.* Wiesbaden: VS Verlag.

Knight, F. H. 1964 [1921]. *Risk, Uncertainty and Profit.* New York: Augustus M. Kelley.

Kriesi, H., E. Grande, R. Lachat, M. Dolezal, S. Bornschier, and T. Frey. 2008. *West European Politics in the Age of Globalization.* Cambridge: Cambridge University Press.

Krohn, W. and J. Weyer. 1989. "Die Gesellschaft als Labor. Die Erzeugung sozialer Risiken durch riskante Forschung." *Soziale Welt* 40: 349–73.

Loon, J. V. 2002. *Risk and Technological Culture.* London: Routledge.

May, S. 2007. "Sicherheit—Prävention—neue Risiken. Zum Wandel moderner Staatlichkeit und ihrer rechtlicher Handlungsformen." *Vorgänge* 46: 92–109.

Meyer, O. W. et al., 1997. "World society and the Nation State." *American Journal of Sociology* 103 (1).

Pauly, L. W. 2009. "The Old and the New Politics of International Financial Stability." *Journal of Common Market Studies* 47(5): 955–75.

Perrow, C. 1984. *Normal Accidents. Living with High-risk Technologies.* New York: Basic Books.

Porter, T. 2005. "The Private Production of Public Goods: Private and Public Norms in Global Governance." In *Complex Sovereignty. Reconstituting Political Authority in the 21st Century.* Edited by E. Grande and L. W. Pauly. Toronto: Toronto University Press. 217–37.

Prantl, H. 2007. "Der große Rüssel. Jeder Bürger wird zum Ausländer im eigenen Land: Vom Umbau des Rechtsstaats in einen Präventionsstaat." *Süddeutsche Zeitung 21/22. April 2007*: 15.

Preuss, U. K. 1994. "Risikovorsorge als Staatsaufgabe." In *Staatsaufgaben.* Edited by D. Grimm. Baden-Baden: Nomos. 523–51.

Rosenau, J. N. and E. O. Czempiel (eds) 1992. *Governance without Government. Order and Change in World Politics.* Cambridge: Cambridge University Press.

Sassen, S. 2006. *Territory—Authority—Rights. From Medieval to Global Assemblages.* Princeton: Princeton University Press.

Schmitt, C. 2006. *Political Theology. Four Chapters on the Concept of Sovereignty.* Chicago: University of Chicago Press.

Shonfield, A. 1965. *Modern Capitalism.* Oxford: Oxford University Press.

Slaughter, A. M. 2004. *A New World Order.* Princeton: Princeton University Press.

Wehling, P. 2006. *Im Schatten des Wissens? Perspektiven der Soziologie des Nichtwissens.* Constance: UVK.

Welzer, H. 2008. *Klimakriege. Wofür im 21. Jahrhundert getötet wird.* Frankfurt: S. Fischer.

Zielonka, J. 2006. *Europe as Empire. The Nature of the Enlarged European Union.* Oxford: Oxford University Press.

Zürn, M. 1998. *Regieren jenseits des Nationalstaats. Globalisierung und Denationalisierung als Chance.* Frankfurt: Suhrkamp.

— 2001. "Politik in der postnationalen Konstellation. Über das Elend des methodologischen Nationalismus." In *Politik in einer entgrenzten Welt.* Edited by C. Landfried. Cologne: Verlag Wissenschaft und Politik. 181–204.

# 3

# World Risk Society and National Democracy

Michael Zürn
*Social Science Research Center*

"Risk society" means "that in the course of the exponentially growing productive forces in the modernization process, hazards and potential threats have been unleashed to an extent previously unknown" (Beck 1992, 19). As a consequence, the border-transcending character of economic transactions and civilization risks (as in the exemplary case of climate change) devalues the instruments of nation-states and the basic institutions of industrial society—the "risk society" necessarily mutates into the "world risk society" (Beck 2009).

Against this background, Edgar Grande (2010) has argued that global risks and the rise of the world risk society require new forms of preventive governance which transcend the functional limitations and territorial boundaries of the nation-state. I want to extend this argument: the simultaneous demand for and resistance to forms of preventive governance lead to a politicization of international institutions and thus transforms not only the basic rules of world politics, but also the functioning of national democracies in the western part of the world.

In order to develop this argument I want to proceed in four steps. In the first step, I will show that the inherent features of global risks and the related notion of preventive governance have created a demand for intrusive international regulations. Secondly, since intrusive international institutions exercise power by definition, they become contested and lead to the politicization of international institutions and affairs. This politicization however is selective and thus, thirdly, has far-reaching implications for the democratic institutions of the Western nation-state.

## Global risks and new international institutions

In his contribution to this volume, Edgar Grande (2010, 44) defines global risks by referring to the following features: they are made by humans; they are both already present in reality and present in our thoughts as an anticipation of future developments; they are incalculable; they are global in scope; and they are unlimited in magnitude.

Three of these features of global risks are especially important for the type of regulation required. Since global risks come with an enormous level of uncertainty and are unlimited in magnitude, the concept of *preventive governance* is brought to the fore. Since global risks are unlimited in magnitude and global in scope, there is a demand for governance beyond the nation-state, that is *global governance*.

My thesis therefore is that global risks create regulatory problems which, functionally speaking, require new kinds of *transnational* or *international* regulation. To the extent that this functional demand is met, new types of regulations emerge, which undermine the notion of territorial sovereignty. This becomes manifest when one contrasts typical traditional multilateral institutions with new international institutions in the age of global risks. The GATT regime is a good example of a traditional international institution. Its form of regulation has three distinctive features.

1. States are the ultimate and exclusive target group of regulation. They are issued directives to not increase customs tariffs or to apply them judiciously. The objective of regulations is therefore to influence state behavior in order to resolve the problem in question.
2. Such regulations take effect at the borders between states, and in this sense, they primarily constitute a form of interface management, regulating the transit of goods and "bads" from one national society to another.
3. There is a relatively high degree of certainty as to the effects of such regulations. The actors are able to make relatively precise, empirically sound predictions about the economic consequences of their tariffs.

International institutions for managing global risks have different features. International regimes for overcoming global environmental problems are typical examples here.

1. The ultimate target groups for regulations issued by international institutions are largely societal actors. While states act as intermediaries between international institutions and target groups, societal actors such as consumers and businesses are, in the end, the ones who must alter their behavior in order, say, to reduce $CO_2$ or CFC emissions.
2. New international institutions are no longer merely concerned with interface management. The reduction of pollutants requires regulations that take effect behind national borders, within national societies. In this sense, anticipated international climate regimes regulate behind-the-border issues.
3. These new international institutions are for the most part concerned with finding solutions to highly complex problems. There is, therefore, a high degree of uncertainty as to the ecological and economic consequences of, say, a particular climate regime. The same is not only true of other environmental regimes, but also of financial agreements and regulations on product safety as well as security issues.

In order to successfully tackle highly complex behind-the-border issues (Kahler 1995) with societal actors as the ultimate target groups, these new kinds of international institutions require a more sophisticated institutional design (Zürn 2004). The conventional international obligation not to increase import duties on certain goods is, in retrospect, in many ways a very simple form of regulation. By contrast, the obligation to reduce $CO_2$ emissions by 30 percent has much broader ramifications. Since the ultimate target group of regulations is not the state, but societal actors (such as people who drive cars and the automotive industry), reducting $CO_2$ is not simply a matter of executive prerogative. Unlike most other international regimes, its failure is possible even if signatory governments fully intend to reduce $CO_2$ emissions. Substantial financial, administrative, and technological resources are needed to fulfill such an obligation. What is more, monitoring compliance of such behind-the-border issues is significantly more difficult than with at-the-border issues. In addition, the problem itself is so complex that discussions about appropriate forms of regulation are permanently overshadowed by questions as to the real causes and the actual degree of, for instance, global warming.

A dense network of international regulations and organizations of unprecedented quality and quantity has therefore developed. While it is more than doubtful that the existing set of transnational and international regulations are effective in terms of fully meeting functional demands, they have nevertheless altered the landscape of political institutions significantly. The quantitative growth of international regulation conceived broadly is indicated by the number of United Nations registered international agreements which grew from a total of 8776 treaties in 1960 to 63,419 as of March 25, 2010. If we limit our consideration to the most important multilateral agreements officially drawn up and countersigned in the United Nations, we still find a comparable level of growth: 942 such agreements in 1969 and 6154 in 2010 (see http://treaties. un.org/Pages/Home.aspx?lang=en).

Many of these new international regulations are far more intrusive than conventional international institutions. Two institutional developments are responsible for this qualitative change. On one hand, states have increasingly delegated to international institutions their autonomous power to make decisions. The secretariat of the International Atomic Energy Agency, for instance, monitors regulations, and the World Bank and many other international organizations implement policies autonomously. The most significant development in this respect however is the rise of international dispute settlement bodies. Given the law-making that is required in any case of jurisdiction, the increase in international judicial bodies is especially remarkable (Bogdandy and Venzke 2010). In 1960, there were only 27 quasi-judicial bodies worldwide; by 2004, this number had grown to 97. If we narrow the definition and include only those bodies that meet all the prerequisites for formal judicial proceedings, then only five such bodies existed worldwide in 1960, climbing to 28 by 2004 (see www.pict-pcti.org/matrix/matrixintro.html; see also Alter 2009). A specific look at international environmental regimes shows that about 30 percent of all policy functions are delegated to international organizations. Given the rise of international treaties, the absolute number of such policy functions autonomously performed by international organizations has grown significantly (Green and Colgan 2010, 7).

On the other hand, international institutions without such a formal delegation of power can undermine the consensus principle as well, when decisions are made on the basis of some form of majority voting. Majoritarian decision-making increases the ability of international institutions to act, by canceling the vetoes of individual states and overcoming blockades. Today, roughly two-thirds of all international organizations with the participation of at least one great power are able to decide by majority vote (Blake and Payton 2008). A detailed investigation into international environmental regimes reveals a similar but more differentiated picture. In the area of international environmental policies, there are many cases of decision by majority vote that have been stipulated by agreement. In practice, however, states are actually more strongly consensus oriented in their approach to international environmental problems. Consensus decisions were only prescribed in 20.2 percent of the cases investigated; but in practice, 58.4 percent of all decisions were arrived at through consensus (Breitmeier et al. 2006, 125). Even if decision by majority vote is employed far less often than formally allowed, it nevertheless exerts pressure on veto players and increases their readiness to seek compromise.

To be sure, these trends do not indicate that these new political institutions suffice in terms of appropriately regulating global risks. They do, however, indicate a shift in political authority. Given the extent to which these new international institutions intrude into the affairs of national societies, the notion of "delegated, and therefore controlled authority" (Kahler 2004) in the principal and agent sense no longer holds. Agents—new international institutions with transnational and supranational institutional features—are at best, answerable to a few governments, but they are not answerable to all the societies into which they intrude and certainly not to a transnational society.

## New international institutions and their politicization

Since the new international institutions are intrusive and exercise authority, they become sites of political contestation. The outcome of international negotiations is no longer welcomed merely because a result has been attained. There is a need to justify the procedures for obtaining results in international political processes and their content, but above all the corresponding assignment of authority. The "right to justification" (Forst 2007) is now demanded of international institutions as well. It is called for by numerous, so-called anti-globalization groups such as ATTAC (the Association for the Taxation of Financial Transactions and for Citizens' Action) and the governments of emerging powers as well as by the resistance organized at the national level against the perceived undermining of democratic sovereignty, for example, in referendums on European integration.

However, such activities are not alone in focusing attention on international institutions and treaties. Only part of the current discussion on international institutions is concerned with opposition. Many transnational nongovernmental organizations and social movements are calling for stronger international and transnational organizations to satisfy the need for regulation.[1] For example, many environmental groups advocate a central world environmental organization and drastic intensification of climate policy measures at the international level, or the strengthening of international development policy. Many governments in the North and the South also aim for stronger regulations, for instance, of the financial markets. There is hence a growing demand for stronger international institutions as well.

I refer to this double movement of increasing protests against international institutions and their more intensive utilization as *politicization*. The current politicization of international institutions thus points to a development in which there are challenges to both the deregulation of national governments, which comes from a liberalized international environment, and to international re-regulation in the technocratic mode of executive multilateralism.[2]

A number of indicators point to such a development and reveal that the politicization of international institutions and affairs does indeed take place. First, on the level of individual attitudes, we can see growing recognition of the desirability and importance of international institutions. A considerable percentage of the population believes international institutions are of key importance to an increasing number of problems. Fifty-five percent of the German population believes that the adverse consequences of globalization can best be handled by international institutions (Mau 2007). Solutions to the biggest problems of our time, such as climate change, the financial crisis, the proliferation of weapons of mass destruction, or the fight against terrorism are therefore expected from international institutions and not from the nation-state, which only 11 percent of the population believes to have the necessary problem-solving competence. In view of the denationalization of problems, international institutions are therefore considered fundamentally *desirable*.[3]

Moreover and against this background, many groups make use of favorable responses to turn international institutions—that is, their policies and procedures—into a political topic. An obvious example would be the activities of the anti-globalization movement—a hybrid mix of local action groups, trade unions, political parties, church groups, and nongovernmental organizations. Their particularly effective mode

---

[1]  Terminologically I follow the established practice in international relations, using "international" to refer to societal activities taking place between states and "transnational" to refer to societal cross-border activities. International problems are accordingly the result of dynamics between states, whereas transnational problems are the consequence of cross-border societal activities; international institutions are set up and carried by states; transnational institutions, in contrast, are societally self-regulating.

[2]  "Executive multilateralism" describes a decision-making mode in which governmental representatives (mainly cabinet ministers) from different countries coordinate their policies internationally, but with little national parliamentary control and away from public scrutiny (Zürn 2004, 264). This mode of decision-making was built based on a functional or technocratic justification of the outcomes of negotiations and the permissive consensus that international coordination enjoyed in most societies (Steffek 2011).

[3]  See Ecker-Ehrhardt and Weßels (2011) and Zürn (2011) for more detailed analyses of this development.

of expression is transnational protest, such as the protests that have occurred on the fringes of major government conferences. The growth of these and similar protest events has been impressive. Whereas in the early 1990s, there were fewer than 5 a year, by 2005 the number had risen steadily to just under 35 (Rucht 2011; see also Gronau et al. 2009).

However, the politicization of international institutions cannot be reduced to the critique of globalization. We must also consider the activities of nongovernmental organizations in the environmental, human rights, and development policy fields that address changes in international governance with a mixture of information campaigns, direct persuasion, and media scandals. The success of such norm entrepreneurs (Finnemore and Sikkink 1998; Liese 2006) lies not least in the politicization of the object of decision-making, arousing broad public interest in the demands addressed to institutions. Examples are security policy campaigns in favor of the establishment of an international criminal court or against the production and spread of landmines or small arms. Some campaigns in the human rights and environmental fields also seek to generate public pressure against national and international institutions. The total number of transnational NGOs, which has risen dramatically over the past three decades, indicates the growth of such activities, even though many of these organizations are concerned with implementation and monitoring (Willets 2002).

The politicization of international affairs through classical interest groups and associations is also worth noting. An analysis of how political pressure groups react to denationalized problems shows, on the whole, that associations are increasingly directing their attention to international institutions (Zürn and Walter 2005). The growing presence of interest representatives in governance centers beyond the nation-state, such as Brussels, Geneva, or New York, can be taken as evidence that the associations are focusing more strongly on international institutions (Eising 2009; Greenwood 2007). Finally, the re-emergence of organized resistance to the existing global order by states that complain about Western dominance can be also seen as a politicization of international institutions.

The extent of this politicization, to draw an interim conclusion, is considerable. The increasing politicization of international institutions is apparent both in individual attitudes and in the behavior of societal and political actors. Although the political debate on cross-border problems and the mandates and decisions of international institutions are not omnipresent, they have been expanding. There is politicizing by local action groups and a multiplicity of civil society organizations, companies, and party associations. They politicize in the media, in the streets, and in the forums of political institutions themselves.


## The selectivity of international politicization

It is however not the case that all global issues can be easily politicized. Politicization depends on a number of conditions and thus remains highly selective.

*Sociocultural factors:* James Rosenau made the argument early on that individual and global developments are closely interrelated (Rosenau 1990) and that a skills revolution had a decisive impact on the view of international politics in many societies. Better education has increased the understanding of international processes, and skills are developing for cross-border economic, cultural, and political engagement (Mau 2007). Education, as well as transnational contacts, thus promote the cultivation of a "cosmopolitan perspective" (Beck 2004; Beck and Grande 2007) and encourage "cognitive mobilization" (Inglehart 1970). Among other things, such cognitive mobilization involves the diffusion of ways of thinking in society, that is, substantive orientations toward certain attitudinal patterns and global-order models in which the world is seen as a largely integrated universe of action and where all observations and information are organized accordingly. The societal response to NGO campaigns therefore depends very much on the cognitive mobilization of a public willing to accept as plausible and credible the transnational state of affairs alleged by the campaigns.

What is more, an essential part of politicization is grounded in normative ideas, more precisely in universalistic notions of a humanity with mutual rights and duties (Held 1995; Lu 2000); witness the campaigns conducted by human rights activists (Finnemore and Sikkink 1998; Deitelhoff 2006) and the politicization of globalization critics who strongly emphasize issues of equity (Della Porta and Tarrow 2005). There is much to suggest that cognitive mobilization creates important sociocultural conditions for politicization through analytical and normative ideas, and that these conditions have significantly improved in recent years in the course of such long-term processes as the expansion of education and cross-border networking.

*Institutional factors:* However important so-called sociocultural factors may be, they cannot fully explain concrete instances of politicization, since the global educational revolution has more of an ongoing and long-term impact. Concrete instances of politicization therefore require an institutional setting if they are to manifest themselves in politically relevant forums. The mere existence of international forums is in this sense the basic institutional prerequisite. They provide "coral reefs" (Tarrow 2001) for communication and networking. Anti-globalization protests are considerably facilitated by prominently attended major conferences such as the World Economic Forum, G8/G20 summits, or EU Council meetings. They offer a focal point for bundling many separate activities (Bedoyan et al. 2004). These studies thus point to an important condition for exercising effective political influence, which Claus Offe (1972), on the basis of the theory of collective action (Olsen 1965), has subsumed under the heading "organizational ability."

*Media and technological capacities:* According to Offe (1972), there is a need not only for organizational ability but also for political conflict competence, that is, the effective exercise of political influence is also based on the ability to inhibit system-relevant performance. What appears to be decisive is the ability to throw sand in the works of international institutions by blaming and shaming or, on the opposite extreme, generating support for international policies. The institutional conditions for the politicization of international affairs therefore include access to politically relevant communication forums, that is, particularly the media and the publics that are essentially produced by them. They create the key echo chambers of the transnational politicization process, whose selectiveness essentially determines the presence of their criticism through their analysis of various agents of politicization.

Some anti-globalization movements comply with the selection rules of the media by organizing spectacular large-scale demonstrations that generate "news value" such as relevance and negativity through large numbers of participants and often violent confrontations with security forces (McCarthy et al. 1996). However, such protests struggle with attracting news coverage that goes beyond figures on attendance, arrests, or casualties—the cause itself is often more or less ignored. Some NGOs, in contrast, such as Oxfam, Amnesty International, or Greenpeace have acquired considerable stature of their own in the public mind; they have long since become respected authorities in their fields and hence important sources for journalists who can present them to the public as credible experts (Ecker-Ehrhardt 2009). Moreover, most prominent NGOs have decidedly better access through the observer status they enjoy in many bodies or their good working contacts with international bureaucracies and government or ministry delegations. To some extent, they can make their demands at the international level directly and on the spot or at least through national governments.

All these modes of access are based on a high degree of transnational networking. Influential actors in international governance must be able to show presence in many places at the same time and to bundle this diversity appropriately. Without the new communication and transport technologies, all nongovernmental organizations— however privileged they may be—would scarcely be able to manage this. Without the internet, the political effectiveness of many transnational nongovernmental organizations and their campaigns would be more or less inconceivable (Dahlgren 2005). Nor should the development of international travel be underestimated. If airfares still cost as much as two or three decades ago, there would not have been 150,000 anti-globalization activists at Porto Allegre. The networking of the world, although it creates denationalized problems, nevertheless promotes world-societal links among political actors.

However, fares are still expensive and the technical prerequisites for using the internet are still not globally available. For many people in the world—and thus people affected by international governance—the internet remains more or less out of reach (Norris 2001), favoring the "North" over the political "South" in its politicization potential (Jäger 2007). This is also true of access to international institutions, which in the final analysis remains limited to resource-rich organizations from the highly industrialized countries. Furthermore, the governments with a seat at the table and decisive implementation resources at their disposal are best positioned. The new opportunity structures have their own selectivity and this reproduces existing inequalities in political representation.

## Implications for the future of national democracy

The politicization of international affairs has significant effects on the politics and policies of international negotiations and institutions. I just want to mention a few of them (for a broader exploration see Zürn 2011a): The politicization of international negotiation processes can produce new policies which could not prevail in the mode of executive multilateralism. At the same time, the ratification and implementation of negotiation outcomes will no longer be rubber-stamped by national parliaments for implementation by national administrative authorities. Moreover, international institutions that are strongly politicized will be less likely to be captured by special interests and less likely to be used as instruments by executive decision-makers to circumvent domestic opposition, but may reinforce existing representational inequalities.

However, the politicization of international institutions and affairs also has important implications for the future of the working of national democracies. In the remainder of this chapter, I would like to focus on the effects of the politicization of international institutions and affairs.

First off, the politicization of international affairs points to the possibility that politicians and the national media drastically underestimate the willingness and capacity of the people and their civil-society associations in the political discourse on denationalized problems and international institutions. The widespread tendency of the political class as well as the media to avoid exposing the public to the challenging complexity of international affairs, cultivating instead the myth of national omnipotence along with the associated highly symbolic but often hollow domestic discourses that repeat a series of well-worn positions, is based on false assumptions. There is a growing willingness to politicize the global dimension and this development is hampered by well-established political processes at the national level and the tendency to present the voter with simple truths. In the long term, we may find that the political forces that are most successful are the ones that respond to denationalized problems politically and not technocratically, which use governance beyond the nation-state not only instrumentally for short-term gains—as in blame-shifting and credit claiming (Moravcsik 1994)—but also consider it an essential component of a value-charged political order.

It follows that the widespread dissatisfaction with the state of national democracy and its depoliticization needs to be relativized. The most important points in this criticism are the dramatic decline in membership in all large parties, falling voter turnout, substanceless election campaigns and parliamentary debates, and political reporting that concentrates on questions of claims and intrigues devoid of political content. But this view remains one-sided, for the growing willingness to commit oneself to specific goals in transnational organizations may possibly replace engagement in national politics. This is certainly not a zero-sum game, but the analysis strengthens the intuition that politicization is directed toward what is important, namely the exercise of public authority. In short, politics is not dying out as is often feared: it is emigrating (Beck 2004, 321).

This also contradicts the theses of a post-democratic age unless one limits the concept of democracy exclusively to the institutionalized confrontation between left and right in the context of a nationally constituted parliamentary democracy (Crouch 2008; Mouffe 2007). But if the democratic principle implies that everyone significantly affected by a decision should have a say, then the shift of the political discourse to international institutions that are exercising increasing authority is valid.

Secondly, Grande and Kriesi (2009, 2011) rightly point out that the focus of "cosmopolitan" criticisms of globalization and NGO campaigns leads many observers to underestimate the potential of the anti-cosmopolitan politicization of international institutions. The rise of right-wing populist parties over the past two decades is evidence of this anti-cosmopolitan potential, as is the now manifest resistance to greater European integration.

The "cosmopolitan perspective" may thus be widespread at the transnational and international levels, but it is opposed by the decidedly "communitarian perspective" adopted by a considerable proportion of people who take a critical view of cultural heterogeneity and social as well as political openness. Although the anti-cosmopolitan perspective is nurtured largely by "globalization losers," groups who have lost or fear losing jobs or status through economic expansion and who lack the media and technological capacities for transnational organization, the communitarian standpoint is not restricted to globalization losers. It is grounded not only in poor education and a failure to comprehend complexity but also, like cosmopolitanism, in understandable beliefs about the importance of boundaries and the advantages of homogeneity (see, for example, Putnam 2007). Both cosmopolitanism and communitarianism have reductionist offshoots that play a major role in political practice. Like the right-wing, populist, nationalistic position that reduces communitarianism to an ideology and exploits it instrumentally, there is a globalist position that in its economic bias ignores the element of global concern and thus reduces cosmopolitanism to a class consciousness of frequent travelers (Calhoun 2003). It is this equivalence of positions—cosmopolitanism and globalism on the one hand and communitarianism and nationalism on the other—that possibly makes this debate the critical divide of the twenty-first century.[4]

The equivalence of standpoints in this debate is however accompanied by greater asymmetry in opportunities for influence. Although the politicization of international institutions deprives executive multilateralism of its exclusivity, politicized but not

---

[4]  It would therefore be wrong to reduce nationalist criticism of international institutions to a backward-looking resistance to the challenges a transnational and complex world presents for local and national customs. Such a standpoint, which sees world-societal functional systems in opposition to local political communities, underestimates the reflexivity of political discourse at the beginning of the twenty-first century. We must unite criticism of the deficient legitimacy of existing international institutions and criticism of the missing regulation of world-societal processes: they are two sides of the same coin. With reference to Carl Schmitt (1932), Chantal Mouffe (2007) criticizes the theory of reflexive modernity (Ulrich Beck, Anthony Giddens) from the point of view of antagonal theories of democracy, claiming that it overestimates dialogistic procedures and ignores the core of politics, namely fundamental, identity-forming conflicts. This criticism may not be unjustified. However, both sides in the debate appear to overlook the formative power of the difference between the cosmopolitan/globalist position and the communitarian/nationalistic position. To a considerable extent, it structures the political discourse within and beyond the nation-state.

fully democratized international institutions nevertheless reproduce selectivity. The preference accorded to the views and interests of developed industrial societies is perpetuated in international institutions thanks to the importance of cognitive skills and the structural advantage of universalistic positions. At issue are not only the advantages of deregulating market-creating positions over market-correcting policies (see with varying emphasis Streeck 1997; Crouch 2008; Scharpf 2009), but also those of giving broader preference to universalistic, deterritorialized standpoints as opposed to communitarian, limiting standpoints.

To the extent that cosmopolitan positions dominate political arenas beyond the nation-state and use them mainly for purposes of agenda-setting and compliance with international norms within nation-states, they can strengthen their position in national political arenas without necessarily being in the majority position. At the same time, communitarian political forces are put on the defensive and appear parochial. To the extent that this hypothesis holds, it provides an explanation for the growing distance between the positions of political, economic, and cultural elites, and those of mass publics and electorates in the age of globalization.

At the end of the day, this asymmetry weakens both. What is needed, therefore, is greater internationalization of the national discourse, which also appears to be socioculturally feasible. But selectivities beyond the nation-state also need to be reduced. This can only be achieved by also reforming international institutions in the direction of procedural universalism. A reform of international institutions with the aim to reduce asymmetries in interest representation and selectivity in the application of rules is required. If this does not succeed, the cosmopolitan outlook can all too easily degenerate into a cosmopolitanism of the few—which would do no service to democracy.

# Bibliography

Alter, K. J. 2009. *The European Court's Political Power. Selected Essays*. Oxford: Oxford University Press.

Beck, U. 1992. *Risk Society*. Cambridge: Polity Press.

— 2004. *Der kosmopolitische Blick oder: Krieg ist Frieden*. Frankfurt: Suhrkamp.

— 2009. *World at Risk*. Cambridge: Polity Press.

Beck, U. and E. Grande. 2007. *Das kosmopolitische Europa*. Frankfurt: Suhrkamp.

Bedoyan, I., P. Van Aelst, and S. Walgrave. 2004. "Limitations and Possibilities of Transnational Mobilization: The Case of EU Summit Protesters in Brussels 2001." *Mobilization* 9(1): 39–54.

Blake, D. and A. Payton. 2008. "Voting Rules in International Organizations: Reflections of Power or Facilitators of Cooperation?" Paper Presented at ISA's 49th Annual Convention, San Francisco, CA, March 26–29, 2008.

Bogdandy, A. V. and I. Venzke. 2010. "Zur Herrschaft internationaler Gerichte: Eine Untersuchung internationaler öffentlicher Gewalt und ihrer demokratischen Rechtfertigung." *Zeitschrift für ausländisches öffentliches Recht und Völkerrecht* 70(1): 1–49.

Breitmeier, H., O. R. Young, and M. Zürn. 2006. *Analyzing International Environmental Regimes. From Case Study to Database.* Cambridge, MA: MIT Press.

Calhoun, C. 2003. "The Class Consciousness of Frequent Travellers: Towards a Critique of Actually Existing Cosmopolitanism." In *Debating Cosmopolitics.* Edited by Daniele Archibugi. London: Verso. 86–116.

Crouch, C. 2008. *Postdemokratie.* Frankfurt: Suhrkamp.

Dahlgren, P. 2005. "The Internet, Public Spheres, and Political Communication: Dispersion and Deliberation." *Political Communication* 22(2): 147–62.

Deitelhoff, N. 2006. *Überzeugung in der Politik. Grundzüge einer Diskurstheorie internationalen Regierens.* Frankfurt: Suhrkamp.

Della Porta, D. and S. Tarrow (eds) 2005. *Transnational Protest and Global Activism.* Lanham: Rowman & Littlefield.

Ecker-Ehrhardt, M. 2009. "Inter- und transnationale Organisationen als symbolische Autoritäten der Mediendemokratie." In *Politik in der Mediendemokratie. PVS— Sonderheft 42/2009.* Edited by F. Marcinkowski and B. Pfetsch. Wiesbaden: VS Verlag für Sozialwissenschaften. 585–608.

Ecker-Ehrhardt, M. and B. Weßels. 2011. "Input- oder Output-Politisierung Internationaler Organisationen? Der kritische Blick der Bürger auf Demokratie und Leistung." In *Gesellschaftliche Politisierung und internationale Institutionen.* Edited by M. Zürn and M. Ecker-Ehrhardt. Berlin: Suhrkamp. 36–61.

Eising, R. 2009. *The Political Economy of State-Business Relations in Europe: Interest Mediation, Capitalism and EU Policy Making.* London: Routledge.

Finnemore, M. and K. Sikkink. 1998. "International Norm Dynamics and Political Change." *International Organization* 52(4): 887–917.

Forst, R. 2007. *Das Recht auf Rechtfertigung. Elemente einer konstruktivistischen Theorie der Gerechtigkeit.* Frankfurt: Suhrkamp.

Grande, E. 2010. "Global Risks and Preventive Governance." Paper Presented at Governing Global Risks—Munich Center on Governance. April 23–24, 2010.

Grande, E. and H. Kriesi. 2011. "Das Doppelgesicht der Politisierung. Zur Transformation politischer Konfliktstrukturen im Prozess der Globalisierung." In *Gesellschaftliche Politisierung und internationale Institutionen.* Edited by M. Zürn and M. Ecker-Ehrhardt. Frankfurt: Suhrkamp. 84–108.

Green, J. F. and J. Colgan. 2010. "Is There Really a Power Shift? Delegating Authority in Global Environmental Politics." Paper Presented at Standing Group on International Relations—7th Pan-European Conference on IR, Stockholm, September 9–11, 2010.

Greenwood, J. 2007. *Interest Representation in the European Union.* Basingstoke: Palgrave Macmillan.

Gronau, J., M. Nonhoff, S. Schneider, and F. Nullmeier. 2009. "Spiele ohne Brot? Die Legitimationskrise der G8." *Leviathan* 37(1): 117–43.

Held, D. 1995. *Democracy and the Global Order. From the Modern State to Cosmopolitical Governance.* Cambridge: Polity Press.

Inglehart, R. 1970. "Cognitive Mobilization and European Identity." *Comparative Politics* 3(1): 47–70.

Jäger, H. M. 2007. "*Global Civil Society* and the Political Depoliticization of Global Governance." *International Political Sociology* 1(3): 257–77.

Kahler, M. 1995. *International Institutions and the Political Economy of Integration.* Washington, DC: Brookings Institution.— 2004. "Defining Accountability up: The Global Economic Multilaterals." *Government and Opposition* 39(2): 132–58.

Kriesi, H., E. Grande, R. Lachat, and M. Dolezal. 2009. *West European Politics in the Age of Globalization*. Cambridge: Cambridge University Press.

Liese, A. 2006. *Staaten am Pranger. Zur Wirkung internationaler Regime auf innerstaatliche Menschenrechtspolitik*. Wiesbaden: VS Verlag für Sozialwissenschaften.

Lu, C. 2000. "The One and Many Faces of Cosmopolitanism." *The Journal of Political Philosophy* 8(2): 244–67.

Mau, S. 2007. *Transnationale Vergesellschaftung. Die Entgrenzung sozialer Lebenswelten*. Frankfurt: Campus Verlag.

McCarthy, J. D., C. McPhail, and J. Smith. 1996. "Images of Protest: Dimensions of Selection Bias in Media Coverage of Washington Demonstrations, 1982 and 1991." *American Sociological Review* 61(3): 478–99.

Moravcsik, A. 1994. *Why the European Community Strengthens the State: Domestic Politics and International Cooperation*. Cambridge: Harvard University Press Harvard University, Center for European Studies, Working Paper Series 52.

Mouffe, C. 2007. *Über das Politische wider die kosmopolitische Illusion*. Frankfurt: Suhrkamp.

Norris, P. 2001. *Digital Divide: Civic Engagement, Information Poverty, and the Internet Worldwide*. Cambridge: Cambridge University Press.

Offe, C. 1972. "Klassenherrschaft und politisches System. Zur Selektivität politischer Institutionen." In *Strukturprobleme des kapitalistischen Staates*. Edited by C. Offe. Frankfurt: Suhrkamp. 65–107.

Olsen, M. 1965. *The Logic of Collective Action: Public Goods and the Theory of Groups*. Cambridge: Harvard University Press.

Putnam, R. D. 2007. "E Pluribus Unum: Diversity and Community in the Twenty-first Century—The 2006 Johan Skytte Prize Lecture." *Scandinavian Political Studies* 30(2): 137–74.

Rosenau, J. N. 1990. *Turbulence in World Politics. A Theory of Change and Continuity*. Princeton: Princeton University Press.

Rucht, D. 2011. "Globalisierungskritische Proteste als Herausforderung an die internationale Politik." In *Gesellschaftliche Politisierung und internationale Institutionen*. Edited by M. Zürn and M. Ecker-Ehrhardt. Frankfurt: Suhrkamp.

Scharpf, F. W. 2009. "Legitimität im europäischen Mehrebenensystem." *Leviathan* 37(2): 244–80.

Schmitt, C. 1932. *Der Begriff des Politischen*. München: Duncker und Humblot.

Steffek, J. 2011. "Mandatskonflikte, Liberalismuskritik und die Politisierung von GATT und WTO." In *Gesellschaftliche Politisierung und internationale Institutionen*. Edited by M. Zürn and M. Ecker-Ehrhardt. Frankfurt: Suhrkamp. 213–39.

Streeck, W. 1997. "Vom Binnenmarkt zum Bundesstaat? Überlegungen zur politischen Ökonomie der europäischen Sozialpolitik." In *Standort Europa: Europäische Sozialpolitik*. Edited by S. Leibfried and P. Pierson. Frankfurt: Suhrkamp. 369–422.

Tarrow, S. 2001. "Transnational Politics: Contention and Institutions in International Politics." *Annual Review of Political Science* 4(1): 1–20.

Willets, P. 2002. "The Growth in the Number of NGOs in Consultative Status with the Economic and Social Council of the United Nations." Available at www.staff.city.ac.uk/p.willetts/NGOS/NGO-GRPH.HTM. [Accessed September 20, 2010].

Zürn, M. 2004. "Global Governance under Legitimacy Pressure." *Government and Opposition* 39(2): 260–87.

— 2011a. *The Politicization of World Politics and Its Effects on Democracy: Ten Hypotheses.* Unpublished paper.

— 2011b. "Vier Modelle globaler Ordnung in kosmpolitischer Absicht." *Politische Vierteljahresschrift* 52(1): i.p.

Zürn, M. and G. Walter (eds) 2005. *Globalizing Interests: Pressure Groups and Denationalization*. Albany: State University of New York Press.

# 4

# (How) Do We Need to Change Political Philosophy to Take Risk into Account?

Daniel M. Weinstock
*University of Montréal*

Is there something radically new about the kinds of risks that modern societies face today? If so, do these differences require that we rethink the tasks of the modern state? And how should political philosophy respond to these changes? Are the conceptual resources and arguments that have occupied the state in the modern era inadequate to address the new imperatives it faces?

This essay is a modest contribution to answering these questions. My principal conclusion is that these questions are, as posed, too coarse-grained. Many distinct realities have been defined as "risks" by social theorists and philosophers. Once we unpack the concept, we will see that it refers to a heterogeneous set of factors that characterize our modern condition and the dangers that we moderns face. Some are familiar, and others are not. Furthermore, among the senses of the term that point to new challenges, we find meanings that do not admit a single answer to any of the aforementioned questions.

A political philosophy of risk must therefore begin by "exploding" the notion of risk in order to identify its constituent, finer-grained concepts. Accordingly, this is the task to which I will devote the first section of this chapter. I will then, in a second section, identify meanings that have been given to the notion of risk that do not, in my opinion, point to any radically novel features of our (post-)modern world. In a third section, I will identify meanings that are arguably novel, but suggest that the tasks they set for political philosophy are quite varied. I will in other words argue that there is no *single* manner in which risk changes the way political philosophers should construe their task.

**1.** As Sven Ove Hansson has shown, the concept of "risk" was already polysemic even before talk of the "risk society" and its challenges became popular in academic and policy circles. Risk, as Hansonn defines it, refers rather prosaically to any unwanted event. The ambiguity of the term stems from the fact that we have used it in a rather undisciplined manner to refer to the event itself, to its causes, to its probability, to the expected disutility associated with it, or to the process that attends decision-making in conditions of uncertainty (Hansonn 2011).

It would be difficult to imagine that someone might make use of the term "risk" if they did not want to refer in some way or other to unwanted events. But if risk is understood in any of the manners just canvassed, there is clearly nothing new about it. We face risks every day, and it has clearly been part of the modern state's central mandate to protect against serious damages. The very image of the "social safety net" that is routinely used to illustrate the functions of the welfare states makes plain that its job is to prevent serious harm from befalling its citizens. Indeed, François Ewald has argued in one of the most penetrating analyses we possess of the welfare state and its emergence that its very *raison d'être* has from its inception had to do with the management of risk (Ewald 1986).

This family of definitions of risk clearly does not account for the apocalyptic tones and the urgent calls for new ways of thinking about the state and the economy that have become prevalent in much modern writing about risk. A survey of the literature reveals that the conceptions of risk that animate talk of a "risk society" or of a "world of risk" reveals quite plainly that contemporary theorists are not referring just to any "unwanted events" when they use the word. What follows is almost certainly a non-exhaustive listing of the most relevant properties of the subset of "unwanted events" that the new theorists of risk have in mind.

*Scope.* According to many theorists of risk, what is distinctive about the kinds of risks that call for reconceptualization in political theory is that they cannot be contained within traditional nation-state boundaries. Risks are continental, even global, but they are certainly no longer purely national. The dimension of scope can be further refined by noting that a risk can transcend the scope of the nation-state in any (or all) of the following ways. First, a risk to which citizens of a nation-state are vulnerable might *originate* outside of the jurisdiction of a nation-state. Second, the risk in question can be one that is *faced* by citizens of more than one nation-state. And third, the policy tools needed in order to *address* risks may require the collaboration of other states or of transnational agents or both. These different ways of refining the idea that modern risks are transnational in scope are moreover logically independent, and empirically, we can point to risks that have been characterized by one of these scope extensions, but not the others.[1]

*Severity.* Some theorists believe that there are now risks that confront humanity in an unprecedented way which call for changes in the way we conceive of the tasks of the state and of political philosophy. One of the factors that must be kept in mind about these risks is the severity of apprehended costs. In other words, what is at issue today is not that human beings face risks, but that these risks might potentially impose unprecedented costs. Thus, it is not risk per se but rather *catastrophic* risk that requires that we rethink the way in which we conceive of our politics. Now, catastrophe itself is a polysemic term. Catastrophic risks can be limited to risks

---

[1]  The allegedly global scope of modern risks is a main theme of Ulrich Beck's *World at Risk* (2008).

threatening the very possibility of life on the planet, the kind of risk that Richard Posner discusses in his book *Catastrophe: Risk and Response*.[2] These include such low-probability but potentially apocalyptic events as asteroid collisions with the Earth, accidents at particle accelerator facilities, and the like. But the idea of catastrophic risk has also been employed to encompass events that would give rise to large-scale loss of life, such as pandemics of virulent viral strains, societal dislocation due to dramatic atmospheric events, or large-scale terrorist strikes. Moving down the scale, risks of economic upheavals caused by the bursting of financial "bubbles" and losses of life on the scale of those wrought by terrorist strikes such as the attacks in the United States on September 11, 2001, are seen by some theorists as sufficiently extensive that we must speak of an entirely new kind of risk.

*Complexity.* One aspect of the risks that face modern societies that has generated talk of a new era of risk has to do with causal complexity. It is, in other words, difficult to clearly identify the precise causes of some unwanted events. Unwanted events are often the result of concatenations of causal factors that are difficult to disentangle. What is more, cause and effect relations are often spread out over long periods of time, since many modern threats have long latency periods, which further complicates the attempt to assign causal responsibility (to say nothing of moral and legal responsibility). In addition, where causal attribution is difficult, so is causal control. Thus, the novelty of some of the risks that we face has to do with the fact that even prudent policy-makers will find it difficult to activate the appropriate causal levers or to identify causal responsibility-bearers.

*Uncertainty.* According to some risk theorists, it is the uncertainty that attaches to many possible unwanted events that makes modern risk qualitatively distinct from risks of the past. Determining the devaluation of a risk is typically thought to require the assigning of a probability to the unwanted event. When an unwanted event is *uncertain*, such assignments are difficult or impossible.

*Technology.* According to some theorists, one of the novel characteristics of present-day risks is that they are largely man-made. That is, they are the unintended consequences of technologies and industrial processes developed ostensibly to promote human welfare, but which have proven to give rise to consequences that more than offset whatever advantages they generate (Shrader-Frechette 1991).

*Irreversibility.* Some people believe that the crucial aspect of the threats to which the modern era of risk makes us vulnerable is that they cannot be undone. This can mean either one or both of two things. The damage that would be created when a risk occurs would be permanent. It can also mean that there is no way to be compensated for these damages nor can technological fixes be found to circumvent their effects (Beck 2001, 41; Ewald 1986, 418).

A first point to be made about this list, other than to point out that it is quite obviously not exhaustive, is that its elements are logically distinct. Severity, scope, complexity, uncertainty, irreversibility, and level of human, technological, causal responsibility can vary independently of one another.

---

[2] See Posner (2004). For another attempt at isolating a distinct category of truly "catastrophic" or "disastrous" risks, see Zack (2009).

That being said, the dimensions of risk that are seen as the harbingers of a new era of risk are typically not taken to occur in complete isolation. Rather, they usually combine several of these features contingently. What is more, it is assumed by all risk theorists that the risks that call for changes in our ways of thinking about the responsibilities of the state and of political philosophy will always be of significant, though perhaps not catastrophic, severity. Severity is, in other words, an ingredient of all the kinds of risks that are taken to characterize our modern "risk societies."

To use technology as a dimension that occurs differently depending on the risk at issue, risks born of terrorist threats or of certain strains of influenza are causally related to technology in indirect ways. The means at the disposal of terrorists are clearly a function of existing levels of technological development, and the careers of viruses are connected causally to levels of technology in different ways. The crossing of the species barrier is made easier according to some accounts by certain practices of animal husbandry, and speed of transmission varies according to levels of economic integration and modes of transportation. But they are not causally related to technology and to industrial processes in the same way, say, as global warming is related to the greenhouse gas emissions created by modern industrial processes.

At any rate, it seems clear to me that attending to these separable, quite distinct dimensions of different unwanted events reveals, first, that some of them have been with us for a long time, and second, that those types of risk that do seem to characterize the modern era do not necessarily point toward the same kinds of political solutions. I now turn my attention to fleshing out these two points.

**2.** Modern states have clearly had to face large-scale risks to the health and welfare of their populations from the moment of their inception. For example, infectious disease has been a scourge upon human populations at every period of human history, and modern policy-makers have seen the eradication, or at the very least, the limitation of the cost in terms of human lives afflicted by viral and bacterial disease as a priority at least since the nineteenth century. Many familiar aspects of modern urban planning have resulted from the attempt in a number of European cities to understand, and then to halt, the spread of diseases such as cholera. Modern water filtration systems that provide safe drinking water to millions in cities around the world owe their origins to the fight against water-borne diseases.[3]

Attending to the particularities of the risk that infectious disease represents in terms of the categorization offered in the previous section reveals that it shares many characteristics with "newer" risks. In other words, many of the features that theorists of the "new risks" view as distinctively modern clearly attach to infectious diseases, which are anything but resolutely modern.

For example, while some viral pandemics, such as the Hong Kong flu of 1968 or the so-called swine flu of 2009–10 did not cause the levels of loss of life that would warrant the use of the term "catastrophic," others clearly have. Most obviously, the Spanish Flu of 1918–19 caused tens of millions of deaths around the world. And it has been all too easy for the European settler populations of North America to forget that

---

[3]  The story is well told by Steven Johnson (2006).

many aboriginal nations were all but wiped out by the cocktail of viruses that were communicated to them, often intentionally, by white settlers, and against which they had no native immunity.

The global reach of infectious disease is not a feature of the modern period either, as the Spanish Flu pandemic eloquently testifies, though it has arguably been intensified by economic globalization and by modern forms of transportation. As for uncertainty and complexity, they are a feature of the fight against infectious disease today just as they were in the past. Epidemics and pandemics often result from the combination of animal and human viral strains into a single virus. Epidemiologists and virologists concede that it is difficult, if not impossible, to predict when such a combination will occur. What is more, viruses are rapidly mutating entities, and probabilistic models aimed at predicting their mutations are shot through with uncertainty. Finally, though viral and bacterial infections have single underlying causes that are not too difficult to identify, transmission vectors—the identification of which is as important to halting the spread of infection as is the mapping of the genetic make-up of the virus or bacterium—has historically proven much more difficult. (The key to understanding the 1854 cholera outbreak in London was figuring out that the cholera virus is water-borne rather than air-borne.)

Thus infectious disease provides us with an example of a source of risk that has existed well before the advent of the era of risk and that possesses some of the features that are taken to characterize this newer era of risk.

There can be no doubt that modern technology has created risk scenarios that would have been inconceivable just a generation ago. The infinitesimally small risks of serious accidents at modern supercollider facilities that would, as Sir Martin Rees describes it, "transform the entire planet into an inert hyperdense sphere about one hundred meters across," are plainly the result of distinctively modern technologies (Rees 2004).

It would however be overly simplistic to hold that we are only now entering a period in which the technological achievements of mankind have begun to generate corresponding risks. Industrialization has wrought environmental risks from its earliest phases. Earlier phases of the process of industrialization were rife with serious respiratory diseases that resulted from unregulated factory emissions and industrial by-products, and such diseases are still most prevalent in countries that have yet to regulate such emissions adequately.

Many of the catastrophic risks we face today, risks that are severe in their consequences, whose occurrences are often shrouded in uncertainty and whose effects are often transnational, even when they are not truly global, are moreover independent of any technological causes, even when their effects are mediated and often even worsened by technological vectors. Earthquakes and tsunamis, hurricanes and floods, most often have entirely or largely natural causes.

We might in fact ask ourselves the following question: given that the history of risk is marked both by continuities and by contrasts, rather than by the kinds of ruptures that the contemporary risk discourse sometimes suggests, what accounts for the fact that our perception, both specialist and public, is that we now live in an unparalleled era of risk?

I offer the following two explanatory hypotheses.

First, the knowledge and technology that states presently wield in order both to understand the causes of potential large-scale damages and to act both on those causes and on the consequences of the risk's having occured is much greater today than it was in earlier eras (e.g. to return to some of the examples given above, the early warning systems that are presently at our disposal to predict the onset of earthquakes and of severe meteorological events are far more sophisticated than those that would have been at the disposal of decision-makers just a generation ago). The epistemic gap under which previous generations of policy-makers, political philosophers, and politicians had to labor were such that they had no choice but to manifest greater fatalism in the face of the prospect of large-scale harms.

A first hypothesis that bears exploring is accordingly that the sense that we presently have, which is reflected in the academic literature as well as in public consciousness, that we live in an era of risks incommensurably greater than ever before may actually stem from the fact that our capacity to limit the impact of risks has increased, and we therefore perceive our inability to fully master them as something of an affront to our technological capacity. The greater our sense that we are able to control our environment, the greater our outrage and fear when it turns out that we cannot, and that even more ironically some of the greatest risks we face are due to our attempts at achieving such control.

A second hypothesis has to do with the patterns of distribution of the harms that modern catastrophes have generated. In his path-breaking book *The Risk Society*, Ulrich Beck makes the point that one of the distinctive traits of the modern era is that the affluent can no longer effectively insulate themselves from "new risks" (2001, 66). A human, all-too-human, explanation of the attention paid to risk today would point to the fact that risks are more likely to reach the top of the policy-making agenda when the rich and powerful are affected by them.

Be that as it may, the point I would like to make in this section is quite limited: once we break down the very broad and encompassing concept of risk into more epistemically tractable components, we can see that it is at least an exaggeration to claim that we presently live in an era of risk wholly unlike any that humankind has ever had to face.

**3.** I now want to turn my attention briefly to three dimensions of modern risks which, on the assumption that they are new and that they call for radical changes in the way in which we construe the role of the state, actually seem to exercise theoretical pressure in opposite directions. The first has to do with the increasing global scope of risk, and the second has to do with its arguably greater complexity.

I have suggested above that there may not be as much new under the sun with respect to risk as some of the exponents of the "risk society" have led us to believe. The prospect of infectious disease and of natural disasters, and to some degree of the unintended consequences of natural disasters, all bear many of the properties that contemporary risks do, and they have been part of the policy-making landscape at least since the birth of the modern state.

Aspects of modern risk that have arguably increased in the modern era have to do with *complexity* and with *scope*. Economic finances and economic globalization have made people's economic livelihoods increasingly vulnerable to the actions and decisions of individuals and states situated very far away. The clearest example of a risk that has attained global proportions is the environment, and in particular, the effects of climate change. Rising ocean temperatures caused by greenhouse gas emissions have led to more violent hurricanes and tropical storms, which have caused death and destruction in societies that lie in the path of those weather events. The melting of the polar ice cap is contributing to very disquieting increases in sea and ocean levels, the impact of which is projected to create hundreds of thousands, and perhaps even millions, of climate refugees in the very near future.

It is impossible to isolate a single agent that is responsible for the dramatic climate events we are presently witnessing. The causes of global climate change are truly global. Nor can the effects of climate change be geographically contained. Some regions of the globe are at greater risk from rising water levels and from desertification in the short term, but the environmental refugees that these processes will create will represent a problem even for regions that are not directly affected, both as a matter of fact and as a matter of justice (Westra 2009). It is inconceivable that the warming of the atmosphere that has led to the situation in which we now find ourselves can be addressed by a single national agent or by a plurality of agents acting in an uncoordinated manner. The risks posed by global warming are thus paradigmatic of the emergence of risks that are truly global in character, and that transcend the carrying capacity of even the most powerful and technologically developed states. They represent in Stephen Gardiner's words "a test for contemporary institutions and theories" (2010).

The following claims seem fairly uncontroversial. First, both the economic impacts of globalization and the impact of climate change upon the livability of certain parts of the planet raise issues of fairness. Even a moderate version of the "all affected principle"[4] leads to the conclusion that those who have predictable uncompensated and unconsented externalities visited upon them through other people's actions have a legitimate claim of fairness against the other people, either to cease the actions in question, or to offer compensation for the disruptions their actions have caused. Second, contemporary theories of liberal democracy and of liberal justice, as well as the practices and institutions of existing liberal democracies, focused as they are on the nation-state and its interests and claims of justice, present members as the appropriate locus for discussions of justice, but they are ill-equipped to deal with such claims, that are very often transnational (and intergenerational) in nature.

Therefore, political philosophy, and the nation-states that have for much of the modern history of political philosophy represented the paradigm case of the political agent, must change so as to imagine political institutions that might encompass the interests and legitimate claims (including a claim to democratic voice) of citizens of all the countries that are affected by global climate change. The exact nature of the changes that the rise of global risks should have upon political philosophy is not an issue that I take up within the limited confines of this chapter.[5] The point I want to make is that,

---

[4]   The all-affected principle claims that all people affected by a policy ought morally to have some say with respect to that policy. For a statement and defense of the principle, see Goodin (2007).

[5]   I have made a small contribution to this question in my "The (Real) World of Global Democracy," in *Journal of Social Philosophy*, 37(1), 2006, 6–26.

to the extent that new risks involve a widening of the range of the causes of risks, as well as the range of people affected by risks, and the range of actors that need to be involved in devising appropriate institutional policy and institutional responses to risk, then what is called for is a widening of our conception of democracy and of justice. Mechanisms must be found whereby the claims of those affected by financial and industrial policies with global economic and environmental impact are heard, and theories of justice (and matching institutions) must be devised wherein the relevant range of interests are fairly weighed to generate fair outcomes.

Let us assume for the sake of argument that modern risks are also characterized by their *irreversibility*. That is, the damages with which they threaten us cannot be undone, or reversed by the passage of time, nor can technological fixes be found that might lessen the loss of welfare that is imposed upon human beings when the risk in question occurs.

If the global reach of modern risks forces us to expand our conceptions of democracy and of justice spatially, irreversibility would lead us to deepen them diachronically. The irreversible nature of modern risks points toward the need to take into account not just the legitimate claims of contemporaneous people, wherever they might find themselves, as long as they are affected by the damage that the occurrence of unwanted events create, but also those of *future generations*, whose interests and rights are irreversibly affected by decisions taken by prior generations.

The question of how to represent and give voice to the legitimate claims of future generations in a just fashion is a fiendishly difficult philosophical puzzle that has occupied the minds of some of the greatest philosophers of the postwar period, including John Rawls (1971) and Derek Parfit (1983). It has turned among other things on the just rate at which the future can be discounted in our present reckoning of the weight to give to temporally disparate interests. It is also complicated by the fact that present policies will impact the identity of the people who live in the future; some theorists suggest that this makes it difficult to compare different present policy options with respect to their future impacts. My intention as above is not to come down on one side or the other of the debate as to the proper way in which to extend our theories of democracy and justice intergenerationally. It is more modestly to point to a direction that must be taken by political philosophers intent on understanding the way in which new risks must reshape the agenda of political philosophers.

The globalization of risk would therefore seem to call for an expansion of democratic mechanisms beyond the nation-state, and for conceptions of justice that take into account the rights and interests of all those affected by the actions of the nation-states most responsible for global warming. But another dimension which is said to warrant a fundamental rethinking of the way in which the state manages risk and the way political philosophers think about the requirements of democracy has to do with the great complexity that attends modern risks.

Modern risks—and here risks wrought by climate change might serve as a paradigm case—are said to be complex in a variety of ways. First, the causal factors at play in creating the climate events that threaten the well-being of people around the planet are various, and they interact in complex ways. Second, the results of the causal operation of multifarious factors are also shrouded in uncertainty. Small differences in impact can mean the difference between climate change that, though causing hardship for people living in the hardest hit regions, is nonetheless not beyond the carrying capacity of modern states, versus scenarios that would truly be catastrophic and that would quite literally make certain regions of the world that are at present quite densely populated uninhabitable.

Some people argue that ordinary citizens simply lack the cognitive sophistication to deal with complex risks. Cass Sunstein, who is at present President Obama's chief regulator, has argued in a number of books that when faced with risks, people generally tend to reach for heuristics that allow them to simplify the task of reasoning about unwanted future events that are marked by causal and statistical complexity. Additionally, populations as a whole tend to be vulnerable to a series of collective flaws in reasoning that result from "cascade" effects and from the communicable nature of fear. As a result, if they are given too much of a decision-making role, they will tend to make costly mistakes, by succumbing to heuristics rather than engaging in the kind of sober, cost–benefit analysis that Sunstein recommends (2002, 2005, 2009). Rather than calling for an enlargement of the way in which institutions of justice and democratic decision-making processes are designed, the complexity inherent in modern-day risks requires, according to Sunstein, affording more discretion to experts who, having identified the errors in reasoning to which common folk are prone, can better resist those errors. They will then reach decisions in the cold light of facts and probabilities rather than in the heat produced by fear and collective dysfunctions of reasoning.

Now, the conclusions drawn by Sunstein about the impact that modern risks should have upon the way in which democracies go about their business have been contested by some. For example, Martin Kusch has argued that Sunstein's work ignores the biases and simplifying heuristics to which scientific "experts" are themselves vulnerable. As is the case for any group, pressures to conform that push people to trust the judgment of others within the group without questioning their epistemic authority can easily make themselves felt within a scientific community. It is always easier to "go along" with consensuses that have been arrived at by others than it is to take an independent stand on the facts. Furthermore, very practical considerations that are absent from the modes of reasoning of ordinary citizens such as pressures related to funding or political pressures can make themselves felt among communities of experts and distort judgment to a significant degree (Kusch 2007).

In addition, what may seem like simple cognitive disagreements that might arise between citizens and experts, where experts would appear at first glance to be able to claim epistemic privilege, may actually involve conflicts of value. As Sven Ove Hansson and others have pointed out, when cognitive criteria are transferred into debates about risk assessment, they raise normative issues, related to issues such as thresholds of risk tolerance (Hanson 2007). As Kritin Shrader Frechette has argued repeatedly, the public's refusal to view cost/benefit analyses as definitional of a rational approach to risk management need not be construed as a failure of rationality. Rather, the public may have legitimate normative reasons to feel that certain decisions should be made outside the cold, hard logic of cost/benefit analysis (Schrader Frechette 1991).

My intention here, as with the problems of scope and irreversibility, is not to settle the issue between advocates of an expert-driven approach emphasizing methods such as cost–benefit analysis and those who believe that popular views about risk should not be considered epistemically inferior. My goal, as in the previous cases, is to point to a space within which political philosophers intent on redefining the mandate of political philosophy in the light of new risks will have to engage.

# Conclusion

My goals in this chapter are modest. First, I have attempted to show that the current tendency to define risk as the kernel of a new paradigm for political philosophy (and for the politics of modern liberal democracies) suffers from excessive generality. The notion of risk does not point to a single reality. Rather, the dimensions of future unwanted events that it denotes are plural, in that they are marked by a variety of properties that do not always, or even typically, occur together.

Second, I have attempted to show that once we deconstruct the concept of risk, we can see that it does not point toward a clean break with the political or philosophical past. Many of the features that characterize "new risks" are in fact also features of "old risks," such as infectious disease.

Third, and perhaps most importantly as far as defining a research agenda for the future is concerned, to the extent that there *are* starkly new risks, they point not in one, but in several directions at once. Those of us who attend to the challenges that modern risks represent will need to think in particular about the ways in which modern risks force us to think about ways in which theories of justice and democracy can be extended *outward* to reach all people affected by any given risk regardless of nationality and *forward* into the future, to account for the impact potentially risky policies taken today have on the interests of future generations. It must also take up the thorny issue about the extent to which decisions about risk, especially complex, potentially catastrophic risks, are best left to experts, and the extent to which they must be taken up by representative democratic bodies.

Not only does taking risk into account give rise to a plurality of distinct research questions for political philosophy, a quick consideration of the debates to which I briefly alluded suggests the disquieting possibility that the answers to these questions may be in conflict with one another. There may in other words be aspects of risk that point toward a greater place for experts and others that call for a deepening and broadening of democracy. How these different demands might be reconciled so as to give rise to a coherent and satisfactory political philosophy of risk is a question to which political philosophers must now urgently devote their attention.

# Bibliography

Beck, U. 2001. *La société du risqué*. Paris: Flammarion.

— 2008. *World at Risk*. Oxford: Polity.

Ewald, F. 1986. *L'État Providence*. Paris: Le Seuil.

Gardiner, S. M. 2010. "Climate Change as a Global Test for Contemporary Institutions and Theories." In *Climate Change, Ethics and Human Security*. Edited by K. O'Brien et al. Cambridge: Cambridge University Press. 555–600.

Goodin, R. 2007. "Enfranchising All Affected Interests, and its Alternatives." In *Philosophy and Public Affairs* 35(1): 40–68.

Hansonn, S. O. 2007. "Risk and Ethics: Three Approaches." In *Risk. Philosophical Perspectives*. Edited by T. Lewens. London: Routledge. 21–35.

— 2011. "Risk." In *Stanford Encyclopedia of Philosophy*. http://plato.stanford.edu/entries/risk/ [Accessed February 3].

Johnson, S. 2006. *The Ghost Map*. New York: Penguin Books.

Kusch, M. 2007. "Towards a Political Philosophy of Risk: Experts and Publics in Deliberative Democracy." In *Risk. Philosophical Perspectives*. Edited by T. Lewens. London: Routledge. 131–55.

Parfit, D. 1983. "Energy Policy and the Further Future: The Identity Problem." In *Energy and the Future*. Edited by D. Maclean and P. Brown. Totowa, NJ: Rowman & Allanheld. 166–79.

Posner, R. 2004. *Catastrophe. Risk and Response*. Oxford: Oxford University Press.

Rawls, J. 1971. *A Theory of Justice*. Cambridge: Harvard University Press.

Rees, M. 2004. *Our Final Hour*. New York: Basic Books.

Shrader-Frechette, K. S. 1991. *Risk and Rationality. Philosophical Foundations for Populist Reforms*. Berkeley: University of California Press.

Sunstein, C. 2002. *Risk and Reason*. Cambridge: Cambridge University Press.

— 2005. *Laws of Fear*. Cambridge: Cambridge University Press.

— 2009. *Worst-Case Scenarios*. Cambridge: Harvard University Press.

Weinstock, D. 2006. "The (Real) World of Global Democracy." *Journal of Social Philosophy* 37(1): 6–26.

Westra, L. 2009. *Environmental Justice and the Rights of Ecological Refugees*. Virginia: Earthscan.

Zack, N. 2009. *Ethics for Disaster*. Plymouth, UK: Rowman & Littlefield.

# 5

# Global Risks and Popular Sovereignties

Ignacio Aymerich Ojea
*University Jaume I and CIEDH*

## Risk as a legitimation of power

The question I intend to raise is far less ambitious than the general statement that underlies this seminar: the governance of global risks. My interest focuses on the legal (or, more accurately, socio-legal) dimension of governance and especially on the legal system's ability to reduce uncertainty by ensuring predictability of the sequence of individual actions, especially in a globalized society. Consistent with the usual way of thinking, we tend to consider response to risk in terms of increasing the capacity of rational control over processes since a characteristic of the rule of law is that all action is subject to the principles of legality; the governance of risk is largely a question of legal certainty. Yet it is possible that the increased rational predictability afforded by rational legal systems since the time of rationalist *jus naturalism* brings about a new type of risk requiring a different type of approach. To address the issue comprehensively, I propose an alternative way of thinking about sovereignty, a different perspective that may, in my opinion, afford another vision of the risks generated immanently in social action's trend toward rationalism.

It is first necessary to define the framework where the problem arises. The discourse through which political power seeks to legitimize itself has always linked the necessity of government with the ability to confront and meet collective risks. Political power and risk are thus united like two sides of a page: government is necessary because there are risks to confront. Throughout history, there have been various types of risks: there have not only been military threats but also threats of epidemics, famine, or unfavorable economic outlooks; risks that disease, corruption, injustice, and religious condemnation will spread, just like the risk of losing collective identity or remaining isolated; certain risks which are hypothetical, imaginary, and simulated. According to the risk presented, the type of government needed for the task will also vary. The equation in which power and risk are articulated may then function as a stable structure, and a historic evolution of forms of risk and government would be the variables of this equation.

Following this general outline, the processes of social change in the modern age could be interpreted as another milestone in the series of historic variations of the relationship between power and risk. According to this argument, we usually present the political transformation that took place after the French and American Revolutions as a change at the top: wherever there used to be an absolute monarchy, there is now democratically elected power. And the new method of organizing power is explained (as Herbert Spencer did, for example) by new types of social challenges and risks: the axis of public management, which focused on the military defense of territory, is moving toward other tasks such as the promotion of industrial and commercial progress. The emergence of modern forms of public and private administration has to do with these new tasks.

For this explanation to be consistent, it must hinge on the classical concept of sovereignty. The usual granting of the origin of this concept to Bodin links it to legislature. Indeed, sovereignty is defined as the absolute and perpetual power of a republic and its absolute nature is united with the power to enact and repeal laws. That is to say that first, there is a pyramidal political structure with legislative power at the top. Sovereign power is identified with the authority to set norms that determine the behavior of lower levels of the pyramid. The actions of individuals, corporations, or political authorities underneath the sovereign are subject to legislative control and are, in effect, predictable. Non-compliance is expected and linked to penalties. Second, normative power is sovereign because it is not subject to a higher power.

On this stable structure, we then have the historic variable of democratization as a change in the way of legitimizing whoever holds supreme legislative power. But in any case, the sovereign holds a position where it is no longer accountable to any higher power: an absolute monarchy does not need to justify its legislative decisions, nor do sovereign people need to justify their choice regarding the election of a parliament that will exercise legislative power. Let us study this development a little more closely.

## Social rationalization and legal regulation

I want to focus on two key processes of social change occurring in the modern age: the rationalization of social action and the expansion of civil liberties. For the former, various authors' descriptions could be used, but I think that Norbert Elias' description is particularly useful. According to his reconstruction of historic development, during early stages of social evolution, the dominant type of risk for individuals represents an uncertainty where their lives as well as their physical integrity are often threatened. Both the non-controllable power of nature and the instability of the modes of organization of political power involve constant risk. Only progress in the social division of work (already described by Durkheim) will allow human interaction to become less aggressive. Stable forms of political organization that assume the role of guaranteeing security prospects in the longer term can then appear: "... only a very high degree of functional division allows the creation of stable financial and political monopolies with highly specialized monopolist administrations, i.e. establishing Western-style states, which gradually bring security into the life of the individual" (Elias 1993, 514).

But the social division of labor implies a greater interdependence of the activities of each individual with respect to the actions of others. This is possible only if individuals increase their ability to predict the consequences of their actions in the general framework formed by social interaction, as well as their ability to predict the consequences of the actions of others. Each individual socialization process is becoming more complex, and it takes longer to make people capable of assuming this predictability. In this way, "social functions have gradually differentiated as a consequence of the increasing pressure of social competence. The more functions differ, the more their numbers increase, as does the quantity of individuals on whom others continuously depend in order to carry out the simplest and most mundane actions. It is necessary to adjust the behavior of a growing number of individuals, and we must organize the network of actions better and more rigidly so that individual action can then manage to carry out its social function. The individual is forced to organize his behavior in a more and more differentiated, regular and stable manner" (Elias 1993, 451). In this context, rationalization of social interaction means that in societies that have a greater division of labor, we need a greater capacity for rational control of one's own behavior and a rational prediction of the behavior of others.

But not everything is based on individual capacities. Mutual expectations can be stabilized to become predictable only if they have a sufficient system of guarantees, and this system can only function effectively if it is of a legal nature. As noted by Habermas (following Weber), this guarantee occurs basically in areas where a rationalized administration allows individuals strategic action that is just as rationalized, that is in rational bureaucracy of the state and of the company: "Formal law, based on the principle of transforming all social relationships into a legal one constitutes organizational means, not only of capitalist economy and of the modern state, but also of their mutual relationship" (Habermas 1992, 216). Only modern law, characterized by the principle of legality, by the fact that all social relationships are ruled by law, and by the fact that it is formally calculable, is able to satisfy the institutionalization of strategic action areas in state bureaucracy as well as in the market, thus allowing the generalization of individual rational action. This is crucial in order to provide legal guarantees to a capitalist-free market system in which agents can act guided by the security that the consequences of the action can be predicted.

Teubner argues that contemporary law has evolved from territorial differentiation, based on state sovereignty over a territory to sectorial differentiation, and the reason for this is that evolution toward transnational social relations generates a demand for regulatory standards that cannot be satisfied either by state institutions or international institutions. This is why (as shown in the case of *lex mercatoria*) various private institutions create an autonomous right claiming global validity, a right that comes from the fact that very diverse social sectors create their own system of rights (Teubner

2005, 121). But in this case, the sectorial differentiation to which Teubner refers focuses on transnational social relations of a fundamentally economic sort. We are coming back to the starting point mentioned by Elias: the division of labor. And indeed, economic globalization is one case where we can best highlight the rationalization of social interaction.

For example, think about the electronic purchase of a product manufactured in East Asia by someone living in Europe, a contractual relationship which would have been impossible not so long ago. It takes a very precise and complex coordination of actions involving the buyer, the Internet service provider, the company that provides safe electronic payment, various logistics and transportation companies, customs and tax authorities, any subcontractors, insurance or translation companies that may also participate, labor and health inspectors, and at the end of the chain, the producer. None of those involved would do anything if the risk of losing money were not minimized by the legal safeguards that protect the whole process. And the detailed identification of respective responsibilities, and how they should be claimed, cannot rely on a simple agreement between parties, an agreement that would be overly complex to determine in each specific case. Hence the demand for security presses toward stable normative regulation which, as Teubner said, is even generated by the private institutions that are involved. Opportunities that arise through such a concatenation of actions not only increase access to new consumer products, but also simultaneously change producers' strategies. Anyone working in an economic sector whose goods are likely to be sold at the global level must be able to predict which potential benefits can come from an already ubiquitous competition. The production process must be designed to enhance the ability to rationally predict a greater number of possible actions by a greater number of agents.

An example like this one may be representative of how the rationalization of social action gives rise to globalization in the economic field, but not all cases belong to the sphere of the economy. Here is an example of another kind: on July 27, 2009, the United Nations Committee on Human Rights approved a report convicting Spain of racial discrimination. The facts motivating this resolution were (in short) that a national police officer carried out an identity check on a person of color. The officer only checked the papers of one person in the crowded train station. The plaintiff asked the officer why he was the only one asked to submit his papers, and the officer told him that identity checks had be carried out because of the large number of immigrants living illegally in Spain and that he was ordered to do so especially with people of color. The plaintiff alleged that this course of action constituted racial discrimination and filed a complaint about it. The dismissal and subsequent appeal then came to the Spanish Constitutional Court, which did not find any discrimination. However, the Committee on Human Rights ruled that the plaintiff had received discriminatory treatment because his racial characteristics were a determining factor for the officer's suspicions of illegal conduct. In this case, there is a chain of responsibilities between the plaintiff and the final resolution protecting the right to nondiscrimination. The police officer's action could have been motivated solely by personal bias, by an order from a superior, by a general order given by senior police officials, by a law, or it could even have been illegal but not determined as such by a lower court or, in turn, by higher courts and so on (which actually happened) until it was presented in a court responsible for guaranteeing fundamental human rights. Whatever the case, we assume that it is possible to rationally reconstruct the chain of responsibility to determine the point where the infringement of rights occurred.

Whether dealing with economic actions or administrative decisions, it appears in both cases that individuals must be capable of responsibility in the etymological sense of the word: they must be able to answer for and explain the reasons for their actions when asked. As long as we are dealing with normatively regulated actions, they must be able to respond under a restricted system of possible arguments. If the delivery person makes a delivery error or if a police authority gives an illegal order, the interconnection of actions that follow can be reconstructed rationally to determine the point of failure. This is how, in the rationalization of both economic and administrative actions, individuals can make predictions about how the concatenation of other people's actions affects them. This complex pattern is only possible if responsibilities are defined in legal terms, but the extension of these long chains of action allows interdependencies between individual actions to extend to a global scale. In this way, law becomes an essential element of social control and therefore a rational and essential way to control risk.

From a legal-normative point of view, the description of a legal system able to predict the concatenations of rights and obligations to form long chains of interdependence of individual actions could be made in Kelsenian terms regarding the formal validity of norms, but obviously, this description does not encompass everything. If markets enjoy varying degrees of legal security existing in different countries (as revealed by the reports of *International Transparency* on corruption), what is important is not whether there are legal norms in force prohibiting it, but rather the extent to which these norms actually work, and the extent to which individuals organize their behavior according to internalize norms. For this reason, an analysis of the legal system, in terms of its ability to bring predictability to social interaction, is research of a sociological-legal rather than a legal-dogmatic nature.

## Interdependence and liberalism

We have studied the first of the processes of change characteristic of the modern age: social rationalization. But as Durkheim noted above, increasing the rational interdependence among individuals resulting from the division of labor does not imply—as paradoxical as this may seem—a reduction in individual autonomy; quite the contrary. The more interdependence increases, the greater the autonomy. Niklas Luhmann describes it as follows: "Any differentiated society that has reached such a level of development and that cannot be sufficiently coordinated from a central point must be based on personalities as a nodal point of social requirements. This leads to more investment in the individual. This is why its demands are socially legitimized.

A greater sensitivity to the personal motivations of behavior and needs is being developed. Tact, tolerance and the ability for psychological understanding are gaining ground perceptibly. Cases where it is possible to treat others with rudeness and where no one around shows their disapproval are becoming increasingly rare. Even criminal law and penal procedures are becoming more humanized" (Luhmann 1974, 55).

As Elias also argues, it is not only that individuals *can* make more choices, but also that they *must* make more choices. A wider range of products and services on the market requires an individualization of selection criteria. Greater professional diversification requires a more considered choice of one's own role. The succession of choice distinguishes individuals. The awareness of the choice between various alternatives in all areas (religion, emotion, profession, ideology, consumption, etc.) involves a gradual internalization of behavioral control and, therefore, a weakening of previous social controls. Javier Noya exposes this in the following way: "If social controls are considered in this way, individualization—the internalization of behavioral control—i.e. the sovereign individual, or 'strong subject,' is the only possible basis of this cultural bonding. Social bonding forces a 'DIY' culture. This is why the normative ambiguity on individuals and their rights is actually inappropriate. The polymorphic complexity of cultural diversity (or, for others, social diversity) requires the principle of individual autonomy as a solid and indivisible basis" (Noya 1996, 279–80).

This is why the recognition of civil liberties and human rights in the modern age is so widespread, leading to the great declarations of rights beginning with those passed in France in 1789 and culminating with the international system of the United Nations from 1948 to 1966. Now, at the head of the normative system, we place guarantees of certain fundamental rights which do not detract whatsoever from the law's ability to ensure the predictability of action. As we saw in the case of racial discrimination, we can make a rational reconstruction of the concatenation of actions to the point of determining the breach of a right, thus requiring corresponding responsibilities. The idea of sovereignty is not compromised, since it is the sovereign legislative power which proclaims these catalogs of rights.

## Sovereignty or popular sovereignties?

This whole explanation can be put on hold if we move from a unitary concept of sovereignty to a different, pluralistic one, as is the case when one wonders what kind of decisions are not legally subject to a duty of justification and are, in this sense, sovereign. *Sovereignty*, thus redefined, would always mean this power over which there is no other, but there is no reason to imagine a social pyramid with only a vertical alignment. Despite the fact that individual actions are linked together by long chains including long and complex sequences of action, there are certain actions that are outside the network. In a society where there are civil liberties, no one is obligated to justify their emotional choices, their consumer preferences, their choice regarding their profession or religious creed, to name only a few. The lack of obligation to justify signifies that there is no legal obligation to respond rationally or to predict the way one's own action intersects with the actions of others and the extent to which one must be able to vouch for possible chain reactions. Therefore, the type of stable social relations arising from the direction in which people solve their sovereign decisions remains subject to uncertainty. This uncertainty generates unique risks. It is no longer simply a matter of government power legitimizing itself vis-à-vis the people by its ability to confront risks outside the political community, since part of the risk is now inside the community itself: with the effective development of the system of fundamental rights, it has become constitutive.

Therefore, while the interdependence of individual actions increases and extends over the entire planet, all *gaps* and courses of actions that are beyond the need of rational justification and thus, the type of predictability that the legal system can make, are also increasing. We cannot require anyone to justify their votes in an election and the vote can be exercised completely irrationally without requiring any individual to be held personally responsible for it. But this unpredictable decision, along with many others like it, can lead (as, indeed, has already happened) to the triumph of populist or corrupt options or aggressive militarism, thereby generating new risks. Neither the Serbian electors of Milosevic nor investors in pension funds that fueled speculative bubbles were forced to predict the consequences of their individual actions.

I would like to consider the choice between unitary/pluralistic sovereignty in the particular case of the right to political participation. When looking at interweaving social actions through the prism of single popular sovereignty, the assumption that a legal public decision must be democratic (and the term "democracy" here refers to a decision in which everyone takes part in public affairs) slips in inadvertently. On this point, Charles Taylor has updated Hegel's argument regarding absolute freedom. "This condition, which we call universal and total participation, is one in which everyone has a say on the whole decision" (Taylor 1983, 201). The ideal of democratic decision implies that we all simultaneously decide (in a single act of decision) on the whole. Sovereignty is not divided, precisely because of the simultaneity that turns the act of deciding into a single act and because of the condition—in line with Rousseau's general will—that the decision should refer to the entire community.

However, we can have a different vision of things if we view them from the perspective of pluralistic sovereignties. Consider, for example, the case of Bell, who chose to devote himself to technical research and invented the telephone. The invention began to spread and an increasing number of people decided to subscribe to the service offered by the Bell Company. Gradually, the majority of communications changed to the point where the invention was disseminated among the masses. At the end of the process, everyone had freely made a decision that, when added to other decisions, transformed the system of social relations. But we do not consider this a democratic decision. It is not democratic, but it allows us to see things from another point of view. The changing conditions of public life were modified freely, but not through an act of unitary sovereignty.

Indeed, regarding the right to political participation in the strictest sense, it is not possible to demand an explanation as to why people assume a more or less heightened level of involvement. Weber describes it as follows: "In all political associations of some weight (i.e. those that extend beyond the area of the circle of tasks of a small rural township), where periodic elections are produced to appoint leaders, political enterprise is necessarily an enterprise of those *interested*. This means that a relatively small number of people interested primarily in politics, that is in participating in political power, is created through open recruitment, a group of activists; they present themselves or make their protégés electoral candidates, go fund-raising, and try to gather votes. It is inconceivable that in large organizations, elections can take place properly without this activity. In practical terms, this means the citizens who are entitled to vote are divided into active and passive political actors, and as the difference is based on free will, we cannot eliminate it, not even by means of any type of disciplinary action" (Weber 1985, 840-1). Since it is based on free will, as Weber said, nobody can be required to rationally justify such behavior, and wherever compulsory voting has been tried, the norm has not made citizens show an equivalent interest in public affairs.

So we could consider making a catalog of individual actions that are beyond the predictability brought by the legal system, although defining the quantity of these actions is of minimal importance. It is clear that in addition to the example already mentioned above, we could add all decisions relating to identity. The fact that, in the medium- and long-term, a differentiated national identity or sense of belonging as an ethnic minority in the People's Republic will ultimately prevail for each of the Uighurs in China will not be fully controllable in terms of legal obligations (although the People's Republic wants it to be). It was not fully controllable in the case of East Timor either. Other countries cannot prevent someone in India from choosing to be a computer technician. Nor can we control people's voting behavior in the Bible Belt of the United States, or the sedentary habits of the developed countries in spite of the associated health risks, or expenditure made on consumer goods at a time when economic activity requires a greater investment in industrial equipment, or as many other examples as we can conceive.

## Governing from uncertainty

A parallel could be made between the type of governance risk represented by the generalization of civil liberties and the risks represented by Heisenberg's uncertainty principle in quantum physics (for any given particle, we cannot accurately and simultaneously determine certain pairs of variables, such as position and momentum) or the theory of uncertainty in economics (highlighted by Knight and by other authors such as Schackle and Marschak). In the area of governance, a lack of actions that are beyond rational predictability brought about by the legal system can be generally unimportant if they are not generalized, but when they are, they may come to accumulate systemic risks. Economists can explain what drives one individual to consume and another to invest savings in financial products, but this explanation is very different from the explanation that the people who have legal obligations must be able to provide. Given that the choice between consumption and savings is a decision that requires no justification, people do not develop the habit of thinking about the ripple effects of such preferences. When globalization makes the growing interdependency of individual actions reach a global scale, the accumulation of such decisions generates high levels of real risk. A hypothetical public official who had the foresight to predict the financial crisis and would have halted the use of high-risk speculative products could find themselves confronted with the dilemma that, in the next election, a rival party might collect the vote of an electorate that is displeased with having limits put on potential profit. Neither the decisions to invest in high-risk products nor the vote for one action or the other requires a justification from the individual. Both irrational decisions would seize rational control from authorities on both sides.

Attempts at reducing uncertainty by narrowing the margins of civil liberties do not lead to easier governance. Using data, Amartya Sen argues that there has never been a famine in multiparty democracies (2000, 221). This is not because multiparty democracies correspond to rich countries since the data show that the correlation also exists in *poor* democracies. Instead, the famines suffered by Sudan and Ethiopia from 1979 to 1984 were due to the political immunity of their respective authoritarian regimes, which did not suffer the pressure that would have forced them to predict risk and adopt effective measures. The case of North Korea, which is unable to feed its population yet whose military spending is excessive, is much more serious.

This is why Hegel's aforementioned argument on absolute liberty is pertinent. When the idea of popular sovereignty is taken to extremes, the decision about the type of society in which we want to live forces everything to be solved *democratically*. Through a single constituent decision (revolution), people define the regime and no individual decision can change it. Therefore, all activity is subject to centralized programs, and any individual's decision to choose a course of action other than the official course because of personal preference is "antidemocratic" (counter-revolutionary). With such a detailed program, predictability should be at a maximum and risks at a minimum, but this is not the case. Hegel observed this in the bloody path adopted, for a time, by the French Revolution, and described it in a chapter of *Phenomenology of Spirit* called "Absolute Liberty or Terror." History has sufficed to show that such regimes are not effective at avoiding risks in public life. We can find proof in the famines in North Korea as well as in Ukraine under Stalin, and the risk of facing imprisonment, torture, or discrimination is much higher than in other societies. The attempt to eliminate uncertainty by reducing civil liberties should be dismissed not only on grounds of illegitimacy, but also in terms of risk management, where experience shows that this path should be forever abandoned.

Therefore, everything seems to indicate that the risk is real, and that it has very much been so for a long time, as Ulrich Beck has pointed out repeatedly. The contribution of the predictability of social action performed by legal systems has increased exponentially since the modern age and has not only made possible the creation of transnational sequences of individual action but has also generated its own specific risks. The cumulative effect of alternatives of unforeseeable individual action increases when these actions are better spread as a result of globalization. Market behavior is a good example of this, but it is not the only one. Given these risks, the possibilities of the traditional normative response are already scarce, and in the era of the knowledge society, will require reconsidering legal security in a globalized society, starting from other bases.

# Bibliography

Elias, N. 1993. *El proceso de la civilización. Investigaciones sociogenéticas y psicogenéticas.* México: Fondo de Cultura Económica.

Habermas, J. 1992. *Teoría de la acción comunicativa.* Madrid: Taurus.

Knight, F. H. 1921. *Risk, Uncertainty and Profit.* Boston: Hart, Schaffner & Marx.

Luhmann, N. 1974. *Grundrechte als Institution. Ein Beitrag zur politischen Soziologie.* Berlin: Duncker & Humboldt.

Noya, Miranda J. 1996. "Ambivalencia, consenso e igualdad." In *Complejidad y teoría social.* Edited by A. Pérez-Agote and I. Sánchez de la Yncera1. Madrid: CIS. 259–82.

Sen, A. 2000. *Desarrollo y libertad.* Barcelona: Planeta.

Taylor, C. 1983. *Hegel y la sociedad moderna.* México: Fondo de Cultura Económica.

Teubner, G. 2005. *El derecho como sistema autopoiético de la sociedad global.* Bogotá: Universidad Externado de Colombia.

Weber, M. 1985. *Wirtschaft und Gesellschaft. Grundriss der verstehenden Soziologie.* Tübingen: Mohr Siebeck.

# Part II

# Representation of Risks: Categories, Affects, Motivations

# 6

# The Dark Horizon of the Future: Opacity, Disaster, and Responsibility

Christophe Bouton

*University of Bordeaux 3/ Institut Universitaire de France*

According to François Hartog, we are now living in a system of historicity focused on the present—"presentism" (2003). "Presentism" has replaced the modern system of historicity, "futurism," which generally prevailed from 1789 to 1989. Breaking from the concept of history as *magistra vitae*, itself belonging to "pastism," "futurism" was characterized by the predominance of the horizon of expectations over the field of experience from which it had broken. In "presentism," the two categories have merged into a perpetual present that quickly forgets the past and no longer anticipates the future. Has "presentism" become the dominant category of historical experience? I would fine-tune this thesis by saying that Western societies are also distinguished by a concern for the future. This is manifested in different ways: by the preoccupation for the fate of future generations, theorized over 30 years ago by Hans Jonas, and by being obsessed by risks. Quoting Ulrich Beck, "risk societies" are societies fixated on short- and long-term risks, and thus on the future—because risk is a *future* dreaded event. Societies are so preoccupied with the future because they themselves generate a large portion of these risks, and they feel as if they can effect future scenarios.

In this contribution, I would like to identify certain categories with which current societies represent the future: because the reflections and actions of groups and individuals are focused on more or less explicit categories which outline the representation of the future, the framework where future events are comprehended.

## Novelty, progress, acceleration, feasibility

First, we must go back to the representation of the future which characterizes modern times, according to the German historian Reinhart Koselleck. From the second half of the eighteenth century, during the Enlightenment, representations of the future changed drastically. Four new categories were required to plot the future: novelty, the promise of progress, acceleration, and action. (1) The new future is actually characterized by the strength of novelty, by its unpredictability. Instead of copying the past, it constantly creates totally new events. The old model of *Historia magistra vitae*, which claimed that the past constituted a series of examples to imitate, has become null and void. The "horizon of expectations" broadened and broke away from the "field of experience" (Koselleck 1990a, 37–62, 307–29). For most thinkers of this era, history never repeats the past; it invents the future. (2) The category of progress replaced the category of the cycle, and persisted until at least Marx, who affirmed that history progresses, even if it is for the worst. The future is the hallmark of improvement. People expect the future to be a different experience, one that is better than what they have already been through. (3) By bringing newness, the future constantly changes the landscape of the present so that history seems to be speeding up. Sweeping changes no longer spread out over decades or centuries, but rush in instead, one after the other. The French Revolution illustrates this new experience of history. In his speech on May 10, 1793, Robespierre declared "The time has come to call upon each to realize his own destiny. The progress of human Reason laid the basis for this great Revolution, and you shall now assume the particular duty of hastening its pace" (Koselleck 1990b, 22). (4) The future conceived in this way is not a mere expectation, but a task, a mission to carry out. People think *they can "make" history*, that they can construct their own future. This is what Koselleck calls the category of the "feasibility" or "availability" of history (1990c, 233–47). History has become "makeable" and producible by people.

Today we are discovering that this four-part representation of the future contains an inherent contradiction that has gradually revealed itself. There is a tension between the feasibility of the future, on the one hand, and its newness linked to its acceleration, on the other. The more the future presents newness, the more it becomes unpredictable, and the less it is makeable. The more it puts pressure on the present, the more history accelerates, and the less it is controllable. In order to accomplish a task, we must have predictive knowledge of the future. To anticipate the future, we must have the time to understand the present.

## Opacity

The first inescapable observation is that the category of the opacity of the future overrides the idea of novelty or at least competes with it. People act in a thicker and thicker fog: "all of us, individuals and institutions, must strengthen our capacity for predictions and the study of the future. But at the same time, the future has never seemed as enigmatic as it does right now" (Innerarity, 58). The future has become obscured and seems to be not only more and more unpredictable, but also darker and more foreboding. What are the reasons for this?

The sense that the future is murky stems partly from the mission, inherent to our modernity, of controlling the future. For Marcel Gauchet, modern democracy was established with the intention of "governing history" (2007, 45–8). In order to govern, we must be able to anticipate and find prospective methods. In France, a good example of this can be found in Condorcet's *Tableau historique* (1998, 10ème livre) and more recently in the *Commissariat général au plan* which was replaced in 2006 by the *Centre d'analyse stratégique*. However, the more one tries to know the future, the more one discovers that it is unpredictable, that it evades any attempt at being predicted. Knowledge increases ignorance. The more instruments capable of predicting there are at our disposal, the more we notice that the future resists them. In this way, attempts at prediction end up revealing the unpredictable. The future has surely always been unpredictable, but this has never been more greatly recognized than it is today.

However, other details may justify the idea that the future is more unpredictable than before. I will mention the large gap between our predictive knowledge and our ability to modify nature. This is Jonas's thesis. Prometheus is "definitely unchained" (1998, 15). Technological processes have become automated and develop frantically to the point where they cannot be stopped. Human freedom is confined to the beginning of the process, to the very choice of implementing new processes. The process then has its own inertia and becomes irreversible and abandons those who started it. People become not only the passive spectators of their creation, but also prisoners of the processes that they themselves have triggered. Jonas said that "technology's seizure of power" is "a totally anonymous and compelling revolution that nobody ever planned" (1998, 245). We are powerless to control technological processes because we are blind to their consequences. Knowledge is no longer what it was from antiquity to the Enlightenment, that is, synonymous with the power man has over the world. Human action has changed profoundly. With the invention of increasingly efficient techniques, human capacity to disrupt nature has become much greater than its capacity to predict the effects of its actions. The more we transform the world, the less we can predict or control it.

We are in a paradoxical situation: "we know more on the one hand, less on the other, about the future than our pre-modern ancestors." The future is more predictable in the sense that physical developments have led to the increase in people's ability to predict. Yet it is simultaneously more unpredictable in the sense that the modern world is perpetually changing. Therefore, it is impossible to use the field of experience of the past to sketch out the future's horizon of expectations. We must "start out with the new, without being able to calculate it" (1998, 231).

The growing opacity of the future can also be explained by the phenomenon of globalization. Societies' evolutions are linked to each other, making them more complex and more unpredictable. In order to anticipate the future of a state, we must take into account the situation of many other states.

Finally, the future is unpredictable because of the acceleration of history.[1] The rather vague category of acceleration actually means that the number of political, cultural, social, technical, or scientific changes that appear in a given unit of time (years, decades,

---

[1] Nora defines the "acceleration of History" as "a more and more rapid disappearance into a definitively dead past" (1997a, 23).

centuries) are continually on the rise (Rosa 2005). There is an increase of events which appear and disappear more and more quickly. Unpredictability increases from the fact that there are more new events to anticipate and that the time needed to anticipate them before their arrival is becoming shorter and shorter. Faced with a situation where the consequences of actions are often irreversible, lasting, and unpredictable, we should make sound political decisions based on rational expectations. Yet acceleration reduces the period of time necessary for such resolutions. Scarcely do new events peek over the future horizon than they are already here, crowding out events occupying the present to a quickly forgotten past. The slowness of the democratic process is ill-suited to the logic of urgency (Laïdi 2000). Thus, "torrential, exponential acceleration" (Jonas 1998, 246) imposes itself upon humankind like fate (which cannot be stopped) and constantly obscures the future. History happens too quickly for us to predict and thus create.

## Indeterminacy

The obscurity of the future is compounded by its indeterminacy. The future is indeterminate in the sense that *many scenarios are possible*. Indeterminacy is not uncertainty or the absence of knowledge. Indeterminacy means that even if we manage to know several possible future scenarios, we cannot know with certainty which one will happen. At best, we can establish probabilities for each of them. It seems to me, from a formal standpoint, that the most pertinent current scientific model to describe the future conceived thusly is provided by quantum mechanics, which has overtaken the determinist paradigm (Heisenberg 2000, 150). Let us recall that Heisenberg distinguishes three periods in the history of scientific determinism. The indeterminacy of the knowledge of the present state of a particle leads to an indeterminacy of the knowledge of its future state; it renders any exact prediction of its future state impossible (Bitbol 1998, 312). However, this indeterminacy is not total since prediction is feasible in the form of probability. Quantum mechanics predicts several possibilities in observing a particle, with a rate of probability applied to each one of them. Schrödinger's equation describes the evolution of these probabilities over time. Predictability is limited, but it still exists since probabilities describe a range of future results.

This schema applies *mutatis mutandis* to the macroscopic future of human societies, with the substantial difference that the probabilities therein cannot be calculated using mathematical equations. The impossibility of completely knowing all the factors of a present situation leads to an impossibility of unequivocally determining the future. We can find several possible scenarios, but we cannot tell which one will come about. We sometimes have probabilities, even if they are difficult to establish. This indeterminacy of the future is included in the notion of risk. Risk means "a latent induced effect" (Beck 2008, 26). It is a possible consequence to a present situation, a threat, a future event that should be prevented. Concerning risks related to the chemical industry, Beck notes that they "take indeterminable, unpredictable paths": "supposed causality still remains more or less uncertain and transitory" (2008, 50–1). And there are often several causalities at stake that converge to produce damaging health effects. Scientific estimations are therefore merely "statements of probability." Indeterminacy increases by the fact that, concerning the evaluation of risks, scientists do not always remain objective, they live in "long-term cohabitation" with the economy, politics, and ethics (2008, 53). This situation can just as easily lead to an underestimation as an overestimation of risks. Scientists whose research is funded by pharmaceutical laboratories, for example, may have an incentive to encourage the diagnosis of a pandemic in order to sell vaccines to the masses.

## Disaster

The category of novelty, without being denied, has been challenged by the categories of opacity and indeterminacy. The landscape of the future grows even darker because the category of progress, typical of the representation of the future in modern times, was balanced out in the twentieth century by the category of disaster. It would be wrong to believe that the idea of progress has disappeared; it remains in a sober and limited form, in surgery and medicine, for example. But the future is now thought of more as a threat than as a guaranteed improvement. Hope for the *Grand soir* has been replaced by the fear of great disaster. This ubiquity of disaster, saturating the expectation horizon of Western societies, is summarized by Günther Anders's statement "Hiroshima is everywhere." In other words, "the possibility of Apocalypse may be our fault. But we do not know what we are doing" (2008, 324).

We might wonder if this declaration is excessive or merely linked to the historical context of the Cold War. Today, the threat of worldwide nuclear war has subsided, but other, real and possible disasters have taken the forefront. This category is applied to very diverse events, from economic crises to tsunamis. The risk society is "a society of catastrophe" (Beck 2008, 43, 143). A disaster is an event which is notable for the magnitude of its destructive effects, an event which has harmful consequences for a large portion of the population (nuclear explosions, chemical pollution, pandemic, etc.). The difference between a simple risk and a catastrophic risk lies in short- and long-term impacts on the population. The notion of violence and suddenness seems to make up a part of the concept of disaster. Yet there exist progressive disasters which are nearly invisible at their beginnings, such as acid rain that slowly destroys forests, or global warming that may lead to rising sea levels, forcing millions of coastal people to emigrate.

Throughout history, humanity has confronted disasters such as plagues, cholera, and earthquakes. The menacing influence of the climate is nothing new either. In the past, harsh winters, sweltering summers, and the famines that ensued have played a determining role in the history of peoples (Leroy-Ladurie 2004–9). What is new today, beyond the magnitude of the warming that has been measured, is the fact that humans can be considered the origin of this natural threat. Arendt emphasizes that, throughout the twentieth century, the idea of production has spread little by little to nature, erasing its boundary with history (Arendt 1989, 79). Through technology, people make nature as much as they do history. Philosophers think especially about the fabrication of the nuclear bomb, which introduces a natural process the Earth has never known. But the production of a hole in the ozone layer is another way for people to (involuntarily) change nature. Supported by the vast majority of current scientific work on the subject, the discovery of the direct link between the use of greenhouse gases and global warming squares with the idea of people's possible control over the natural history of the Earth because we hope we can undo anything we have done.

The category of disaster plunges our present era into gloominess, of which the Cormac McCarty's novel *The Road* is but one reflection among many.[2] The future abounds with multiple possible disasters: ecological, terrorist, nuclear, epidemiological, health, humanitarian, financial, airline, climatic, etc. We can also add to this list the innumerable disasters cleverly sensationalized and broadcast by the media, like the accident that trapped 33 Chilean miners underground for several weeks in September–October, 2010, attracting more journalists than the attacks on September 11, 2001![3] It is not easy to determine the criteria for calling an event a disaster. These criteria are partially determined by the media, which often favors one disaster over another. In France, even the legal term "natural disaster" is difficult to define absolutely. It may be declared when a specific region is struck by an extraordinary weather-related or geological natural phenomenon (storms, floods, avalanches, landslides, earthquakes, etc.). But this situation is left to the discretion of the authorities, and sometimes leads to heated debate, especially when it comes to financial issues related to insurance indemnities. The category of "natural disasters" is actually not natural, in the sense that its application adheres to meticulously studied scientific, legal, and media processes.

I would like to emphasize here that the category of disaster is balanced out by "feasibility," which continues to increase in power. The future darkened by various threats of disaster can be modified and changed, in addition to being "feasible" and "changeable" by people. Randomness and fate are replaced by risk, something which can be considered and removed. Future disaster is "a fate that we can *choose* to distance ourselves from"; "it means acting *as if* we were dealing with a particular destiny, in order to better divert its course." We must "predict the future in order to change it" (Dupuy 2004, 63, 161). What is "changing the future," if not exerting lucid influence on the course of events and on certain aspects of the history of the world—helping us to guide and make future history? The future is "a pathway with many forks" and can be described in the form of alternatives, like a decision-tree (184). It is represented as an arborescence of more or less probable possibilities.

At the time of the Lisbon Earthquake in 1755, we did not usually think of disasters as something caused by people. Today, we tend to think the opposite, that nearly all

---

[2]   On a different note, we could cite numerous blockbuster movies which depict the end of humanity by disasters of exceptional magnitude. The latest one, to date, is Roland Emmerich's *2012*.

[3]   I would like to thank Dominic Desroches for this commentary about the media's response to disaster.

disasters imply human responsibility and can, therefore, be foretold. The boundary between natural and human disasters (those caused by human activity) becomes vague. The watchword is to "predict disaster," meaning both to anticipate and to avoid it, acting upon its causes or at least its effects. There are very few disasters for which people can be freed from any liability.

The Chernobyl nuclear disaster in 1986? This was the result of a culmination of malfunctions (such as a lack of any confinement enclosure) and human error (safety procedures were not carried out).

The tsunami in 2004? Until proven otherwise, humans are in no way responsible for the movement of tectonic plates. But in reality, we can always set up measuring instruments, alert systems, and seismically retrofit houses and other structures. So, in a certain respect, even if we cannot foretell the causes, we can at least anticipate the effects of this kind of disaster.

Global warming? Greenhouse gases are responsible for the rise in observable temperatures, and as a result, their decrease should prevent future disaster.

In a very different way, economic disaster is also worth mentioning, that is the subprime crisis of 2008. These financial instruments were originally meant to reduce risks. These types of mortgages were granted to persons with low borrowing capacity and were effectively transformed into marketable securities. Banks shared these risks with other financial institutions that bought the securities. But securitization had the inverse effect of extending risk, with a domino effect: the accumulation of the borrowers' personal bankruptcy sullied the accounts of the banks, which had bought up these debts on a massive scale, etc. So was this disaster unavoidable? For certain economists, the subprime crisis showed instead that "our system effectively makes us 'firefighting arsonists,' constantly putting out the fires we ourselves set" (Giraud and Renouard 2009, 19). Bank managers are even more responsible for the crisis, as reported by certain specialists. The President of the Central European Bank, Jean-Claude Trichet, thus made his concerns public on several occasions in 2006, 2007, and 2008.

These economists believe that, if we cannot abolish capitalism completely, we can and should still "reform" it: "*it would be fitting to choose, together, which type of capitalism we want to develop for the future. This choice falls within the responsibility of democratic debate, but certainly not any economic fate whatsoever (whether it be the so-called market laws or laws of history)*" (Giraud and Renouard 2009, 317).

## Responsibility

The last category of the future I would like to bring up is that of "responsibility," something very difficult to define. Even though the future may be obscure, indeterminate, and menacing, we can act upon it, remove catastrophic scenarios, select options that are judged as preferable. In short, we are responsible for this future.

Hans Jonas was the first to highlight the importance of this responsibility for future generations. The ignorance inherent to human action is the fate of our modernity. This unprecedented situation demands the ethics of responsibility whose main goal is to limit our power, for want of broadening our knowledge:

> The gap between the strength of predictive knowledge and the ability of doing leads to a new ethical problem. Recognizing this ignorance then becomes the other slope of the obligation of knowing and this recognition then becomes part of the ethics that must teach ever more necessary self-control of our excessive power. (1998, 33)

This type of analysis probably inspired the principle of precaution. When in doubt, it is best to envision the worst-case scenario. Other authors have used dialectical reasoning: it is precisely because the future has become more uncertain, indeterminate, surprising, and inventive that it leaves room for human decision and action. A predicted future, one that is planned out in advance, would not leave the slightest room for initiative (Innerarity 2012; Gauchet 2007, 126–7).

If we place this thesis in a historical perspective, we could say that the category of responsibility has taken the place of the "feasibility" of history, which, during the twentieth century, was marred by totalitarian regimes. At the dawn of the twenty-first century, the future no longer resembles the one that began in modern times. Let us look back at the four categories put forth by Koselleck. Acceleration has become synonymous with opacity, novelty has been taken over by indetermination, progress has been eclipsed by disaster, and feasibility has been transformed into responsibility. People do not design and produce history like they could a product for sale, but they are responsible for it in an especially prospective manner insofar as these decisions may affect the future course of events. This forward-looking responsibility is collective and political, even if political decisions then translate into individual and private actions. It is an answer to the increasing gloominess of the future.

# Bibliography

Anders, G. 2008. *Hiroshima est partout*. Paris: Seuil.

Arendt, H. 1989. "Le concept d'histoire." In *La Crise de la culture*. Paris: Gallimard.

Beck, U. 2008. *La Société du risque*. Trans. L. Bernardi. Paris: Flammarion.

Bitbol, M. 1998. *L'aveuglante proximité du reel*. Paris: Flammarion.

Condorcet. 1998. *Esquisse d'un tableau historique des progrès de l'esprit humain*. Paris: Garnier-Flammarion.

Dupuy, J. P. 2004. *Pour un catastrophisme éclairé*. Paris: Seuil.

Gauchet, M. 2007. *L'avènement de la démocratie. I. La révolution moderne*. Paris: Gallimard.

Giraud, G. and C. Renouard (eds) 2009. *20 propositions pour réformer le capitalisme*. Paris: Flammarion.

Hartog, F. 2003. *Régimes d'historicité. Présentisme et expérience du temps*. Paris: Seuil.

Heisenberg, W. 2000. "Physique de l'atome et loi de causalité." In *La nature dans la physique contemporaine*. Paris: Éditions Gallimard.

Innerarity, D. 2012. *The Future and its Enemies: In Defense of Political Hope.* Trans. S. Kingery, Palo Alto: Stanford University Press.

Jonas, H. 1998. *Le Principe Responsabilité.* Trans. J. Greisch. Paris: Flammarion.

Koselleck, R. 1990a. "'*Historia magistra vitae.*' De la dissolution du '*topos*' dans l'histoire moderne en mouvement' et 'Champ d'expérience' et 'horizon d'attente': Deux catégories historiques." In *Le Futur passé. Contribution à la sémantique des temps historiques.* Paris: Éditions de l'EHESS. 37–62.

— 1990b. "Le futur passé des Temps modernes." In *Le Futur passé, Contribution à la sémantique des temps historiques.* Paris: Éditions de l'EHESS.

— 1990c. "Du caractère disponible de l'histoire." In *Le Futur passé, Contribution à la sémantique des temps historiques.* Paris: Éditions de l'EHESS.

Laïdi, Z. 2000. *Le sacre du présent.* Paris: Champs-Flammarion.

Leroy-Ladurie, E. 2004, 2006, 2009. *Histoire humaine et comparée du climat* (t. 1, Canicules et glaciers, XIIIᵉ–XVIIIᵉ siècles ; t. 2, Disettes et révolutions ; t. 3, Le réchauffement de 1860 à nos jours, avec le concours de G. Séchet). Paris: Fayard.

Nora, P. 1997. *Lieux de mémoire.* t. 1. Paris: Gallimard.

Rosa, H. 2005. *Beschleunigung, Die Veränderung der Zeitstrukturen in der Moderne.* Frankfurt: Suhrkamp.

# 7

# Re-Learning to Fear: The Perception of Risks in the Global Age

Elena Pulcini

*University of Florence*

It is more complex than it seems to define the notion of *global risks*. For that reason, it is better to start from the notion of *risk* that has been taken up by contemporary reflection on the epoch-making transformation of late modernity.[1]

In his well-known *Risikogesellschaft*, Ulrich Beck (1986, 1998) distinguishes the notion of *risk* from the notion of *danger* by emphasizing the fact that the primary characteristic of risk is that it is the *result of human action and decisions*. Indeed, the notion of risk is closely connected to the notion of calculability, and the possibility to calculate the potentially harmful effects of human action. But this original meaning is progressively lost when risk increasingly concerns the effects produced by scientific and technological development. In fact, Beck states, technology produces undesired and unknown effects that are unforeseeable and often irreversible, leading to the collapse of all claims that they can be calculated. Therefore, the risks of late modernity (mainly identified by Beck as environmental risks, which I will come back to) have a "new quality," in that they produce "the threat of self-destruction of all life on Earth" (Beck 1986, 21).

1. Now the question is: why? How did we end up in this situation? If we do not want to demonize technology, we need to look deeper and concentrate our reflections on the *subject*: on the hegemonic model of subjectivity in modernity, on its passions and its pathologies. This is where philosophy can make a valuable contribution. I am thinking in particular of the twentieth-century philosophy of technology, of authors such as Günther Anders (1956) and Hans Jonas (1979). With the dizzying development of technology, they tell us, the *homo faber*, that is, the Promethean subject of modernity, blessed with rationality and planning ability, has experienced a sort of corruption. As a result, this subject has lost his purpose and sense of action, becoming, as Anders calls him, a *homo*

---

[1] For an in-depth treatment of the topics dealt with in this chapter, see my book (Pulcini 2011a).

*creator*. The *homo creator*'s action, projected toward new unlimited goals and conquests, has ended up producing unforeseen and undesired consequences, which are increasingly resistant to all human capacities of control. Thus, the Promethean ability to foresee and govern the future that was peculiar to early modernity is distorted. The result is that risk is pushed into the ungovernable dimension of uncertainty.

Contemporary reflection in fact highlights the progressive shift in the notion of risk toward the notion of "uncertainty" (Lupton 1999, 13; De Marchi et al. 2001, 63), in regard to those events whose effects become difficult, if not impossible, to know and calculate.[2] "Risk was supposed to be a way of regulating the future, of normalizing it, and bringing it under our dominion," says Giddens on this matter. "Things haven't turned out that way. Our very attempts to control the future tend to rebound upon us, forcing us to look for different ways of relating to uncertainty" (Giddens 1999, 25–6).

Uncertainty and uncontrollability, and the probability of their negative influence on the future, are therefore the two aspects that many of the "new risks" have in common.

This is without a doubt the case, to give two significant examples, of the dangers connected to the two great technological revolutions of our age: *genetic engineering* and *information technology* (Habermas 2001; Virilio 1998). It is legitimate to take biotechnologies and the IT revolution as macroscopically exemplary cases of risk-producing technology, but it is also true that these two factors of the contemporary world cannot be denied their intrinsically *positive* potentials. Suffice it to think of an alternative and solidary use of the Internet, the new glue and medium of emancipatory movements (the Seattle movement of 1999, the Amsterdam community network, Avaaz.org, etc.), liable to become, as Castells suggests, embryonic testimonies of a new civil society and subjects of a future information democracy (2001, ch. V). Or in the case of biotechnologies, suffice it to recall the comforting promises we have been given by embryonic stem cell research. In short, there are at least two sides implicit in these two sectors of technological development, which means that they cannot be uniquely labeled as hazards or pure sources of risk. That is, they show an undeniable *ambivalence*, which makes them, at the same time, promoters of an improvement in the human condition and generators of harm. There is still room, above all if upheld by the stance of late modern (or radicalized modern) critique and reflection, for that "trust" in expert systems seen by Giddens as an inevitable ingredient of social existence (1990, ch. III).

Instead, today we are faced with a dimension of risk in which this ambivalence is lost entirely in favor of the *negative* pole. What I am talking about are the so-called *environmental risks*, whose birth is marked by Hiroshima and the nuclear bomb (De

---

[2]  In this connection, Cerutti (2007) rejects the same notion of *risk* (which implies the rationally manageable possibility of a harmful event) and instead speaks of two global *threats* (nuclear weapons and man-made climate change) which he proposes to deal with as global *challenges* since they remain in the realm of uncertainty. While bearing in mind this significant distinction, I nevertheless keep to the sociological notion of global risks, since it allows me to deal with the problem of risk perception and the strategies implemented by the subject; although I will then essentially concentrate on what Cerutti indeed defines as the two global challenges *par excellence*.

Marchi et al. 2001, 12), but which since then have multiplied dramatically. As a result, the idea of risk, which nevertheless has "the possibility of a positive and desired result," has shifted once and for all toward the idea of *uncertainty*. This, as I have already noted, "takes us to a negative, undesired outcome, associated with the idea of loss, damage, and catastrophe" (63) and seems to defy every possibility of control and rational calculation.

Nuclear accidents and climate change, lethal viruses (Bovine Spongiform Encephalopathy (mad cow disease), bird flu, Severe Acute Respiratory Syndrome (SARS)) and radioactive waste, electromagnetic pollution and a loss of biodiversity are the unforeseen and undesired effects of technological action. They cause alterations in the natural environment, exposing not only humankind (our health and assets), but all living things, to potentially irreversible harm. They are unprecedented threats that profoundly change the picture of modernity, but that, at the same time, originate from this very basis; through the perversion of the *homo faber* into a *homo creator*, they are the undesired consequences of those same tools (such as technology) meant to free human beings from insecurity, need, and fear.

In other words, this means that the "goods" are definitely overwhelmed by the "bads," the negative effects of technology. This prompts legitimate skepticism as to the possibility of combating this process through further and more sophisticated uses of technology itself (according to the *technological fix* principle) (De Marchi et al. 2001, 49; D'Andrea 2004, 25–8). Whether triggered by the normal operations of production activities that generate toxic and polluting substances or by their malfunctioning (accidents with oil tankers, the Seveso disaster), by uncontrollable interactions among technological applications and the social and environmental context (Genetically Modified Organisms (GMOs)), or by add-on effects generated by everyday consumption and lifestyles, the resulting harm does not only involve those who are responsible for it and the workers in the field, but also crosses geographical and political boundaries to affect the surrounding area (Chernobyl) or even distinct areas from where they were originally produced (Bhopal).

The *common* feature is their unpredictable and undetermined nature, the impossibility of circumscribing them in space or time, uncertainty as to their causes, the inability to forecast their consequences and possible remedies, the difficulty of pointing the finger of blame. But above all, it is their potentially *global* nature, that is, the possibility that their negative consequences may affect the whole planet, exposing humankind and all living things to the danger of radical degradation and destruction. It is no coincidence that this is the central issue addressed by the two authors, Beck and Giddens, who first traced the risk profile of late modernity.

As we shall see, what I am referring to are the two quintessential global risks—the *nuclear threat* and *global warming*—which bring all people, the whole of humankind, together in a condition of vulnerability.

Now, what evidently derives from this is a state of general *insecurity*. This results in a widespread feeling of *fear* which exposes the individuals in the global society to a dizzy feeling of impotence and disorientation, to the specter of "losing control" over events and their very lives themselves (Bauman 1998, 1999).

This primordial passion, from which humanity seemed in part to have freed itself by putting its faith in institutional strategies and the control mechanisms of liberal and democratic societies, therefore comes back to occupy the social scene, nourished by the undetermined nature of widespread threats that are often invisible and difficult to control.

**2.** But what kind of fear is this? In other words: what are we talking about when we speak of *fear* in the global age?

We can certainly answer that it is no longer the fear that Hobbes (1985) spoke of at the beginning of modernity, the fear prompted by the *certainty* of danger (fear of the other and violent death), which is immediately transformed into rational and productive action. And it is not premodern fear either (fear of nature and the outside world); indeed, it is true, as Beck says, that the undetermined, uncontrollable, and invisible nature of global risks would seem to restore men to ancestral and archaic fears, characterized by a sort of impotent fatalism (Beck 1988, ch. 4); but contrary to the dangers of premodern societies, late-modern risk is the product of human action (Lupton 1999, 71).

The change in the nature and the sources of danger has an impact on the physiognomy and the phenomenology of fear. Hence, the definition of fear today seems to escape traditional parameters.

Nevertheless, there is a preliminary road we could follow in this sense. We could bring up the distinction between *fear* and *anxiety*. This pair of concepts is found first of all in Freud's thinking and, at the philosophical level, in Heidegger, both making the same distinction between them: *fear* is the fear of a definite object, of a particular danger, while *anxiety* is anxiety toward an indefinite object, toward an uncertain danger (Freud 1977, 100–1; Heidegger 1989, 174). Even if, for Freud, anxiety originates from an instinct, and it has an existential nature for Heidegger, both correspond in emphasizing the indefinite nature of the object and the danger: fear is fear of a real, impending threat so recognizable that it can be avoided, while anxiety is instead a fear without a place or object. Therefore, due to the indefinite and elusive nature of the danger acting on individuals with the disorienting power of the *Unheimlich* (*uncanny*) and giving them the sensation of impotence, anxiety seems to be a suitable label for the new, undefined, and widespread fears that permeate the global, open, borderless society, with no clearly identifiable set of rules.

Nevertheless, in my opinion, even the concept of anxiety proves to be inadequate in this sense. Indeed, although they are prompted by undetermined, often invisible and incalculable elusive dangers located in the future, the new fears of the global age *have an object all the same*: the disquiet toward nuclear power or environmental decay are evidently feelings that do not come from an inner source, whether instinctual or existential, but from *external* events, produced by the very actions of humankind and the form of our social relations.

Therefore, the fears of the global age do not seem to be definable either using Hobbesian fear, since they derive from indefinite objects and dangers, or using the anxiety of Freud (or Heidegger), since they are nevertheless prompted by an external object. In this sense, the definition of "liquid fear" proposed by Zygmunt Bauman seems to give an effective description of the current transformations of this passion (Bauman 2006). It is an indistinct and widespread fear, generated by a feeling of insecurity and a perception of losing control over events. A fear that permeates the global age, produced by real dangers, but at the same time lacking a clear and immediately recognizable cause.

But what I wish to highlight is that, precisely because it is generated by a danger that is paradoxically both real and indefinite, concrete and phantasmal, fear seems to have lost that *productive* function pertaining to its modern configuration. So much so that the recently suggested definition of *unproductive* fear seems to be wholly pertinent: a fear lacking in positive effects, an implosive and paralyzing fear (Galli 1991).

**3.** Let us take a look at the reasons why. What I would like to uphold is that the indefinite nature of the threats produces a distortion in the *perception* of the danger since it allows us to implement defense strategies. As we will see now, these are *denial* and *self-deception*.

It is no coincidence that sociology and risk psychology agree on the importance of its indefinite nature and emphasize that what has a decisive influence on the way risk is perceived are its very characteristics (Lupton 1999; De Marchi et al. 2001; Savadori et al. 2005; Djalma Vitali 1994). Ulrich Beck had already stressed the fact that the often invisible nature of global risks, the unforeseeable nature of their effects, and the merely potential nature of the harm that they cause mean that they escape our perception and require a type of reflection that interprets the new scenarios through knowledge that is on a par with the new challenges.

But in reality the problem is even more complex. It is not that the risk is not seen; instead, we are faced with processes in which the *perception and assessment* of risk is *distorted*, and this affects both the emotional and cognitive spheres and, above all, *how they interact with each other*.

A field that is without doubt attentive to this problem is cognitive psychology which, starting from the classic studies by Chauncey Starr (1969) and then Fischoff and Slovic, and on the basis of what is called the psychometric paradigm, has come up with complex cognitive maps aimed at providing a list of variables with an influence on the subjective perception of risk (Starr 1969; Fischoff et al. 1978; Slovic et al. 1982; Slovic 2000). For example, these show that preoccupation in the face of threats (whether they derive from particular activities, substances, or technologies) grows in tandem with certain characteristics, including the involuntary nature of risks, the impossibility of controlling them, their ability to cause irreversible damage, and their originating from an unknown source. But above all, these maps emphasize the fact that individuals are prone to making distorted assessments and judgments of the risks to which they are exposed. For example, individuals tend to overestimate remote and exceptional risks and to underestimate less serious ones which are however more common and frequent; to overestimate threats publicized by the media even if they are occasional; to consider dangers faced voluntarily as more acceptable than dangers to which we are subjected or that are wholly unprecedented and unfamiliar; and to feel fear in the face of very vivid events (September 11, 2001), while at the same time having little capacity for a historic memory to link these events together.

The virtue of this approach is that it recognizes the impact of subjective aspects and the uncertainty factor in defining the concept of risk, and it pinpoints the presence of non-rational responses; however, its limits lie in its strong assumption of the notion of probability. For example, Mary Douglas claims that this approach ignores the social and institutional context and the symbolic-cultural factors that influence the perception of threats (1992). Thus, she again puts forward the idea of an individualistic and de-contextualized social actor based on an abstract idea of rationality.

But above all, I would like to suggest that the limit of this approach is that it does not take into account *why*, that is, the underlying reasons that pollute the correct perception and assessment of risks.

In this connection, some authors have used the reassessment of the role of the *emotions*, which in recent decades has greatly undermined the hegemonic paradigm of rationality,[3] to emphasize that cognitive and emotional factors must go together to recognize the existence of a risk and to assess the possible consequences (Savadori 2005). They uphold that the information entering our cognitive system can only have an effective impact on how we act if it manages to create images in our psyche laden with emotivity. This means that although we may know perfectly well that there are particular threats, it does not involve our emotions; we can only be deemed effectively aware of the risks and thus be suitably mobilized if our knowledge is transformed into the capacity to "feel," to react emotionally, and to imagine the possible effects.

Now, the current problem with global risks seems precisely to be triggered by the *imbalance between knowing and feeling*. Anders grasped this perfectly when he spoke of a "Promethean gap." With this expression he alludes to the split between the faculties, primarily the *split* between the power to do/to produce and the ability to foresee which characterizes the *homo creator*. Paradoxically, Anders says, the immense human power to produce and create that is possible because of developments in technology is matched by an inability to imagine the consequences (1956, Introduction, Part IV). Our imagination and our emotions are no longer on a par with our unlimited power. We can no longer keep *up-to-date* with our Promethean productivity and with the world that we built: "[. . .] we are on the brink of building a world that we cannot keep up with and in order to catch hold of it totally exorbitant requirements are made of our imagination, our emotions, and our responsibility" (Introduction). Prompted by this "schizophrenia" (Part IV, ch. 4), which is where the fundamental *pathology* of our era lies, is the paradoxical combination of power and impotence, activity and passivity, knowledge and unawareness that exposes the contemporary subject not only to previously unheard-of risks, but also and above all, to the impossibility to recognize their destructive potential.

This pathology appears particularly evident in the risk *par excellence* of the technological age, the risk that threatens not only the quality of individuals' lives (as happens, for example, in the case of the possible effects of biotechnology), but the very survival of humankind on the planet: that is, the risk produced by the creation

---

[3]   The obligatory reference is to Damasio (1994). But on the cognitive role of the emotions, see also Elster (1999) and M. Nussbaum (2003). I also refer to my book (Pulcini 2011b).

of the nuclear bomb, which we can recognize as the first effectively *global* challenge (Cerutti 2007). We built the bomb, Anders says. *We know* that it is not just a means but a monstrous *unicum* that can bring human life on earth to an end. And yet, this does not touch our emotivity. Because our *knowledge* does not correspond to a *feeling*: the split between producing and imagining is doubled into the split between knowing and feeling, between the *cognitive sphere* and the *emotional sphere*. Indeed, there is no one who does not know what the bomb is and who does not know of its possible catastrophic consequences; but, Anders adds, this *knowledge* does not generate reactions, it does not transform into action, because it does not suitably correspond to a feeling, to an awareness with an emotional basis.

Therefore, although the very destruction of humankind and all living things has become possible, there is, surprisingly, no fear (Anders 1956, part IV, ch. 3). Today *fear has become unavailable to us*; or rather, we are *anesthetizing* fear. And this anesthetic mechanism works in direct proportion to the enormity of the risk and what is at stake. While it is indeed true that at the very most we are able to imagine our own death, we are not able to imagine the death of tens of thousands of people. We are able to destroy a whole city without batting an eyelid, but we cannot imagine the terrible scenario of the *day after*. Hence, it is inevitable that we are wholly incapable of perceiving the destruction of the whole of humankind. Although the end of humanity has become possible and although we are ourselves responsible for this, the psyche recoils at the very idea of this possibility, therefore inhibiting the emergence of fear at the outset.

**4.** In my opinion, Anders' diagnosis of the *anesthetizing* of fear and the split between knowing and feeling corresponds precisely to that peculiar defense mechanism defined by Freud as the "denial of reality."

Denial (*Verleugnung*) is not repression (*Verdrängung*); it is a more complex and subtle mechanism. While with repression the subject pushes particular ideas linked to an instinct into his unconscious, denial means that, despite rationally recognizing a painful and difficult situation, the Self prevents it from reaching the emotional sphere. Repression is a defense against *internal drives*, while denial is a defense against the incitements of the *external reality* (Cohen 2001), which we recognize *rationally*, but do not feel or partake of *emotionally*. This is transformed into that peculiar ambivalence between "knowing and not-knowing" which belongs precisely to denial; an ambivalence that Anders had already caught onto and clearly underlined (Anders 1956, part IV, ch. 3).

The sociologist Stanley Cohen recently used the concept of *denial* to diagnose a series of phenomena that characterize contemporary society: "people, organizations, governments or whole societies are presented with information that is too disturbing, threatening or anomalous to be fully absorbed or openly acknowledged. The information is therefore somehow repressed, disavowed, pushed aside or reinterpreted. Or else the information 'registers' well enough, but its implications—cognitive, emotional or moral—are evaded, neutralized or rationalized away" (Cohen 2001, 1). There are many forms of denial, he says, and the psyche needs this defense mechanism. But the form that is most disconcerting and problematic, since it may, as is the case today, affect whole cultures, is precisely the one in which the subjects of denial are *at the same time aware and unaware*. In other words, they are placed in that gap between consciousness and unconsciousness which does allow access to reality, but in such a way as to ignore it since it is too frightening or painful or simply too unpleasant to accept. "We are vaguely aware," Cohen says, highlighting the ambivalence of denial, of choosing not to look at the facts, "but not quite conscious of just what it is we are evading. We know but at the same time we don't know" (5).

But that is not the extent of the complex dynamics of denial. In addition to the classically Freudian meaning that Cohen can take credit for bringing back to our attention, we can make out a variant of this defense mechanism that is, in some way, *more active*. This variant consists not only of withdrawing and sheltering ourselves in a sort of emotional indifference from a situation that is inconvenient or painful for the psyche, but also of lying to ourselves in order to believe something that responds not to our rational assessment, but to our desires. This is *self-deception*, a defense mechanism whose definition as "the most extreme form of the paradox of irrationality" (Davidson 1982) is no fluke.

Self-deception is what indeed drives individuals to form a belief that contrasts with the information at their disposal, since their *desires* interfere with their vision of reality and cause them to act differently than their own rational judgment would suggest. In other words, it consists of believing something because we want it to be true. It converges in this way, although there are differences, with the dynamic of *wishful thinking* (Davidson 1985, 1998; Pears 1985). Like denial, meant, so to speak, in its *pure* form, self-deception presupposes an *Ichspaltung*, a split subject. Finally, like denial, it is an ambivalent phenomenon since it acts in the gap between consciousness and unconsciousness and thereby creates a paradoxical situation of knowing and not-knowing (Cohen 2001, 65).

What I would like to suggest is that these two defense mechanisms allow us to explain different emotional reactions in the face of what I have defined as the two fundamental global risks: the *nuclear threat* and *global warming*.

In other words, while denial appears, as we have seen, to effectively explain the lack of perception and the anesthetizing of fear in the face of the *nuclear threat*, self-deception, in my opinion, may prove pertinent in order to understand the complex emotional response that individuals give to the other global risks mentioned above: that is, the twofold environmental risk of *global warming* and the *depletion of the ozone layer*.[4] Here, the undetermined nature that characterizes the nuclear risk is greatly augmented, due to the fact that global warming and the depletion of the ozone layer have wider margins of uncertainty, created by their inertia and the impossibility of measuring and predicting their future development, and therefore calculating their possible effects and the ultimate deadline for any countermeasures with any certainty. Their elusiveness and invisibility, further boosted by the difficulty of attribution, mean that, despite alarming international reports on the climate and reliable scientific

---

[4]  Here I would like to point out that, with the Montreal Protocol of 1987, some solutions were found for the second problem (relating to the risk of depletion of the ozone layer). These solutions were made possible by the fact that they did not require, as would be the case for a response to global warming, costs and sacrifices at the economic level or in terms of lifestyle.

forecasts on devastating future damage, which are also receiving increasing media attention, people overall seem to fail to fully grasp the phenomenon. We, therefore, often shrug off this excessively catastrophic outlook with distant irony. We resign ourselves to powerlessness or express our enlightened faith that technology will put everything right.

In other words, though known and rationally recognized, risk does not produce enough emotional involvement to give rise to effective answers. At most, it causes a widespread and generic feeling of anxiety and disquiet which ends up imploding, sucked in by the much more real concerns of everyday life.

The causes of this paradoxical situation can first of all be traced back to a location *within the same fear dynamic*, an essential aspect of which Hobbes grasped in his diagnosis. He tells us that fear, as the necessary and vital passion allowing us to respond to the immediate danger (of death), loses its effectiveness when the danger and the harm that could result from it shift to the *future*; that is, when temporal distance is inserted between the present action (founded on destructive passions) and its possible consequences, so as to rid the problem of all certainty and inevitability. As a result, it may be deemed a remote and avoidable possibility, so it does not make sense, nor is it worth it, to mobilize immediately. In other words, in this case the fear is not able to defeat present-day passions.

Hobbes's intuition is all the more apt in the case of global risks, whose possible harm is even more remote and particularly concerns future generations. That is, fear does not have the strength to change present action (and therefore the underlying desires and passions) when the damage that this action can cause is bad not for ourselves but for "others," who are anonymous, generic, and far off in time. In short, by weakening fear, the future nature of the damage makes it easy for essentially self-preserving individuals, preoccupied with satisfying their own desires, to deceive themselves as to the nature of the risk itself, therefore they minimize it or deny its possible consequences. In this case, the aim is not so much to defend ourselves emotionally against events that are too painful to bear (as in the case of the nuclear threat), but to carry on acting in a way that allows individuals to legitimize and satisfy their current desires, to preserve their lifestyle and not lose consolidated privileges.

In short, individuals resort to self-deception in order not to pay the price of giving up their current desires, assets, and pleasures, further helped, in this self-defensive operation, by the morally innocent, innocuous, and banally everyday nature of the actions that produce the risks.

To sum up, what I wish to emphasize is that, precisely because it is generated by a danger that is at once and paradoxically real and undetermined, concrete and phantasmal, fear seems to have lost its *productive* function, that is, the active and mobilizing function pertaining to its modern and Hobbesian configuration. It has become *unproductive* fear, that is, a fear lacking in positive effects, implosive, and paralyzing. The lack of a productive fear, inhibited by denial and self-deception, is not belied by the cyclical occurrence of crises of panic and collective hysteria which break out upon the sudden appearance of threats (as has always happened from Chernobyl to SARS to bird flu). On the contrary, a *lack* and an *excess of fear* are nothing but two sides of the same coin, the two extreme and "unproductive" forms of the manifestation of *global fear*.

5. Therefore, we need to *learn to fear again*. This requires two fundamental conditions that I can but hint at here, while returning to the philosophical reflection of Anders and Jonas (see Pulcini 2011a, Part 3).

First of all we need a subject who could be defined as reconciled, who recreates a connection between cognitive and emotional functions, between the power to do and to produce, and the capacity to feel and to imagine. This subject, as a consequence, will be able to avoid denying reality.

To use Anders's terms, it is a case of overcoming the Promethean gap, bringing our *ability to feel* back up to the level of the challenges of the global age. First, this requires the ability to reactivate the *imagination* in order to be able to foresee the possible consequences of *homo creator*'s unlimited actions. Imagining the catastrophic scenarios of our actions means becoming aware of the need for a limit, which we must assume in order to reappropriate our future. It means gaining awareness that, for the first time in the history of humankind, the very possibility of future existence depends on our actions and our decisions in the here and now, in our present.

Second, I would like to suggest that only reconciled subjects, that is, subjects who have reestablished contact between their faculties, have the capacity to access a form of productive and mobilizing fear. Nevertheless, it no longer has to be a selfish fear, that is, a *fear of*, such as Hobbes's fear, but instead, as Hans Jonas suggests, a *fear for*: in other words, a fear for the destiny of the world. The global age may give the objective premises for this form of fear as it brings us all together in a single humankind, united by the same challenges and by a single, possible destiny.

It is upon these premises that we lay down the ethical wager concerning the *responsibility* for our actions, as Hans Jonas had already proposed at the dawn of the global age when he underlined the nexus between fear and responsibility. Without fear, meant as fear for the world, today there can be no access to responsibility, in the sense of being aware of the consequences of our actions, the risks to which our actions expose the whole living world.

This means, in other words, that in order to give rise to an *ethics of responsibility*, we need to rediscover the *emotional* foundations of ethics. But I would have to start a whole new chapter about this.

# Bibliography

Anders, G. 1956. *Die Antiquiertheit des Menschen*. Bd. I, München: C. H. Beck.
Bauman, Z. 1998. *Globalization. The Human Consequences*. Cambridge-Oxford: Polity Press-Blackwell Publishers.
— 1999. *In Search of Politics*. Cambridge: Polity Press.
— 2006. *Liquid Fear*. Cambridge: Polity Press.

Beck, U. 1986. *Risikogesellschaft. Auf dem Weg in eine Andere Moderne.* Frankfurt: Suhrkamp.

— 1988. *Gegengifte. Die organisierte Unverantwortlichkeit.* Frankfurt: Suhrkamp.

— 1998. *World Risk Society.* Cambridge: Polity Press.

Castells, M. 2001. *Internet Galaxy: Reflections on the Internet, Business, and Society.* Oxford: Oxford University Press.

Cerutti, F. 2007. *Global Challenges for Leviathan.* Lanham: Lexington/Rowman & Littlefield Publishers.

Cohen, S. 2001. *States of Denial.* Cambridge: Polity Press.

D'Andrea, D. 2004. "Rischi ambientali globali e aporie della modernità." In *Epimeteo e il Golem. Riflessioni su uomo, natura e tecnica nell'età globale.* Edited by D. Belliti. Pisa: ETS. 32–8.

Damasio, A. R. 1994. *Descartes' Error. Emotion, Reason and the Human Brain.* New York: Putman.

Davidson, D. 1982. "Paradoxes of Irrationality." In *Philosophical Essays on Freud.* Edited by R. A. Wollheim and J. Hopkins. Cambridge: Cambridge University Press. 289–305.

— 1985. "Deception and Division." In *Actions and Events.* Edited by E. Lepore and B. McLaughlin. Oxford: Basil Blackwell. 138–48.

— 1998. "Who is Fooled?" In *Self-Deception and Paradoxes of Rationality.* Edited by J. P. Dupuy. Stanford: CSLI Publications. 1–18.

De Marchi, B., L. Pellizzoni, and D. Ungaro. 2001. *Il rischio ambientale.* Bologna: Il Mulino.

Djalma Vitali, E. 1994. *Pericoli e paure. La percezione del rischio tra allarmismo e disinformazione.* Venezia: Marsilio.

Douglas, M. 1992. *Risk and Blame.* London and New York: Routledge.

Elster, J. 1999. *Alchemies of the Mind: Rationality and the Emotions.* Cambridge: Cambridge University Press.

Fischoff, B., P. Slovic, S. Lichtenstein, S. Read, and B. Combs. 1978. "How Safe is Safe Enough? A Psychometric Study of Attitude towards Technological Risks and Benefits." *Policy Sciences* 9: 127–52.

Freud, S. 1977. *Inhibitions, Symptoms and Anxiety.* New York: W. W. Norton & Co.

Galli, C. 1991. *Modernità della paura. Jonas e la responsabilità.* Bologna: Il Mulino.

Giddens, A. 1990. *The Consequences of Modernity.* Cambridge: Polity Press.

— 1999. *Runaway World. How Globalization is Reshaping our Lives.* London: Profile Books.

Habermas, J. 2001. *Die Zukunft der menschlichen Natur.* Frankfurt: Suhrkamp.

Heidegger, M. 1989. *Being and Time.* New York: State University of New York Press.

Hobbes, T. 1985. *Leviathan.* London: Penguin Books.

Jonas, H. 1979. *Das Prinzip Verantwortung.* Frankfurt: Insel.

Lupton, D. 1999. *Risk.* London: Taylor and Francis Books-Routledge.

Nussbaum, M. 2003. *Upheavals of Thought: The Intelligence of Emotions.* Cambridge: Cambridge University Press.

Pears, D. 1985. "The Goals and Strategies of Self-Deception." In *The Multiple Self.* Edited by J. Elster. Cambridge: Cambridge University Press. 79–92.

Pulcini, E. 2011a. *Care of the World. Fear and Responsibility in the Global Age.* The Netherlands: Springer. (Translation of 2009, *La cura del mondo. Paura e responsabilità in età globale,* Torino: Bollati Boringhieri).

— 2011b. *The Individual without Passions. Modern Individualism and the Loss of Social Bond*. Lexington: Lanham (USA). (Translation of 2001, *L'individuo senza passioni. Individualismo moderno e perdita del legame sociale*. Torino: Bollati Boringhieri).

Savadori, L. and R. Rumiati. 2005. *Nuovi rischi, vecchie paure. La percezione del pericolo nella società contemporanea*. Bologna: Il Mulino.

Slovic, P. 2000. *The Perception of Risk*. London: Earthscan.

Slovic, P., B. Fischoff, and S. Liechtenstein. 1982. "Facts versus Fear. Understanding Perceived Risks." In *Judgment under Uncertainty: Heuristics and Biases*. Edited by D. Kahneman, P. Slovic, and A. Tversky. Cambridge: Cambridge University Press. 463–89.

Starr, C. 1969. "Social Benefit Versus Technological Risk." *Science* 165: 1232–8.

Virilio, P. 1998. *La bombe informatique*. Paris: Galilée.

# 8

# Certainty, Risk, and Uncertainty

Serge Champeau
*Bordeaux*

The current economic crisis confronts us not only with "risk" (inherent to any economic activity in a market economy) but also with "certainty" and "uncertainty." From the beginning of the crisis, economic agents, and beyond them, all citizens, have indeed discovered that they can no longer consider themselves as rational agents, *calculating* risks. Instead, they should consider themselves as subjects confronted with certainties (the inevitability of pension reforms and controlling the state budget) and uncertainties (will the common European currency disappear? will another large-scale terrorist attack strike a Western country?) and essentially, as subjects generating various *affects* when faced with inevitability and contingency.

These concepts (certainty, risk, and uncertainty) are nothing new. Before and during the crisis of the 1930s, economists like Knight and Keynes drew attention to the difference between risk, which is calculable, and uncertainty, whose mathematic probability is incalculable (Knight 2008; Keynes 2007). Keynes thought that the next world war or the price of copper in 20 years would end up as an uncertainty, rather than a risk: "we simply do not know" (1937). In his *General Theory*, he noted that with uncertainty, our decisions "can only be taken as a result of animal spirits—of a spontaneous urge to action rather than inaction, and not as the outcome of a weighted average of quantitative benefits multiplied by quantitative probabilities . . ." (2007, ch. 12, VIII). Even if this distinction between risk and uncertainty is often challenged today (it is not firmly established, since there are intermediate states which are neither calculable nor non-calculable), I find it relevant to account for what will be the object of my analysis: a true experience of certainties, risks, and uncertainties at the level of what is known as public opinion. It may be that what seems a risk to the eyes of experts (for the secret service, the next terrorist attacks in Europe) is more or less calculable. However, in the definition of "uncertainty" above, this risk is uncertain in the eyes of citizens. And as we have seen during the recent financial crisis, one of the dimensions of this uncertainty is that even if they know the experts' opinions, citizens cannot quantify the probability of experts' calculations (as all pundits on the recent crisis noticed, irrational exuberance has the effect, among others, of overestimating the truth of these calculations). The distinction between risk and uncertainty, as defined above, is accepted here only as a purely descriptive definition, aimed at realizing a representative opinion (I am aware that public opinion is not homogeneous and that a more precise analysis of this concept is necessary, something which cannot be treated in this chapter). Certain theorists of the current crisis, such as R. A. Posner (2010), who have now rediscovered the theory of uncertainty and incorporated it into stimulating analyses, seem to be using uncertainty in a way similar to mine.

Forgetting about these fundamental distinctions for years is understandable. During a period of relative stability or economic growth, the median area of risk and rational activity indeed takes the spotlight, even if, as many commentators on the crisis such as Akerloff and Shiller (2009) have shown, it is mere façade (the apparent stability may hide "a situation in which confidence has gone beyond normal bounds, in which an increasing fraction of people has lost their normal skepticism about the economic outlook and are ready to believe stories about a new economic boom" (65)). In times of crisis, on the other hand, the extremes of certainty and uncertainty, and the emotional responses they generate, make their existence known to consumers, entrepreneurs, citizens, and to all those whose job it is to try to understand what is happening.

At first glance, this might seem to simply be a return to a normal situation. For a long while, humanity has been more concerned with these extremes than with the median area of risk. Throughout history, cultures have developed a wide range of affects faced with certainty (existence, death, the duty to work, etc.) and with uncertainty (the ultimate end of human existence as well as more concrete matters: epidemic, famine, war, etc.). Astonishment, gratitude, resignation, or revolt, and many other emotional tones have allowed us to understand and tolerate the inevitable—and hope, desperation, or skepticism have bolstered our ability to face contingency. Historians know the complexity of this web of emotions (to take but one example, death has been understood, depending on the culture, as either the certainty of an end or as the uncertainty of a passing-on, and each of these interpretations has led to various emotions). As for philosophers, they have developed elegant analyses on the types of certainty and uncertainty and on the multiplicity of corresponding affects. For example, Heidegger interpreted the certainty of being as the inevitability of that which is radically contingent, without reason: being, the fact that something is—*das Ereignis*—is the event that all beings suppose, an event that is not explainable in the manner in which all other beings and events are, which means that it is not, strictly speaking, an event.[1] Wittgenstein (1971, 150) said that certainty is the inevitability of that which lies beyond necessity and contingency (since the existence of the world is not empirical, for we cannot think of it otherwise; it is, strictly speaking, neither contingent nor necessary, since these two concepts assume a contrast, in this case an opportunity not to be). But these distinctions within the concept of certainty are secondary to the thing that these philosophers have in common: the fact that there is always a link between certainty and affectivity. For Heidegger, any understanding

---

[1]   See Heidegger 1976, for example pages 28–9 on the "ontological difference."

(*Verstehen*) of being (thus any certainty in the sense I just gave) is accompanied by affective tones (*Stimmungen*), which Heidegger placed under the general heading of *Befindlichkeit* (the feelings of being are angst, serenity, or even ennui, which for him is "an attitude of facing time, a feeling of time," 1992, 127). In the same manner, in his first works, Wittgenstein (1971, 1961, prop. 6.44 and 6.45) pointed out the tight bond that exists between certainty (that the world *is*, a certainty that cannot be expressed) and affectivity (amazement in the face of this inexpressible presence of the world). That is to say that for both these authors the sphere of rational calculation is bounded by that of affectivity (or, if we place ourselves on the side of the forms of objectivity rather than subjective experiences, that the sphere of contingent events is bound on one side by the inevitable and on the other by uncertainty).[2]

The impatient reader might wonder how such analyses, which appear to belong to the metaphysical realm, could clear up the phenomenon I am considering here, the economic crisis. We can, however, come to this by saying that the era in which we are living reminds us of something that philosophers often forget: the fact that certainty and uncertainty are not only constants of human existence, as we saw with Heidegger and Wittgenstein, but also that beyond their universal forms, demonstrated by all cultures, they are arranged in particular and contingent patterns during certain economic conditions. For example, certainty today takes forms unknown by past generations. A reform, like pension reform in France, might be considered inevitable not because of fate or providence or historical necessity (what Marx called "alienation," that is the fact that people's free actions in history end up escaping them, solidifying and imposing themselves upon people with the necessity of a natural law (1968, 163)), but rather because faraway and unknown, yet omnipresent experts show that it is necessary. In a recent article on our pension system, Roger Pol-Droit (2010) believes that the unavoidable nature of the reforms generated a complex response with a large number of the French, something that he called, following the psychoanalyst O. Mannoni, "*négaffirmation*": "Yes, I know, but still . . ." Yes, a pension reform (in whatever form it might take) is inevitable and reasonable, but I still find it unacceptable that I should work more than the previous generation, because there may be another solution somewhere, even if we do not know it, etc.[3] It seems to me that this is a new form of objectivity, accompanied by new affects. We have no word to designate a belief in an objective proposition (the pension system is in danger, the state's debt has become unsustainable) forever unverifiable by lay subjects (likening it to a scientific proposition) and marked with doubt (more so that scientific propositions, but at times only slightly more), and more of an ever-possible doubt than a real doubt. For lack of a better term, if we call this new form of objectivity "quasi-objectivity" (we would actually need a more paradoxical term), we could call the affects it engages "quasi-emotions," which are also as numerous as the ontological emotions that our philosophers pointed

---

[2]  This hasty analysis of feelings, which for Heidegger and Wittgenstein come with certainty, should be completed by the analysis of feelings confronted with uncertainty.

[3]  This concept of *négaffirmation* needs to be discussed further. Let us just say that it does not include the strong hypothesis of the unconscious, unlike the Freudian concepts of "disavowal" (*Verleugnung*) and "negation" (*Verneinung*).

out: the quasi-resignation of the convinced (which, as any poll clearly indicates, does not keep them from supporting demonstrations) or the quasi-anger of the opposition (who shout even louder that they "cannot really believe it").[4]

The job of analyzing these affective reactions to new types of certainty is much less advanced than that of different affective reactions to uncertainty. Keynes performs remarkable analyses on these "animal spirits" of optimism and pessimism, as well as many others, in particular what he calls "the uncontrollable and disobedient psychology of the business world" (2007, ch. 22, II). In order to develop Keynes's analyses, we would need to meticulously analyze the quasi-hopes and quasi-fears resulting from the crisis and its uncertainties. For instance, in France it is clear that if we discard minority opinions (on the one hand, those who fight for sustainable development, and on the other, deniers of ecological matters), we find ourselves with an average sentiment (which could still be distinctly subdivided) or a quasi-fear, a paradoxical feeling (a true fear which does not truly fear), leading to paradoxical behaviors (e.g. a strong call to action in favor of the environment accompanied by a rejection of the carbon tax or complaints about energy-saving light bulbs). Of course, we can judge politicians severely when they bring up this paradoxical feeling (in a unique style yet one that is deeply revealing of this paradox: "We've had just about enough of the environment!"[5]), but we must not forget that this sentiment is deeply rooted in both French and, to various degrees, European populations, and it may develop further if the economic crisis persists (we must also not forget that political leaders need not follow the average opinion, but this is another topic).

In this domain, we can hope that these analyses will avoid certain problems that may await them, for instance, bringing the distinction between calculation and affect to the classic opposition between reason and feeling. Saying that cultures develop various affects when confronted with certainty and uncertainty (we need only compare the psychology of the French and the British during the current crisis) does not amount to denouncing affects as irrational (or as cognitive bias). In his analysis of what he called "animal spirits," Keynes highlights the fact that action in an uncertain situation, driven by optimism or by a taste for risk, is far from irrational—and there is no shortage of psychologists and biologists (e.g. Nettle 2006) who work on emphasizing the adaptive nature of risky behaviors (one of the most serious effects of the crisis is reinforcing the aversion to risk, making us forget that not all risks taken translate to irrational exuberance). Affects are more a-rational than irrational and as any individual can verify in his or her own case, they can inhibit just as well as incite. This is why they are and must be the object of particular attention from political and union leaders in contemporary democracies, and more broadly from all those who exert influence on public opinion (experts, journalists, teachers, etc.). Policy making is not a matter of only making technical decisions (based on calculated risks) or only making political

---

4   "All the French are schizophrenic: they know it is the end of an era, that they must change, but without really believing it," Eric Le Boucher, *Les Echos* (October 8, 2010). While the term "schizophrenic" is inappropriate, the intention is clear.
5   Speech by Nicolas Sarkozy, President of the French Republic, before an audience of farmers.

decisions (trying to harmonize various interests). It also means managing affects, that is when faced with new forms of certainty and uncertainty, considering that affective responses are an essential aspect (which only technocrats would wish to eliminate) and that since they may take many forms, becoming valuable auxiliaries to action or inhibiting panics, these affects must be influenced, modified, or even hindered depending on what is considered to be the common good. All affectively motivated actions are not equal. Resigning, revolting, or praying are not similar attitudes . . . When faced with uncertainty, none of these actions is essentially irrational or rational. In a given circumstance, each one can be a means to explore new solutions and escape a difficult situation. The complexity of our world is measured by the fact that the boundary between certain ways of dealing with affects, either efficient or counter-productive, is particularly vague. In matters of immigration or terrorism, reassuring and causing worry are fundamental aspects of political action, but we know how delicate it can be to find a correct balance in this field. This obviously must not move us to inaction, but rather to become aware that the era of simplistic political behaviors toward certainties and uncertainties has passed. For example, we might think that pension reform is necessary, that the one that government has proposed is acceptable and, *at the same time*, think that the angry reactions by a segment of public opinion, grounded or not, are a way of signaling underlying problems in a democracy, even if they have no relationship whatsoever with the pension system, or as a means to encourage the discovery of new ways—and it is probable that such an attitude toward the affects of public opinion will change them in return.

Another major complexity in the political management of public affects lies in the fact that public affects are never controlled by anything but other affects. If the current crisis reminds us that, not only risk, but certainty and uncertainty are as inherent to the human condition (as highlighted by the philosophers above) as to everyday human life and its hazards (which the crisis finally only heightens), then politics cannot be confused with a technique, even the technique most inclined to carefully calculate risks (which it does not always do). And if affects are inherent to social life since it too always includes, not only risk, but also certainty and uncertainty, then it would be vain to think that we might manage these affects technically. This daydream represents a particular form of technocracy: something intelligent enough to understand that works upon human matters, that is affects, yet not intelligent enough to understand that it is made up of the exact same matter (of course there are other fantasies of the technical management of affects, from paternalism to totalitarianism, which I shall not discuss here). In other, more precise words, we cannot control the fears that certainty and uncertainty about the crisis generate with only fear, but with a particular fear, as Roosevelt mentioned during another crisis: the fear of fear ("The only thing we have to fear is fear itself"). In France, and most likely elsewhere, individually and collectively, through public debate, there is nothing more vital than to be able to fear our fears (or to put it as Hume would, to replace our violent passions by calm passions, or as Akerlof and Shiller (2009, 173) say: "our animal spirits can be harnessed creatively to serve the greater good"). Admitting the problems of climate change, the floundering financial system, and also immigration, terrorism, the possible dissolution of national identity, etc. (and not foolishly denying them, as French politicians often do, each selecting pet risks in order to more easily reject or forget the others), trying to develop a reasonable fear for them, and thus a reasonable hope of resolving them, seems to me to be the only path—albeit a narrow one—that the political management of public affects should take.

Let us put this another way: in times of crisis, faced with the danger represented by certain affective reactions (searching for scapegoats—whether immigrants or bankers—or even pessimism and defeatism), we sometimes foster the hope that, with lots of effort and imagination, we can return to the happy medium where we only deal with risks and calculations, or so we would believe. We would then dream of a future where as long as everything was going well, as long as the economy was on the upswing, it would once again be possible for us to occupy our lives with rational calculation (economy, politics) in charge of the domain of risk and reflection upon existence (religion, wisdom, philosophy, or whatever name we might give it) which would tackle the extremes of certainty and uncertainty and the complex affects they produce within us. However, it would be delusional to divide human existence like this, pitting universal constants (the certainty of living and dying, the uncertainty of our ultimate goals) against variable contingencies (the risks inherent to technical, economic, and political activity), or pitting affectivity against calculation. Only the elite, and particularly the intellectual elite, live in a world where culture (which interprets certainty and uncertainty) and technique (which calculates risk) are juxtaposed. Nowadays, the French are confronted with quite concrete certainties and uncertainties in their work and everyday lives (e.g. the certainty that we must partake in the globalization of the economy and the extreme uncertainty of what will become of it, according to the definitions of "certainty" and "uncertainty" given above). They are fostering various affects, which can very well be either our downfall or our salvation. Yet, even though we must calculate, we will not get out of the crisis simply by calculating better and by doing everything to transform the terrifying uncertainties into run-of-the-mill risks. We will only get out if, in politics, we hold both ends of the chain: rational action in one hand and, in the other, the collective management of affects which arise from being exposed to new forms of raw necessity and radical contingency. We know that the first task is difficult and we are only beginning to discover the difficulty of the second (I am reminded particularly of the stimulating analyses by H. Thaler and C. Sunstein in *Nudge*, where the authors argue, when addressing the feelings which overestimate the good or underestimate the bad, in favor of "libertarian paternalism" whereby public authorities encourage citizens through the "gentle power of nudges" to change their feelings and to better satisfy the needs that were explicitly theirs).[6] The current economic crisis will perhaps serve to remind us what politics means and which form it may now take to deal with the quasi-feeling that arises from quasi-certainties and quasi-uncertainties (it should be understood that by "remind us what politics means"

---

[6]  See Thaler and Sunstein (2008, 5–8). See also page 72: "people will need nudges for decisions that are difficult and rare, for which they do not get prompt feedback, and when they have trouble translating aspects of the situation into terms that they can easily understand."

I do not intend the same thing as those, especially in France, who think that the risks and uncertainties which are presented by the crisis point us back to the very simple fact that it is the state's responsibility to manage the economy and society).

# Bibliography

Akerlof, G. A. and R. J. Schiller. 2009. *Animal Spirits*. Princeton: Princeton University Press.

Droit, R. P. 2010. "Retraites: la négaffirmation." *Les Echos* 29/09/2010.

Heidegger, M. 1976. *Acheminement vers la parole*. Paris: Gallimard.

— 1992. *Les concepts fondamentaux de la phénoménologie*. Paris: Gallimard.

Keynes, J. M. 1937. "The General Theory of Employment." *Quarterly Journal of Economics* 51.

— 2007. *The General Theory of Employment, Interest and Money*. Evergreen Edition, Inc. Kindle edition.

Knight, F. H. 2008. *Risk, Uncertainty, and Profit*. Evergreen Edition, Inc. Kindle edition.

Marx, K. 1968. *L'idéologie allemande*. Paris: Editions Sociales.

Nettle, D. 2006. "The Evolution of Personality Variation in Humans and Other Animals." *American Psychologist* 61.

Posner, R. A. 2010. *The Crisis of Capitalist Democracy*. Cambridge: Harvard University Press.

Thaler, R. H. and C. R. Sunstein. 2008. *Nudge*. New Haven and London: Yale University Press.

Wittgeinstein, L. 1961. *Tractatus logico-philosophicus*. Paris: Gallimard.

— 1971. "Conférence sur l'éthique." In *Leçons et conversations*. Paris: Gallimard.

# 9

# Global Warming as a Globalized Risk and Global Threat for Future Generations

Dimitri D'Andrea
*University of Florence*

*"A society that assumes growth as its goal is like a person who considers obesity an ideal."*

(Luigi Pintor)

This contribution attempts to provide an analysis of some of the emotive and cognitive processes that make it so difficult to deal with *global* challenges. The essence and nature of these difficulties vary in relation to the different types of challenges. In this chapter, I will analyze the phenomenon of global warming, while trying to identify the difficulties connected to taking responsibility toward/for future generations. Nevertheless, I will inevitably also have to briefly mention two other global challenges: the risk of a large-scale nuclear conflict and the threat of the depletion of the ozone layer.

## Global challenges and globalized phenomena: Community and interdependence

I would like to start by establishing some distinctions. The first is the difference between global and globalized, between a global phenomenon as something (an event or process) that defines a condition of community and a globalized phenomenon as something (an event or process) that describes a condition of interdependence.

A global phenomenon or process is one that possesses four characteristics:[1]

First, it involves all the individuals on the planet. A global phenomenon outlines a *homogeneous* space: a global challenge is a threat or a risk that does not simply involve

---

[1]  I take this definition of *global* from Cerutti (2007).

a multitude of individuals in different and distant places, but concerns all individuals and all places on earth.

Second, something is global when it not only involves all individuals, but also all individuals in the same way and with the same intensity.

Third, a global challenge (risk or threat) is one that comprises the possibility of damage that cannot be indifferent to anyone. *Global* can only be an event that erases any possible differences in evaluation and every discrepancy in the calculation of the costs and benefits.

Fourth, a global challenge is one that can only be fought if everyone takes part.

Only a phenomenon that has all four of these characteristics can be defined as global. Hence, the adjective global references a particular extension and intensity of risk or threat. A global challenge is a risk or threat that concerns everyone in the same way, cannot be indifferent to anyone, and can only be effectively confronted with a contribution from everyone. A global risk or threat is one that establishes the foundation of an *objective community* of interests, which is so radical as to overcome differences of opinion in the cost–benefit calculation and so universal as to get past partial involvement.

On the contrary, a globalized phenomenon is one that does not involve all the inhabitants on the planet or does not involve them all in the same way. In other words, a globalized phenomenon is one that:

1. involves a large number of individuals who may be located in very distant parts of the planet, but not *all* human beings. In this sense, a globalized phenomenon is one that not only embraces the planet like a net and that, like a net, connects places and people on a planetary scale, but also possesses *areas of non-involvement*, empty spaces (*unsaturated* spaces); or
2. involves human beings in general, but in ways that lead to or cause far-reaching differences between the interests of some and the interests of others, between those who choose to risk and those subject to the danger, between those who risk damage and gain an advantage, on the one hand, and those who only risk damage on the other, between those who are exposed to radical damage and those simply exposed to a nuisance. In this sense, globalized space is a *totally filled* (*saturated*) space, but it is not *homogeneous*: a globalized phenomenon is a phenomenon to which no one is immune, but which for some is a resource and for others only damage, for some a choice and for others destiny, for some a catastrophe and for others a nuisance.

The reason for the distinction between globalized and global phenomena is that only the latter establish an *objective* foundation for the community of mankind. A globalized phenomenon causes an objective situation of *interdependence* (which can also be planetary); a global phenomenon leads to an objective situation of *community*.

The assimilation of phenomena that involve many people scattered all over the planet to truly global phenomena can only be upheld if the possibilities of involvement in the globalized phenomena are the same for everyone, and only if a particular event that does not involve everyone could involve anyone in the same way. In reality, in some of the types of risk that Beck (2007) defines as global (climate change, terrorism, nuclear energy, atomic weapons, economic–financial crises), this uniformity of exposure does not occur: not only for individuals, but also for nations, regions, social groups, etc. Terrorism is a globalized risk because it can strike in many places scattered around the planet, but it is not true that it could strike everywhere, nor that we are all equally likely to become targets. Until the end of this century, climate change will not harm the inhabitants of the planet as a whole. There will be regions that will even benefit from it.

## Risks and threats, present and future generations

The second distinction I intend to propose is between a *risk* and a *threat*. Here the bottom line is drawn by the nature and position of uncertainty. We take the term *risk* to mean the possibility (which at times can be associated with a numeric value) of a harmful future event that may derive from particular processes that are underway or from particular future events. It is a future event that we are not able to predict due to the uncertainty (epistemological or ontological) that surrounds the causes needed to produce it. Therefore, a risk can be defined as the probability of a harmful event conditioned by the production of *further* events and processes to those already underway. In other words, in the case of risk, we do not know if the events (of whatever kind they may be) needed to produce a particular harmful event will actually take place. The uncertainty concerns whether there is—or there will be—sufficient cause.

On the contrary, the notion of *threat* intends to emphasize the prior existence of processes that could produce future harmful events. While the term "risk" refers to the probability (whose entity is also unknown) of a future harmful event, a "threat" refers to a certainty, if no events or decisions take place that could interrupt the current course of events. In the event of a threat, the probability of damage does not refer to the uncertainty of the active cause, but to the uncertainty of an inhibitory event. The probability/possibility contained in a threat relates to the existence of a margin of time for inhibitory factors to burst in. With a risk, something has to happen for a certain event to be produced (and we do not know if that will take place); with a threat, something has to happen (and we do not know if it will take place) for what is already being produced and can, at best, be stopped, to not come into being. A threat refers to the idea of something being inevitable if nothing new happens, if nothing interrupts a process that is already underway.

Finally, a third distinction has to be made referring to the temporal dimension of the challenge. We need to distinguish between risks and threats looming over present generations and risks and threats that will only concern future generations.

# Features of the phenomenon

In order to grasp the reasons it is so difficult to fight global warming, at this point we need to quickly go through some of its features.

1. In the next 100/150 years, the consequences of global warming will not necessarily be harmful, and as already said, they will not even be distributed equally.[2] There will be areas and populations on the planet for whom global warming will have positive effects, favoring human activities in various ways. There will be other areas where the positive effects will go hand in hand with negative effects, and finally there will be areas which will experience negative effects alone. In short, for the next 100/150 years global warming will not have catastrophic effects, it will not have exclusively negative effects, nor will it have the same effects on everybody.

2. If we are to look further into the future, the scenario becomes extremely different. The long-term effects of a lack of policies to curb greenhouse gas emissions will be to produce a change in the ecosystem that could compromise the conditions for the survival of human civilization. The uncertainty as to the "how" and "when" of not necessarily or universally harmful events in the short term would be associated with the certainty of the final disaster, its inevitability if no opportune limits are introduced. In the long term, the increase in greenhouse gas emissions is like building and launching a missile which sooner or later—but inevitably—will strike the earth, jeopardizing human civilization.

3. An essential feature of global warming is that it is extremely inertial. Inertia, typical of complex systems, implies a constitutive imbalance between the decision-makers and those feeling the consequences of those decisions. Complexity produces inertia, and inertia consumes time. What present generations do in the next two decades will make very little difference to what will happen in the next 45 years, but it will have a profound effect on the climate in the second half of this century and in the next.[3]

4. Lastly, global warming is a phenomenon which progresses in a nonlinear fashion. Precisely due to the complex nature of the phenomenon, due to the possibility of feedback and the probability that a change in some elements of the ecosphere could prompt a domino effect, it seems impossible to identify a point of no return with any certainty, a threshold beyond which the process of global warming becomes uncontrollable or generates irreversible and disastrous effects on the

---

[2] "For the next few decades [climate change] will neither affect the planet's inhabitants without distinction or all in the same way, nor will it strike with such radical events as to prompt evaluations and concerns that are necessarily and absolutely the same for all" (Stern 2006).

[3] "The effects of our actions now on future changes in the climate have long lead times. What we do now can have only a limited effect on the climate over the next 40 or 50 years. On the other hand, what we do in the next 10 or 20 years can have a profound effect on the climate in the second half of this century and in the next" (Stern 2006, I).

conditions for human life on the planet. The global warming trend and its impact on the ecosphere and life forms do not proceed in a linear fashion: the greater and more rapid the progress of global warming, the more probable the emergence of sudden events and irreversible catastrophes.

On the basis of these features and the terminology proposed, global warming is the cause of a series of globalized risks in the near future and a global threat to the very survival of human civilization for future generations in a more distant future. It is the factor triggering a series of short- and mid-term risks of neither the size nor the universality to generate a universal convergence of interests to fight it. But it is also a process that will inevitably lead—in a distant future if not fought in time—to the extinction of the conditions that have made human civilization on this planet possible. The risk of harmful events in the short-/mid-term is associated with the threat of disaster in a not immediate future. A disaster deferred in time, but inevitable, if we continue to behave as usual. Something that is also a global threat, and not only a globalized risk, because of:

1. the necessary link between the present cause and the future consequences: the future self-destruction of human civilization has its necessary and sufficient cause in our present way of life;
2. its radical nature: the extinction of human civilization induced by humankind is something that escapes all cost–benefit calculations in terms of the meaning and enormity of the damage;
3. its capacity to involve all human beings in the same way;
4. the need for worldwide cooperation to deal with it effectively.

According to the proposed terminology, the depletion of the ozone layer was also a global threat for future generations, and the very presence of nuclear weapons is a global risk for present generations.[4] While in the case of a nuclear conflict, the production of damage is linked to the appearance of an as-yet unmade human decision, in the case of global warming, destruction in a not-too-distant future of human civilization is the necessary and inevitable consequence if we continue our current lifestyles and behave as at present, unchanged.

## Moral and political implications

These features of the global warming phenomenon give rise to some morally and politically significant consequences.

**1.** First of all, global warming puts us up against an unprecedented version of *responsibility as accountability* for an event that causes someone harm ("responsibility for").

---

[4] For a classification of nuclear weapons as a threat, see Campbell (2003); Morgenthau (1954a; 1954b); Sagan and Waltz (1995).

a. The catastrophic effects caused by global warming are situated in an undetermined future and nevertheless in times and places very distant from the action and individual conduct causing them.

b. The possibility of damage to health and people's activities is the counterproductive and indirect consequence of technology that is in itself harmless. Carbon dioxide is a collateral product of modern industrial civilization and the exponential increase in the availability of goods that characterizes that civilization. The drastic rise in $CO_2$ emissions is linked to the industrial revolution and the massive use of fossil fuels (first coal and then oil) that made it possible and to conduct and lifestyles not directly connected to industrial production such as air traffic and private transport. We are dealing with "good," useful technology that produces catastrophic consequences only indirectly and for extrinsic reasons. Global warming is an undesired consequence of technology and behavior that are in themselves innocent. The individual conduct that contributes to producing the global threat of atmospheric warming does not possess any intrinsic negative quality in moral terms. It is a conduct that in no way anticipates or predicts the enormity and gravity of its consequences.

c. The global threat of global warming for future generations is the consequence of banal and day-to-day individual behavior: from using electrical appliances to transportation for work and free time. The catastrophic effects induced by global warming depend on generalized behavior in everyday individual life. Ulrich Beck effectively highlighted this characteristic of contemporary risks by defining them as the "stowaway passengers of everyday consumption" (1986). In the case of global warming, the radical ill of the future is the result of banal actions that belong to our everyday life. The everyday and banal action of turning on a light bulb or using the car to get around produces the ill of the global threat of global warming for future generations.

d. The global threat of rising atmospheric temperatures for future generations once again puts forward a version of responsibility that modernity used to consider obsolete: collective responsibility. It is only due to its generalized nature that a type of conduct produces harmful consequences for other individuals: it is the diffusion and generalized repetition of a certain action that determines its quality and nature. In a society used to conceiving of responsibility (accountability) in essentially individual terms, individuals find themselves faced with conduct whose moral value does not depend on the conduct itself, but on the fact that it is adopted by a large number of other people. To some extent, it is the others who determine the moral quality of our action. Global warming is a "global environmental threat" for future generations that appears as the indirect and undesired consequence of the generalized use of "good" technology, tools designed to transform the environment to people's advantage and to satisfy innocent and day-to-day needs: the risk of damage for health and people's activity is essentially the unintentional and indirect consequence of the day-to-day and generalized use of technology that is in itself harmless. Above all, these elements make the whole thing difficult to understand and perceive. Global warming proposes a more serious version of the "Promethean Gap" that Günther Anders used to theorize the relationship between late-modern humanity, technology, and the world. The gap between "most of what we can produce and most (embarrassingly little) of what we can imagine," denounced by Anders (1992, 12) in relation to the consequences of a piece of technology—the atomic bomb—which "for the first time has put humanity in the condition to produce its own destruction" (13), is expanded when we have to imagine not the consequences of a weapon of mass destruction, but those of a banal piece of inoffensive, everyday technology. The fact that global warming is rooted in the "economic innocence of day-to-day consumption" makes the catastrophe threatening us doubly unthinkable: unthinkable because it is too big for us to imagine, and unthinkable because it is difficult to trace back to normal everyday life.

e.  Finally, the global environmental threat is also to a large extent a systemically conditioned threat: the result of a complex society in which the single behavior that produces harmful consequences appears as something over which the individual has lost all power. The spiral of more production/more consumption/more speed is the specific logic of a way of producing and a system that seem increasingly ungovernable and, nevertheless, impossible to modify through exclusively individual choices. Speed, mobility, and expanding consumption are first of all economic needs that we cannot avoid without making a more or less far-reaching correction to the systemic logic underlying them. The responsibility for global warming therefore also—and I would say eminently—possesses a holistic and systemic dimension. Individual responsibility extends not only to what we do individually, but also—and I would say, above all—to our choices as to the rules that govern our social lives. It is political responsibility in the broad sense.

To sum up, the harmful consequences for other individuals triggered by our present actions are remote in time and space, indirect and undesired, produced collectively and conditioned systemically. The case of global warming—like the other global threat for future generations, the depletion of the ozone layer—exhibits a paradoxical combination of extended responsibility (in terms of the enormity of the consequences and its extended scope in space and time) with reduced individuality (Jamieson 2007, 475–8). The responsibility is less and less individual, but it relates to effects that are bigger and bigger and more and more distant in space and time. We are responsible for increasingly great and far-off consequences, but we are less and less responsible individually. The responsibility tends to lose its strictly individual nature, but its effects and the extent of consequences become larger. On the one hand, the effects of our actions grow out of proportion in terms of quantity, quality, space, and time, while, on the other, the responsibility is increasingly shared: what generates the catastrophic consequences is not the single conduct as such, but the fact that it is universal. In this scenario, the possibility of intervention actually having an effect on the expected consequences to a large extent depends on that intervention concerning all the conditions for the working of society: its rhythms, its organization, its ends. When we reduce the direct, personal, and empirically and analytically reconstructable nature of the relationship between the single individual's action and the damage caused, the extension of the chains of events that we are accountable for grows out of proportion.

**2.** Secondly, from the dual nature of global warming—global threat and source of globalized risks—it is possible to draw the conclusion that there is no generalized "selfish" motivation for the present generation to fight global warming.

    a. First of all, because the effects of global warming will not be distributed in an equal or uniform manner over the whole planet.

    b. Secondly, because these effects will not be able to lead to a univocal assessment of costs and benefits. The harm that can affect the activities and health of the individuals alive today is, therefore, not so radical and generalized as to form a universal interest in combating climate change. In almost all cases, the harm to the activities and health of human beings produced by global warming will not affect the individuals who are called upon today to make the decisions, nor will it affect them with events of such a nature as to justify an egoistically motivated commitment.

    c. Thirdly, because, due to the inertia and the cumulative character of the phenomenon, the costs and benefits are distributed over different generations.

Our choices on the subject of greenhouse gas emissions will have a significant influence on the state of our atmosphere at the end of this century and the next. The inertial and cumulative nature of the phenomenon leads to a constitutive split between those acting and those who will feel the consequences, between those who will pay the costs and those who may draw benefit. What present generations do in the next decades will produce very little in the way of benefits for themselves, but will have an enormous influence on what will happen in 50 years' time and above all on the condition of the planet at the end of this century and during the next (Stern 2006, 1). The costs of the politics aimed at limiting global warming must be paid by present generations, but the benefits in terms of the damage avoided will be felt by future generations alone.

The fight against global warming is a fight that present generations must uphold wholly to the advantage of future generations.

The motivation behind the choice to fight global warming cannot be either fear of the consequences or a rational calculation of the costs and benefits involved in the different strategies for a single subject.[5] The time delay in the harmful effects of present consumption—the time difference between those who are responsible (cause) for climate change and those who will experience the damage—rejects any strategy based on the hypothesis of a selfish-rational subject such as the one hypothesized in

---

[5]  I developed this thesis more broadly in D'Andrea 2004.

modern political realism beginning with Hobbes. Fear cannot be what motivates the fight against climate change: those who have to choose to restrict emissions are not the same people who will experience the advantages, and those who should pay the costs will not be harmed to an extent that would justify this egocentric choice. When selfish fear constitutes a suitable rationale for the size of the commitment because the harmful events have drawn near and become radical and generalized, in all likelihood it will be too late to avoid worst-case scenarios.

The foundation for a universal commitment against atmospheric warming can only be of a moral nature, can only consist of a conscious assumption of "responsibility toward"[6] future generations. In order to have some hope of successfully combating global warming, we have to hypothesize a morally better subjectivity than the one induced by fear to choose peaceful coexistence.

**3.** Thirdly, taking "responsibility toward" future generations cannot legitimately be postponed or transferred to posterity. Since we are not able to precisely define when the phenomenon will become uncontrollable and irreversible, we cannot pinpoint when it will no longer be morally legitimate to continue to carry on acting "as normal," when the necessary countermeasures will need to be taken. Therefore, we cannot defend a strategy that postpones the adoption of inevitable countermeasures to the last possible minute simply because we do not know when this moment will occur, because our decisions have to account for the absence of precise information as to when our actions will become useless in combating the deterioration of the atmosphere.

Inertia, complexity, and nonlinear progress characterize a degenerative process whose point of no return—the point beyond which all deeds become useless—is impossible to define. These features of global warming transform a future event into a solid basis for today's obligations. The radical nature of the possible catastrophe and the impossibility to fix the point of no return force us to adopt, according to the precautionary principle, drastic reductions in emissions now.

## Indifference and responsibility

By making a comparison to other global challenges, we can make some conjectures about why it is so difficult to take responsibility and commit ourselves to dealing with the challenge of global warming. The following conclusions can be drawn:

1. Some authors (see Jamieson 2007, among others) have attributed the difficulties in launching effective policies against global warming to the unprecedented nature of our responsibility for this phenomenon as described above. The reasons for these difficulties are said to arise from the uncertain and novel nature—indirect/

---

[6] On the distinction between responsibility as accountability and responsibility toward, see Pulcini (2010).

innocent, far off in time/space, cumulative/collective and systemic/holistic—of our responsibility for climate change. In reality, this type of relationship between present behavior and the consequences for future generations also existed in the case of the depletion of the ozone layer, but this did not prevent us, in that case, from finding an effective solution in a relatively short time span.

2.  Another frequently used argument centers around the inefficacy of fear and the fact that the paradigm of modern political realism cannot be applied to the problem of global warming. Only the fear of an imminent physical death would be able to cancel out the emotive differences that cause individuals to desire different things and form different ideas about what is better for them. Only if the consequences of global warming were to expose all individuals to the imminent danger of physical death would fear become effective in motivating the acceptance of policies aimed at fighting the phenomenon. When it is not present generations who are threatened with physical death or are exposed to such radical damage, fear loses its ability to form unanimity and leaves room for a whole range of cost–benefit assessments. Not just any damage, but the radical damage of physical death—the loss of that asset that we all cannot help but desire (life)—makes fear politically productive because it renders it universal and necessary. Fear only works when it relates to something imminent, which threatens everyone's survival. Therefore, we can rely neither on the fear of political realism, nor on the present generations' interest in their self-preservation (Jonas 1974, 20).

This line of argument seems to me to be substantially easy to accept. All the same, it needs to be integrated by two considerations.

1.  The first concerns the efficacy of fear of an imminent physical death. The modern (Hobbesian) political paradigm considers it beyond doubt that common exposure to an imminent risk of physical death is sufficient to motivate individuals to take the necessary measures to escape this incumbent risk. Paradoxically, this is an optimistic assumption. In reality, the existence of an imminent risk of human civilization's self-destruction, which happened in the past—and which is still given in the case of the only true global risk for the present generations (nuclear weapons)—seems to show that the bond between the risk of death and fear is less automatic and direct. Despite there being an objective foundation for a common selfish fear, a strategy aimed at overcoming the risk of a vast-scale nuclear conflict is not even on the agenda. The existence of an objective community of interests as well as the existence of an objective foundation for common action guarantees neither adequate subjective perception nor adequate mobilization. The objective existence of a current shared threat is not sufficient to arouse fear and to mobilize us against the threat. It is not possible to rely on the fear of the individual's imminent physical death (the fear of political realism) for the collective to take responsibility for the future; not because the self-preservation of present individuals is not at stake, but because common exposure to risk is not sufficient to produce risk perception resulting in mobilization to solve the problem.

2. The second concerns the existence of different motivations for fear as the possible basis for policies to fight global warming. The case of ozone layer depletion teaches us that the absence of a direct selfish interest (fear) does not necessarily imply that it is impossible to ward off a threat: moral responsibility is not necessarily an ineffective motivation. Unlike what has happened (to date at least) in the cases of global warming and the risk of nuclear conflict, the threat of ozone layer depletion was dealt with successfully by the international community on the basis of an act of responsibility toward future generations. The reasons seem easy to pinpoint: the destruction of the ozone layer was due to just one cause: the emission into the atmosphere of a single substance (chlorofluorocarbons); there was a technically simple solution: there were a relatively limited number of industrial products that used chlorofluorocarbons and replacement technology was available, and a technical solution was available that performed at the same level and had the same costs.

Simple causes, technically feasible replacements, limited costs, compatibility with the normal workings of the economy and with lifestyles: all these things helped make it possible to *imagine* a solution to the problem. Therefore, the decisive issue seems to be, first and foremost, the ability to imagine a solution, which is the condition for the perception and constant awareness of a problem. Where the imagination sees no possibilities, the problem is repressed. But the imagination is a function of *worldview* (*Weltbild*). The imagination moves within the limits set by a world image. It is the worldview that outlines the imaginable on the one hand, and on the other, the impossible. In the case of nuclear risk, it is the unavailability of a credibly imaginable solution that makes the problem unsolvable and leads to its repression. In a world image centered around war, the exclusive pursuit of power interests and the conflict of egoisms, the risk of a nuclear conflict can be *repressed* but not *resolved*.

But the case of the depletion of the ozone layer allows us to highlight an additional aspect: the central nature of the issue of cost and the nature of what had to be given up in terms of consumption and lifestyles in order to deal with the threat. In current technological conditions, fighting global warming means reducing consumption and mobility. In other words, it means overcoming the authentic economic imperative that is growth. And no country—whether industrialized or developing, Western or not—seems capable of questioning this imperative. Increasing the gross domestic product and economic growth in Europe are also the primary goals of both the Union and single-member states. Reducing consumption does not only contrast with the widespread idea of well-being, it also contrasts with a mode of production in which the expansion of consumption is the necessary but not sufficient condition for the market economy to function in a socially sustainable manner. Reducing consumption in an economy that produces in order to sell means reducing the need for work and reducing employment. Contemporary global capitalism is what best responds in terms of material relations—economic and social in the broad sense—to the modern idea of happiness or, less emphatically, well-being, but it presupposes the tendency toward an unlimited expansion in consumption and a constant acceleration in the rhythm of life.[7]

The problem is not indifference and a lack of responsibility in general, but a lack of willingness to pay the price.[8] Here what is at issue is no longer the imagination, but the material nature of a world in which we feel "at home," the protected and comfortable world of the overabundance of consumer goods that we are not willing to renounce. The unwillingness to even call into question—before giving up—the levels of consumption and well-being that we have acquired is the other root of our difficulties. Here the problem is only in part a problem of imagination. It is rather a problem of the ability to recognize and respect a duty when this involves a (however partial) relinquishment of a material dimension of well-being (acquired or deemed acquirable). The inability of modern Western societies to effectively deal with the problem (now more than 20 years have passed since the first international conference on climate change) is essentially due to the inability to call into question our condition as inhabitants of the "pampering greenhouse" [*Verwöhnungstreibhaus*] (Sloterdijk 2006, 278) that is ultimately responsible for global warming.

While this incapacity is, in my opinion, the dead end where a civilization that has absolutized well-being, growth, and consumption has ended up, outside the West the conditions for taking responsibility toward future generations do not seem to be any more favorable. Indeed, global late modernity is the epoch which has spread modernity beyond the West. The modern technical-economic cosmos, whose genesis required the

---

[7]  Recently, the Stern report became the most significant attempt to show not only the economic advantage of immediate action to fight climate change, but also its lack of economic burden: one percent of the Gross Domestic Product (GDP) a year on condition that we start to act immediately. Besides the issue of the relevance of a calculation in exclusively economic terms when those who pay the costs and those who benefit belong to different generations, the point that I feel I must highlight is that the whole cost assessment is based on a goal to stabilize the concentration of $CO_2$ in the atmosphere at 500–550 ppm: "central estimates of the annual costs of achieving stabilization between 500 and 550 ppm $CO_2e$ are around 1 percent of global GDP, if we start to take strong action now" (Stern 2006, VII). Official estimates received from the same European institutions consider this level of concentration out of sync with achieving the goal of an increase in temperatures equal to or less than 2° Celsius compared to the pre-industrial era. If we suppose that the concentration of $CO_2e$ in the atmosphere is stabilized at a level that gives more certainty of achieving the 2° Celsius goal, the costs are much higher both from an economic viewpoint and more generally in terms of social sustainability. Without precisely pinpointing the quantity, the same Stern report clearly states that: "It would already be very difficult and costly to aim to stabilize at 450 ppm $CO_2e$" (Stern 2006, VII).

[8]  The lack of willingness on an individual level to assume the costs of responsibility is also confirmed on an empirical and by no means conclusive level by the results of a Eurobarometer survey which asked Europeans if they were willing to pay more to have energy produced from renewable resources. Beyond the far-reaching differences from one country to another, the results highlight the difficulty found by Europeans in accepting the economic costs of the fight against climate change: 66 percent of the citizens in the 10 new member states, 51 percent of the 15 old member states, and an average of 54 percent for the 25-member state European Union are not willing to pay more to have energy produced in a sustainable manner. The percentage of those who would be willing to bear economic costs goes down to 24 percent at the mention of the amount that would have to be spent, that is 5 percent more compared to current prices. Despite the percentage being higher (+3 percent) than in a previous survey, only one quarter of Europeans would be willing to pay 5 percent more to have energy from renewable resources (Eurobarometer 2006, 19).

contribution of a particular type of subjectivity, has spread throughout the planet, and shown a "universality" that has led to the establishment of forms of subjectivity that did and continue to pertain very much to the modern Western subject. Capitalism and technology have also imposed their logic and dynamism on populations that had and continue to have a profoundly different image of the world from the typically Western one, in many cases out of tune with the image implicit in capitalism and in the universe of technology and science. On the one hand, this ongoing diversity in forms of subjectivity has worked in favor of the adoption of the modern technical-economic cosmos; on the other hand, the persistence of non-Western images of the world does not seem able to hinder or slow down the quantitative and incremental logic of economics and technology. To sum up, modernity outside the West does not seem to be able to rely on greater resources of sense than Western ones in order to reintroduce a culture of limits. Inside and outside the West, material well-being, economic growth, and expanding consumption constitute the imperatives of politics and the expression summing up individuals' aspirations: staying inside or entering the crystal palace[9] of the society of hyper-consumerism is the only goal truly shared on a planetary scale.

# Bibliography

Anders, G. 1992. *L'uomo è antiquato II*. Torino: Bollati Boringhieri. Translation from 1980. *Die Antiquiertheit des Menschen*, Bd. I., München: C. H. Beck.

Beck, U. 1986. *Risikogesellschaft. Auf dem Weg in eine andere Moderne*. Frankfurt: Suhrkamp.

— 1992. *Risk Society: Towards a New Modernity*. London: Sage.

— 2007. *Weltrisikogesellschaft. Auf der Suche nach der verlorenen Sicherheit*. Frankfurt: Suhrkamp.

Campbell, C. 2003. *Glimmer of a New Leviathan. Total War in the Realism of Niebuhr, Morgenthau and Waltz*. New York: Columbia University Press.

Cerutti, F. 2007. *Global Challenges for Leviathan. A Political Philosophy of Nuclear Weapons and Global Warming*. Lanham: Rowman & Littlefield.

D'Andrea, D. 2004. "Un mondo finito, un mondo comune. Rischi ambientali globali e limiti della paura." In *Etica delle relazioni internazionali*. Edited by S. Maffettone and G. Pellegrino. Lungro di Cosenza: Marco Editore.

Dostoevskij, F. 2005. *Memorie del sottosuolo*. Torino: Einaudi.

Eurobarometer. 2006. *Attitudes towards Energy*, Janvier, n° 247.

Jamieson, D. 2007. "The Moral and Political Challenges of Climate Change." In *Creating a Climate for Change: Communicating Climate Change and Facilitating Social Change*. Edited by S. Moser and L. Dilling. New York: Cambridge University Press.

Jonas, H. 1974. *Philosophical Essays. From Ancient Creed to Technological Man*. Chicago: The University of Chicago Press.

Morgenthau, H. 1954a. "Will it Deter Aggression?" *New Republic* 137, 29/03.

---

[9]  For the origin of the crystal palace image as the symbol of Western civilization see F. Dostoevskij (2005); for the reuse of the image, see P. Sloterdijk (2006, 41–3).

— 1954b. "The Political and Military Strategy of the United States." *Bulletin of the Atomic Scientist*, October.

Pulcini, E. 2010. "The Responsible Subject in the Global Age." *Science and Engineering Ethics* 16: 447–91.

Sagan, S. D. and K. N. Waltz (eds) 1995. *The Spread of Nuclear Weapons: A Debate*. New York/London: Norton.

Sloterdijk, P. 2006. *Il mondo dentro il capital*. Roma: Meltemi. Translation from 2005. *Im Weltinnenraum des Kapitals*. Frankfurt: Suhrkamp Verlag.

Stern, N. 2006. *The Stern Review. The Economics of Climate Change*. www.webcitation. org/5nCeyEYJr.

# Part III

# The Governance of Global Risks

## 10

# A New Political Order for the Twenty-First Century: From State *Governments* to Global *Governance*

Gurutz Jáuregui
*University of the Basque Country*

## Introduction

Until now, all political systems have been focused on the immediate present and have been structured around a territorial area established by national state borders.[1] This double temporal and spatial constraint has begun to break down radically due to the phenomenon of globalization.

Today the idea of determining the future of generations to come by means of actions taken in the present is unacceptable, while it is now too late to do anything about our current problems, which affect the world in which we live today as well as humanity itself, via state-level political action or legislative measures. There is therefore a need to establish a new social accord in line with new realities, a need for spatial and temporal order, for a new agreement that considers the future, but which at the same time must be universal.

Leaving aside questions relating to time and more specifically the future, this chapter shall focus on some of the "spatial" or territorial consequences that globalization has on the present political world order, particularly on democratic systems. To this end some of the challenges faced by certain classical structures and concepts, such as the state, sovereignty, and constitution, shall be analyzed.

First, therefore, the need to superimpose a new, still emerging concept of global or world "governance" on the classic concept of nation-state "government" shall be addressed.

[1] This work has been carried out within the IT-448–07 Consolidated Research Group, financed by the Basque Government-Eusko Jaurlaritza and the DER2008–04499/JURI Research Project financed by the Ministry for Science and Technology.

Secondly, the future of states in the emerging new world order shall be discussed. For this purpose, four (or five) possible models of governance shall be established.

Thirdly, we shall analyze the consequences caused as a result of the new situation, looking at one of the fundamental pillars which still continues to support the present judicial and political systems, that of sovereignty.

Finally, we shall discuss the future of nation-state constitutions from the perspective of a complex judicial system in which it is becoming more and more difficult to distinguish between state law, community law, international law, and transnational law.


## A new social accord for the twenty-first century

The concept of "globalization" has become the buzzword not only in the area of economics and finance but across all social sciences and even in the daily lives of ordinary citizens. Globalization, not just the word but the slogan or saying, is surely the "worst applied, least defined, probably the least understood, most nebulous and politically the most efficient term of recent and foreseeable years" (Beck 1998, 40). Globalization encompasses a diverse range of elements and dimensions; it can be spoken of in the sense of economic globalization, and, sometimes, financial globalization; it can be used to refer to the labor market, communication technology, ecology, civil society, and culture.

Leaving aside these types of partial or specific visions, I believe that the core element that defines the phenomenon of globalization with respect to other historical phenomena is the idea of globalization as a radical transformation of space and time (Giddens 1998, 14). If there are two fundamental characteristics that define our world today, such features are the expansion of space and the acceleration of time.

Globalization is in a space that goes beyond geometry and in which distance is covered effectively in real time. Time and space therefore seem intrinsically linked, with the fate of future generations being intertwined with spaces of globalization. The scope of space and at the same time the chronological dimensions of the future are also increased.

Until relatively recently, all political and judicial systems were, and still largely remain, focused on the immediate present. They have been structured around a territorial area established by national state borders.

This double temporal and spatial constraint has begun to break down radically in recent years. Until recently, we had "colonized" the future in favour of the immediate present. Only in the 1970s did we begin to start to incorporate the future as an element to be considered in our agenda (Innerarity 2012). At present, the need to structure time, by taking into account not only the present but also the future, has become one of the most important challenges in policy and law of the globalization era.

Today we wonder whether it is morally acceptable to pass on to future generations things such as nuclear waste and a damaged environment, but this question leads us seamlessly to the second question of whether it is possible to solve these problems, which affect global land area and humanity, via state-level political action or legislative measures.

There is a necessity therefore to establish a new social agreement in line with new realities, a need for spatial and temporal order, for a new arrangement that considers the future, but which at the same time must be universal. The preservation of many of our shared assets (the environment, peace, sustainability, etc.) or the solution of many of our problems (climate change, nuclear energy, genetic engineering, etc.), can only be guaranteed by tackling the problem simultaneously on two levels, on a temporal intergenerational level and on a spatially global or universal level. There are a growing number of decisions that have to be made regarding the future (environment, energy, technology, etc.) which cannot be resolved within a confined space. The global time and space of the market and technology have come into conflict with the political time and space of democracies, politics, and legislation.

Although we are aware of the impossibility of defying the boundaries of time and space, for the purpose of this discussion I am going to avoid the question of time and focus on some of the "spatial" or territorial consequences of the globalization process.

## From "government" to "governance"

In the current era of globalization, the existence of state political systems that are not subject to external restrictions is unworkable. Democracies seem to be profoundly conditioned by globalization trends. It is therefore quite impossible to isolate or reduce democratic systems to the internal ambit of state borders. Hence there is a need to move from a system of state democracy to a system of supranational democracy or even a global democracy. This is what the most recent theories have called the step from state government to global governance.

The need to address new challenges arising from globalization has given rise to a new political term known as "governance," a term that differs from the classical idea of "government." The difference between the two concepts or terms is twofold. On the one hand it refers to the actual content of what is meant by government, and on the other hand, it refers to the territorial area in which said government is developed.

With regard to the first issue, the concept of "government" fundamentally carries legal, official, and institutional connotations, whereas the issue of "governance" is much broader and assumes a capacity for decision-making and responding to and dealing with conflicts. Governance is, in short, the capacity to govern, a capacity to keep different groups and organizations in place and to meet the minimum requirements of its citizens. This implies a greater involvement in achieving certain specific objectives such as economic development and promoting higher levels of public health. Governance is, in this regard, the particular quality of a political community, according to which government institutions operate effectively within that space in a manner considered legitimate by its citizens, thus allowing the free exercise of political will through the civic obedience of its people.

With regard to the second issue, government is limited to the territorial area of a specific state. Governance however covers a wider territorial area, therefore the distinction between government and governance is particularly pertinent in the current era of globalization. The term "international relations" is too absolute and lacks specific meaning at a time like the present in which, as we shall see, states have ceased to constitute the sole subject of international politics. Globalization is causing the emergence of many other entities or organizations which exert an increasingly strong role. These are organizations that have very diverse content, structure, and scale, but their common feature is that they have an ever-increasing influence within the scope of global politics and the economy. For their part, regional and local governments are increasing their international presence beyond state borders. The same is the case with the development of supranational or global agents which continue to increase in both number and influence. The private sector has also acquired an extraordinary role through different agents such as think tanks, foundations, control agencies, and consultancy councils. To all this must be added the extraordinary influence exerted by an increasingly broad and heterogeneous group of social movements, NGOs, etc., which have injected innovative dynamism to world politics as a whole. All this has led to politics and international relations giving way to politics and relations that are purely and simply global.

This dense network of new organizations, structures, and entities is having a powerful effect on democratic systems. On the one hand, it is now quite impossible to approach the development of democracy solely and exclusively through the state. On the other hand, the presence of these international organizations is not only unfavorable to the development and deepening of the democratic system, but it generally assumes an apparent retreat from democratic levels achieved within the state.

A clear example of this, and not the most poignant, is found in the European Union, an organization in which its institutions are less democratic than many of its component states. A large percentage of the decisions that affect the citizens of these states fall outside of what has been considered the essence of state democracy since the advent of the liberal state: legislative control of the executive branch.

If this happens within the European Union, what can be said of the many other organizations for which no control or accountability exists? Almost all these organizations act entirely independently of their citizens. Their activity is not governed by the rule of democracy but by the logic of technocracy. They are not governed by representatives elected by their citizens, but by a host of economists, managers, engineers, scientists, legal experts, and all kinds of specialists who make decisions for their citizens without being subject to any kind of democratic scrutiny. When the policies designed and implemented by these experts fail and when their mistakes lead to repercussions, often very serious repercussions which affect a large number of citizens, as is unfortunately happening in the case of the current economic crises, no one is held responsible.

The absence of politics is allowing large transnational corporations to carry out, effectively, a seizure of power, in which they are actually taking global control outside of the realm of politics. This activity is allowing transnational corporations to imperceptibly occupy the vital material centers of society, without revolution, without making changes to laws or constitutions, by the simple development of everyday living, and all this while at the same time conditioning and in some cases ignoring the political system, government, parliament, public opinion, judges, etc.

Therefore the democratic state is being replaced by a state of private law, devoid of any philosophical reference to human rights, reduced to a strict code of rules based on performance criteria.

A political system may only be democratic if it is able to act independently of any restriction imposed by another dominant political system or another dominant force or organization. There are two types of restrictions on a political system: internal and external. The former are those that are produced within the specific political system itself and the latter are those coming from systems or organizations located beyond its territorial area.

In the current era of globalization, it is unviable for state political systems not to be subject to external restrictions. The concept of nation-state democracy starts to become more and more of a "contradictio in terminis." A democracy that confines its activity within state boundaries takes the form, in practice, of an "apartheid" democracy.

In addition, the changes produced as a consequence of globalization are causing a genuine lack of order, true international anarchy. We are going through a general crisis of legitimacy, not only with regard to individual states, but also the international order created by them. It is becoming increasingly untenable to maintain the current asymmetrical and unequal system of international relations. The reality of globalization is making it more and more urgent and necessary to implement a true form of global integration based on law.

That is why it is essential to consider the need to shift from a system of state democracy to a system of supranational or even global democracy. Therefore what is required is global governability, governance, meaning a structure that is capable of integrating the activities of the state with the activities of intergovernmental organizations, nongovernmental organizations, and transnational movements. A structure which combines all of the above, mutually influencing one another, in order to produce a system of global governance.

Moreover, all these issues bring immense difficulties. Which of these organizations or bodies should participate in global governance? How should they be structured? Before whom should their actions be accountable? Who shall control their activities? In short, how, within this new complexity of institutions and bodies, can it be made possible to apply the two golden rules of democracy, maintaining control by the ruled over the rulers, and maintaining mutual control among rulers?

# The four models of governance

In view of current positions, it would be appropriate to distinguish, in my opinion, between four distinct models of governance.[2] These are not radically alternative models or models that are hostile to one another, rather they are sometimes complementary models, since they often present common aspects or elements that are barely distinguishable. In any case, I believe it is worth establishing a typology of these models, even if only for illustrative purposes.

## The Westphalian model

As already mentioned, the current political world order is based on the territorial division of sovereign states, each of which holds power and exclusive sovereignty over an established territorial area, defined by one or several border lines of separation. This international order acquired full recognition from the 1648 Treaties of Westphalia, giving rise to the establishment of a "realist" theory of international relations based on three principles: (1) the establishment of a world political order as a society of states; (2) the establishment of coexistence among these states by virtue of which a series of minimum conditions were specified which would allow these states to coexist and organize their own policies within the international order; and (3) the establishment of a mutual regulatory system in which an international authority is not necessary.

Several characteristics stem from these three principles: (1) States are the only entities that are recognized as subject to international law. (2) There is no international legislator capable of establishing valid rules applicable to all. The only valid international law is that produced by the states themselves by means of bilateral and multilateral treaties. (3) There is no jurisdictional authority of an international order that can identify and, if appropriate, punish violations of international law. (4) State sovereignty is absolute and unconditional within the domestic sphere, and the external environment is limited only by treaties or agreements signed with other states. (5) All states are formally equal. The real inequalities that exist between the various states are irrelevant from a legal point of view. (6) Every state has the full right to resort to war or other coercive measures in order to defend its sovereignty and interests.

The Westphalian model was primarily aimed at securing a series of rules that allowed the establishment of peaceful coexistence among all states. However, historical reality

---

[2]  We could even talk of a fifth model, the neoliberal model, rooted in the dogma that all human activity should be subject to the primacy of the global economy. Its fundamental characteristic consists of entrusting governance to the auto-regulatory capacity of the emerging global market and minimizing the presence and actions of political organizations and institutions. This is a possible model, but also an extremely dangerous one. I do not include it here because I believe that it bears no relation to the idea of establishing a multidimensional, polycentric, global society, which is politically capable of acceptably overcoming the great social, economic, political, and cultural challenges faced by the world today. As J. Estefanía highlights, the main lesson of the crisis that we have been going through in recent years is that globalization cannot exist without standards, principles, authority, and limitations.

has shown that this objective has not been satisfied in practice. Experience has shown us that the practice of international relations over the last three centuries has been much closer to the view of the state of nature inspired by Hobbes than the thesis proposed by Kant in his Perpetual Peace project. If one thing has definitively defined international relations during this time, it is the condition of permanent war among states.

Contrary to formulated predictions, the Westphalian model established anything but a uniform system in which all states maintained a situation of perfect equality. Beyond the apparent formal equality, what was really established in practice was a profoundly hierarchical system which produced huge inequalities and injustices, the main victims of which were small non-European countries and civilizations.

In practice, there has always been a clear divergence between the formal division of the world into nation-states and underlying political, military, social, economic, and cultural reality. Apart from the formal division into states, the world has always been organized around certain geostrategic blocks which have developed and changed in accordance with historical circumstances (French–German hostilities in Europe, the British Empire, the United States, the Soviet Union, Southeast Asian, and now China, Brazil, and the European Union). However, such divergence is currently reaching a degree and level that would have been hard to imagine just a few years ago.

The current process of globalization is having a decisive impact on the present state systems currently in force. States are losing power and influence both internally and externally. On the external front, they are giving up spheres of control to certain agents and activities that have arisen from the globalization process regarding issues such as the environment, climate change, information technologies, migration, international terrorism, and organized crime. Internally, we are seeing a surge, or sometimes a revival of solidarity regarding identity, culture, religion, etc., which put the official national identity of these states into question.

This brings with it important consequences regarding political order. The Westphalian model is overwhelmed by the reality of a multipolar world in which there is increasing transnationalism in political decision-making processes. All this significantly effects the principle of state sovereignty. It is now difficult to find or identify a single example of real state sovereignty. Borders are porous and lose their significance when nonstate entities are able to communicate across them. The state is no longer a unitary actor; it has become one of several frameworks in which political differences are negotiated and resolved. Collective action is infringing more and more on the jurisdiction of the state.

International order has, in practice, ceased to be an order based on individual states and has become a rather more complex system. It is clear that the erosion of the state shall not be absolute. In the future, states shall continue to be defined, probably as an essential structure in the framework of future global governance. But the fact remains that the epicenter of this new order will not be individual states but rather transnational institutions. The states shall continue to exercise their activity but not as sovereign entities, rather as components of a more extensive and complex new international political order. The states will not, by themselves, have the capacity to respond to new challenges.

A new multilateral form of politics is becoming increasingly necessary, one that is wholly different from the Westphalian system that has been in place up until now. In this new transnational order, the rigid notion of sovereignty linked to specific geographic areas and spaces must be overcome and a new type of power distribution must be established, in which sovereignty is shared across malleable and flexible times, levels, and spaces.

## The UN model

The creation of the United Nations, in 1945, was a clear step forward compared to the previous world situation. However, the world of 1945 has absolutely no bearing on the international reality of the new millennium. That is why a process to assimilate the United Nations to the new international society is essential. The recent crises in Iraq, Somalia, Bosnia, Rwanda, Kosovo, Afghanistan, and Palestine, to name just a few of the most recent, and the far from adequate role played in these crises by the United Nations are good examples of the profound extent to which formal structures are divorced from reality.

The failure of the United Nations is consubstantial with the model designed in its own constitutional charter. The United Nations model is defined by the following characteristics: (1) Individual states are no longer the sole subjects of international law, with international organizations, especially the United Nations, also being subjects of international law. (2) Some general principles are established regarding international law which are not only binding on all states, but which mandatorily prevail as *ius cogens*, peremptory law for international treaties and norms. (3) The myth of legal equality among all states is broken, a good example being the fact that there are five permanent members of the Security Council. (4) The disagreement with international norms ceases to be a private matter among states, and becomes a public matter that implies and involves humanity as a whole. The punitive use of force is now entrusted to a centralized body, the Security Council.

However the UN model, in practice, affirms the division of the world into powerful states with very specific and complex geopolitical interests. The recognition and enforcement of the power held by these states is demonstrated by the veto power granted to the permanent members of the UN Security Council. This reduces the capacity of the United Nations to act as an autonomous entity in response to pressure from individual states. It can therefore be said that the United Nations enjoys a form of conditional freedom.

The belief that the Security Council and the Secretary General by means of the Security Council has any independent power and superiority over military organizations and the nuclear arsenals of great powers is nothing more than a mirage. There is clear evidence of this in the way in which the five permanent members of the Security Council acted during the Cold War period, and the way in which the United States used and abused the institution and its decisions as a legitimizing smoke screen for its policies of aggression.

Compared to the United Nation's theoretical framework of the formal equality of states under one legitimate and superior power, reality affords us a very different picture altogether. What the United Nations offers in practice, as demonstrated on many occasions, is the appearance of legality, a legal smoke screen with which to cover the brute force exerted by the great powers. Before the UN system, the great powers exercised their force outside the law and in accordance with their power and capacity to rule within the world community. Now the great powers have the legal approval of the United Nations to exercise this tyrannical power. And in the event that such an exhibition of force takes place outside or contrary to the provisions adopted in the UN Charter, the veto power enjoyed by the great powers makes any type of sanction unviable, however serious the transgression might be.

The international political situation which developed after the fall of the soviet empire made the situation, if anything, worse. As is well stated by Zolo, for some years there has been no more than one single star, the United States, at the center of the planetary system of the cosmopolis. The predominance of this star is revealed not only in economic and political spheres but above all in the military sphere. Since the end of the Cold War, the United States has steadily built an international military structure of regional commands; it has signed agreements to establish military bases all over the world and has developed relations with foreign armed forces assuming a US military presence that is both global and permanent. The US armed forces are currently deployed in some 40 countries, maintaining tight control and military contacts, including exchanges and training exercises with almost all European countries, some of the former Soviet states, as well as parts of Asia and Latin-American.

The UN model conceived as a means to ensure peace by the agreement of at least two superpowers has had to undergo drastic simplification. Now ideas concerning world peace must fall in line, inevitably, with the strategy of preserving the status quo that the United States considers suitable for the protection of its interests.

This does not mean however that we find ourselves in a unipolar situation. As Ortega states, the United States is possibly a predominant power, and in some parts of the world perhaps even a hegemonic power, but it exists in a very complex world in which there are also other great powers.

For this reason, and leaving political and strategic situations aside, the fundamental problem of the UN system is the absence of a coercive legal system, both in the legislative and judicial spheres, which is able, in general, to command and oblige states to comply with its resolutions. Thus at a legislative level, sanctions should be determined by the Security Council and any decisions taken should be conditioned by the interests of the members of said Council. Furthermore, the implementation of sanctions decided by the Security Council is decentralized and largely voluntary. This means that such implementations also depend on the degree of political will that the Council's members have to implement said sanctions.

At a judicial level the jurisdictional functions of the International Court of Justice have, in practice, very little influence. As we already know, the International Court of Justice only pronounces its sentences in order to resolve disputes between states that have already accepted its jurisdiction. The International Court of Justice has no international police force with conferred power to impose sanctions against violations of international law. The issuing of such sanctions is, once again, left to the discretional judgment of the Security Council.

It is possible and desirable that the new implementation of the International Criminal Court will produce some significant changes to the current situation. There are several characteristics that define and differentiate this Court with respect to past precedents. With respect to the International Court of Justice, it offers the advantage of being able to judge specific individuals. With respect to other courts, such as those created on an *ad hoc* basis to judge crimes committed in Rwanda and the former Yugoslavia, these offer the advantage of establishing a permanent court.

However, the International Criminal Court continues to rely largely on the will of Security Council member states. The Security Council can endorse the initiation of a process but can also explicitly block it. Given that several permanent members of the Security Council (United States, Russia, and China) have not yet ratified the Statute of the Court, and some like the United States have been actively boycotting it, it is unlikely that the Council will maintain even a minimal operational level in this sense, and it is especially unlikely to do so against the interests of these states.

## The Cosmopolitan model

Defenders of the UN model believe that it has only been implemented to a very limited extent. Therefore they insist on the need to put the intrinsic potential of the model into effect and strengthen its structure. The adaptation of the United Nations to current international reality would require different states to abandon their current structure of imposing their own power in favor of a collective security system which is capable of protecting weaker states from the more powerful ones as well as responding quickly to events that may threaten world peace. But in order for this to happen, the United Nations needs greater power and greater authority in order to exercise proper control of its states. This would replace or at least overlap national democracies with a cosmopolitan global democracy.

Other doctrinal views believe, however, that the United Nations, as with its historical predecessors (Holy Alliance, League of Nations), has an intrinsic incapacity to develop peace in the world. Thus for Zolo, the failure of the UN system does not only derive from the theoretical and practical limitations to which it is subjected, but also from a more profound cause, which is humankind's inherent struggle for hegemony and power, and the consequent struggle of human groups and societies. The UN system would, in this sense, be an excessively idealistic system which does not sufficiently take into account factors relating to the human condition.

Therefore we will see, first, the essential aspects of the cosmopolitan model, in order to address, later, the alternative model, which we could call the complex model.

The characteristics on which the cosmopolitan model is based are principally the following: (1) the primacy of international law over domestic law by means of progressive reduction of state sovereignty; (2) the conversion of international law into a coercive law capable of imposing itself on the state; (3) the development of the theory of legal pacifism, in the sense to which I shall refer later; and (4) the progressive establishment of a world constitution.

The Cosmopolitan model is based largely on the distinction made, more than two centuries ago, by Kant in his essay "Perpetual Peace," between international law and cosmopolitan law. For Kant, the rules of international law that regulate war and peace should only be valid transitorily until legal pacifism has created a cosmopolitan order and thus the abolition of war is achieved.

It is therefore important that the terms "cosmopolitan democracy" and "international democracy" should not be confused. International democracy invokes the idea of creating a system of democratic laws and procedures among states without questioning the domestic constitution of each one. The concept of international order invoked by cosmopolitan democracy goes much further than the mere creation of international laws and procedures and supposes the reformulation of the Kantian idea of a cosmopolitan order suitable for the new world situation. Cosmopolitan democracy seeks to develop domestic and international democracy in parallel.

This involves creating a set of global institutions capable of instructing and disciplining the political regimes of different countries and, where necessary, influencing the domestic affairs of nation-states. Cosmopolitan law should be institutionalized in such a way that it binds different governments together. The international community must be able to force its members, under threat of sanctions, to at least conduct themselves in accordance with the law. Thus the external relationship of international exchange, contractually regulated between states, is transformed into a domestic relationship based on a statute or constitution between members of the organization.

This presumes that it is possible to deprive states of their coercive powers when, for example, they are used against the well-being and safety of their citizens or when used to prevent the development of collaborative relationships among states. The creation of cosmopolitan institutions does not necessarily imply the dissolution of the state; rather it grants a series of powers to these institutions within clearly established areas of activity. States shall have to find a new space, a new means of articulation within the framework of new global democratic law, so that their regulations are but one of many reference points for the development of laws, political reflection, and mobilization.

Proponents of cosmopolitan democracy base their approach on the need for implementing comprehensive reform of the entire system designed in the 1945 Charter. A short- to medium-term reform which focuses on at least five major areas: (1) Compliance by the Security Council with the principles of international law. (2) The reform of the Security Council with regard to the number and composition of and the power of veto granted to the five permanent members. (3) The strengthening of the International Tribunal in The Hague and the granting of compulsory sentencing, as well as the effective implementation of the International Criminal Court. (4) The creation of an economic agency which can coordinate efforts on both a global and regional level. (5) The establishment of an effective and responsible military force that is truly international.

The steps of a more important and definitive proposal for long-term reform are set out below:

1. The development and approval of a new United Nations Charter or Constitution.
2. The creation of legislative power by means of converting the General Assembly into a World Parliament elected by universal suffrage.
3. The reduction of the Security Council to the status of a mere Standing Committee of Parliament.
4. The establishment of an executive power by means of converting the Secretary General into a world government.
5. The development of an international judiciary from the current Hague Tribunal and the various existing international criminal tribunals.
6. The reform of certain financial- and tariff-imposing organizations (International Monetary Fund, World Bank, World Trade Organization, etc.) in order to free them from their current subordination to the economic and financial policies of developed countries and make them serve the comprehensive development of the planet.
7. The granting of real power to exercise overall control over the production and trade of weapons so as to achieve a gradual general disarmament.

These future hypotheses are valid as just that. What is not so clear is their feasibility, at least not in the context of the current world. The Cosmopolitan model is flawed in the sense that it carries a certain naivety and an excessive dose of utopia. It is a model that particularly affects formal, legal, political, and institutional matters, but underestimates the influence of economic and financial factors within the dynamic of international conflict. It does not take into sufficient account the crucial role played by large international and economic institutions and organizations in the current economic globalization process and, consequently, the establishment of power networks on a global scale.

The large economic and financial powers and organizations that are currently dominant will attempt to prevent, in fact they are already doing so, the adoption of changes that may limit or undermine their current degree of power and influence. The establishment of a cosmopolitan model of governance may contribute to some formal control of such organizations and, therefore, may mitigate the most arbitrary or abusive aspects of their dominance, but it will in no way undermine their hold on power.

## The complex model

As I mentioned earlier, we are experiencing a general crisis of legitimacy, not only of states but also of the international order established by them. It is becoming increasingly untenable to maintain the current asymmetrical and unequal system of international relations. The reality of globalization is becoming more urgent and the necessity to implement truly global integration based on law is becoming ever more pressing.

This new international order should be based on a different law, one that is able to place individuals, governments, governmental, and nongovernmental organizations under a new system of legal regulation. The construction of this complex new legal order will allow the coexistence between a global law and an internal law based on a balanced relationship.

This brings us to the perspective of a new horizon, which is the need to assume the progressive development of a new world order. An order based on a complex legal system in which the coexistence of different legal orders would be possible, not necessarily supported by hierarchical relations of superiority and subordination, but by shared criteria, coordination, and subsidiarity.

World democracy requires a constraint or limitation on the sovereignty of states but, contrary to what often happens at present, this limitation cannot, nor should it, be exercised by other states. No state is authorized to determine the sovereignty of another state, as is now happening all too often. The only entities empowered to do so would be transnational organizations or institutions to which international law has previously granted said legitimacy.

This requires that transnational organizations be able to exercise their authority and limit state power, quite the opposite of what is happening at the moment where certain international institutions such as the United Nations have become, by inertial force, a docile instrument in the hands of the most powerful states.

It is not enough, therefore, to develop an international community of democratic states. It is also necessary to structure an international community of democratic societies committed to respecting the law and laws, both inside and outside the borders of different countries. The creation of a complex democratic order requires the active consent of peoples and nations, as well as many other protagonists of the present social, economic, political, cultural, technological, and religious world. The growing complexity of the international environment and the subsequent interdependence among its variables tend to produce a systemic situation which Rosenau defines as "governance without government."

This is a situation in which the absence of a government providing formal authority (government) coexists in the context of the self-regulating aggregating phenomena (governance) of international agents. The world will be, indeed is already becoming, more multipolar, not only in terms of states and groups of states, but also in terms of agents. As Zolo puts it, in situations of high complexity, dynamic systems tend to result in a polycentric policy matrix, which arises from widespread processes of strategic interaction and multilateral negotiations. This matrix resembles more the structure of a network, or a series of networks, than the classic pyramid structure designed by Kelsen.

This would imply, in general and summary form, the creation of a global order consisting of a set of multiple and overlapping networks of power relating to matters such as welfare, culture, civic relations, the economy, relations of coercion, and organized violence, as well as regulatory and legal relations. This requires, of course, an intense coordination and cooperation among the various regional, national, transnational, and international entities that are involved. Realistic coordination has nothing to do with the idea of a formal cosmopolitan government that is supposed to miraculously be able to solve every problem.

All groups and associations would have a certain capacity of self-determination based on the principle of autonomy and the recognition of a set of laws and obligations. A number of legal principles would be established with the purpose of defining the shape and scope of individual and collective action within the various organizations of both the state and the economy and civil society. Within this framework, the creation and application of the law may be developed in a variety of places and at different levels by expanding alongside state, national, regional, and international courts.

Finally, individuals could become members of and participate in the various communities that may affect them and consequently have access to various forms of political participation. In this regard a concept of citizenship should be established that would enable individuals to exercise their membership in different political communities, both local and global.

The ultimate goal of this model would be directed, as proposed by Held, at the consolidation of global democratic law through the enactment of a new Bill of Rights and Obligations, the creation of a global parliament connected to regional parliaments and the national state, the separation of political and economic interests, the enactment of a comprehensive legal system, the implementation of a system of accountability, and control of transnational and international economic agencies to parliaments and assemblies, both at global and regional levels, and the progressive transfer of the coercive capacity of nation-states in favor of global and regional institutions, the ultimate goal being one of demilitarization and overcoming the current system of war.

As we can see, the cosmopolitan model of governance would stand as a third way between the Westphalian and UN model, both of which are obsolete but still supported; but there would be important differences between them in the political monopoly of nation-states and a likely emerging model, which is as predictable as it is scary, namely the establishment of a global state empire. Global governance does not imply turning the world into a new state since there will be no states to compete against one another for exclusive territorial sovereignty, nor should it lead to a new national state on a global level.

This is a hybrid model which bases itself on nation-states while at the same time denying them. It is not an international or supranational state, but a *glocal* state in which the global and local are not mutually exclusive but are instead two sides of the same coin.[3]

In order for this type of democracy to function properly, the establishment of a division and interconnection of power and authority at different levels is essential, both horizontally and vertically. This involves establishing a complex structure based on the logic or principle of subsidiarity, which allows not only a sharing of sovereignty but also shared authority between various bodies or institutions. It would be a new model, capable of uniting the strengths of confederal and federal models, in which it would be possible to limit the monopoly of different states, both domestically and

---

[3]   On the role of cities in the information era, consult the excellent Borja and Castells (1998).

internationally, as subjects of international law, without this necessarily meaning the end of the state itself.

Within this new distribution of power, it will be necessary to establish local or regional, state, national, and international spheres of decision-making. Therefore issues and matters whose management and undertaking result in the direct implication of citizen should be moved to the local–regional level; matters in which a population located in a given territory is affected by collective problems and issues that do not exceed their own borders should be moved to the nation-state level; and matters that require transnational mediation given the interconnection between the state and transnational structures should be moved to the global sphere.

Except for the differences between eras and contexts that have little to do with one another, it should be noted that there is historical precedent for complex governance. For example, the British Commonwealth at the time offered an alternative institutional form of sovereignty, a system in which the states accepted the authority of British institutions in certain areas without losing international legal sovereignty.

## The European Union as a complex model of governance

Another more current, and therefore much more interesting, possibility is the case of the European Union. We all know that the European Union suffers from significant shortfalls from a democratic point of view and is therefore a long way from being a truly democratic model of complex governance. However, from a structural standpoint, the European Union is beginning to take shape as a new emerging model of governance which is different from the classical models used so far.

The European Union has territory, recognition, control, national authority, extra-national authority, and supranational authority. There is no generally accepted term by which to refer to the European Union. Is it a state, community, domain, confederation of states, or a federation of states? On the one hand, while containing certain federal elements, the European Union is not a federal state because it lacks the mechanism reproducing nationality and the state incorporated in any federal construction. On the other hand, it goes beyond simple intergovernmental cooperation, with the exception of certain specific areas. Whatever the truth, it exists and exists comfortably in the midst of an international context that is predominantly populated by sovereign states.

The European Union lacks a specific place of supreme authority. Within it, there are, as I said, supranational state structures and international structures. For example, the European Commission and the European Court of Justice (ECJ) and, to some extent, the European Parliament, are structures of supranational authority.

The ECJ can annul laws and specific decisions of member states, but at the same time, many of the decisions made within the European Union are the result of negotiations between those states. There is no hegemonic actor which is ultimately responsible for making and implementing decisions which bind states together, or any institution capable of implementing constitutional elements such as exercising the monopoly of violence.

There is also no formally centralized structure of charges. The European Union does not have a hierarchy of functions whose apex is a central authority.[4] Most of the division of functions are governed by the horizontal principle of distribution of powers, and not by the vertical principle of hierarchy. Therefore there is a formal and informal network of horizontal interactions and continual negotiations between actors at various levels, each with their own independent power base.

This overlap between the European Union and its member states leads us to a new type of political organization which is yet to be formed, but which has features and basic elements which are radically different from those we have seen thus far. In this regard, the European Union is the basis for a new way to structure a complex, multilateral world order.

With European unification, the traditional principles that have underpinned the Westphalian model and the UN model start to crumble away, or at least weaken, including those states that apparently intended to sustain the cosmopolitan model. Thus, confronted with the coincidence of a sovereign entity and an exclusive territory where this sovereignty is exercised, a multinational political system emerges, which is geographically open and constantly growing. The porosity of borders and the strengthening of mutual interdependence incapacitates even the most powerful states in the Union, making them unable to safeguard the autonomy of their territorial space. This erosion of state capacity occurs in military, political, economic, social, and cultural spheres, both externally and internally.

Against a single and indivisible sovereignty, a shared sovereignty is appearing. In conjunction with state laws, comparable community regulations and, where appropriate, regional laws and regional regulations are emerging. In addition, transnational laws derived from treaties or legally enforceable agreements signed between interregional, cross-border entities, etc., are created.

The idea of the rule of law, understood as the ultimate abstraction of power, is still perfectly valid and continues in full force, but it is now a rule of law that is not solely applied to the nation-state. The mutual relationship between community law, state law, regional law, and transnational law (not to mention international law) means that power and sovereignty are shared among the various authorities and subjects depending on material spheres of power assigned to each one of them. The nation state no longer has exclusivity with regard to supporting legitimacy and implementation of the rule of law, as evidenced by the presence of the European Court of Justice or the European Court of Human Rights.

Within this complex model, states would continue to have their own force and power, but it would be profoundly modified. They would no longer constitute the basic institutional structure of political order and would become, as Castells points out, parts

---

[4]  Since the implementation of the Lisbon Treaty in December 2009, the European Union has a President. However this figure lacks, not only the executive powers of a Prime Minister, but also the symbolic nature of the head of state of a parliamentary democracy.

or nodes of a wider network. A network in which, on the one hand, they share power with transnational organizations, both governmental and nongovernmental, and on the other hand, with infra- or interstate entities. In other words, states would exert their activity not as sovereign entities, but as component parts of a new global political order, which would be much larger and more complex.

## The future of sovereignty

The new situation requires substantial modification to one of the fundamental theoretical paradigms that has until present supported the legitimacy and power of states, that of the notion of sovereignty. The integrating myth of the national state has been defined traditionally by three classic dogmas of sovereignty, those of supremacy, indivisibility, and state unity. In applying these principles, the law and the state have been permanently united. The law, in its classical sense, has always been an emanation of state sovereignty. No rights other than those produced by the state itself are recognized, and international law is accepted only to the extent that it is legitimized by the state.

It is clear that the current globalization process has opened up deep gaps in the formal classical conception of sovereignty understood as supreme, original, and independent. The idea of sacrosanct state sovereignty supported by the corresponding immutability of borders is increasingly under question. An increasingly frequent series of events such as environmental disasters, development of weapons of mass destruction, human rights violations, etc. are causing, on the one hand, questions regarding the principle of sovereignty by means of more frequent interventions, by the international community, of varying intensity, including military interventions, and secondly, the questioning of the classic standards of international law.

This set of facts makes the principle of sovereignty, at least in its indivisible, unlimited, exclusive, and perpetual classical sense, totally obsolete and dead. States will survive in the new world order. What is now more questionable is whether their sovereignty will survive, at least in the classical sense in which this concept has been understood over the last few centuries.

It seems clear that a complex and open society like the present, particularly in the case of Europe, should also have corresponding sovereignty, and therefore, a legal and constitutional arrangement which is both complex and open.

Therefore, the idea of sovereignty shall not go away, but will, in the future, be profoundly altered. There is no question of getting rid of old sovereignties or replacing them with a new global sovereignty, or in our case a new European sovereignty, or replacing constitutions currently in force with new constitutions; what is required is rather an overlap between them.

The eventual adoption of a European constitution offers us two alternatives. Either we continue to maintain the classic thesis of a single sovereignty understood in the triple sense of supreme, original, and independent power, or we opt for the idea that sovereignty can be shared. If we choose the first alternative, we still have to solve the problem of whether such sovereignty should correspond to the European Union or to nation states, in other words, whether we end up with the prevailing logic of integration or sovereignty.

In light of this position, there appears a second alternative, which is opting for shared sovereignty. Assuming that a European constitution is inevitable and that the new European sovereignty will not lead to the extinction of the sovereignty of different states, but to a superposition of sovereignty, then the question arises of what will be the residual sovereignty of the states and what might be the elements of conflict between both sovereignties.

It seems that it is necessary to establish a complex structure based on the logic or principle of subsidiarity, which allows a sharing not only of power but of sovereignty among various entities and institutions. This means a new model, capable of uniting the strengths of confederal and federal models, in which it is possible to limit the monopoly of different states, both domestically and internationally, or in our case within Europe, as subjects of international law, without it necessarily meaning the end of the state.

It is undeniable that the decline of the nation-state as the sole legal and political structure through which the rule of law is configured leads to quite extraordinary crossroads and unforeseeable consequences for both the idea of the constitution and constitutional theory itself. However, I believe that this change does not necessarily mean that constitutions are to be completely dissolved until such a time when they are reduced to a mere historical category.

Regardless of the way in which supranational agencies such as the European Union are comprised in future, its existence will always presuppose that of individual member states and, with them, their respective constitutions. In turn, on the other hand, the future European Union can only effectively undertake its duties if its implementation is decentralized and if it observes the principle of subsidiarity.

It is therefore right to dispel the classical idea that every law necessarily has to emanate from a single source of power, a single sovereignty. In light of this idea, it is necessary to raise the possibility of having a broader or more diffuse law, building a concept of law that allows the possibility of overlap and interaction between different legal systems, without having to necessarily suppose a system of subordination or hierarchy either between them or with third-party systems.

Instead of the monistic, kelsenian view of a legal system understood as a unitary whole, a pluralistic vision capable of maintaining compatibility between systems seems more appropriate, in which states overlap and interact with each other. There are many possible forms and degrees of dependence and independence.

Fortunately, in contemporary international law, the idea that state sovereignty cannot act as an impregnable shield against serious human rights violations is an idea that is becoming increasingly stronger. It is no longer possible to avoid responsibilities under the cover of the euphemism of internal affairs. At this juncture, there is no point in maintaining such a rigid separation between the internal and external. Therefore, any approach in which the principle of national sovereignty prevails over respect for human dignity is radically contrary to the most elementary principles of justice.

This gradual blurring between domestic law and international law offers the prospect of a new horizon to legal experts, one in which the progressive development of a global constitution is necessary. It must be a regulatory constitution made up of a complex legal system which is not necessarily supported by hierarchical relations of superiority and subordination, but by shared criteria, coordination, and subsidiarity. That is, in short, the great challenge of constitutionalism which we face in the twenty-first century.

# Bibliography

Beck, U. 1998. *¿Qué es la globalización?* Barcelona: Paidos.

Borja, J. and M. Castells. 1998. *Local y global*. Madrid: Taurus.

Castells, M. 1998a. *La era de la información. Economía, sociedad y cultura. La sociedad red*. Madrid: Alianza.

— 1998b. *La era de la información. Economía, sociedad y cultura*. El poder de la identidad. Madrid: Alianza.

— 1998c. *La era de la información. Economía, sociedad y cultura. Fin de milenio*. Madrid: Alianza.

Estefanía, J. 2000. *Aquí no puede ocurrir*. Madrid: Taurus.

Giddens, A. 1998. *Más allá de la izquierda y la derecha*. Madrid: Cátedra.

— 1999. *La tercera vía*. Madrid: Taurus.

— 2000. *Un mundo desbocado*. Madrid: Taurus.

Held, D. 1995. *Democracy and the Global Order*. Cambridge: Polity Press.

Innerarity, D. 2012. *The Future and Its Enemies: In Defense of Political Hope*. Tran. S. Kingery. Palo Alto: Stanford University Press.

Jáuregui, G. 2000. *La democracia planetaria*. Oviedo: Editorial Nobel.

— 2004. *La democracia en el siglo XXI*. Oñati: Basque Institute of Public Administration.

Kelsen, H. 1965. *Principios de derecho internacional público*. Buenos Aires: Editorial El Ateneo.

Ortega, A. 2000. *Horizontes cercanos*. Madrid: Taurus.

Rosenau, J. N. and E. O. Czempiel. 1992. *Governance without Government: Order and Change in World Politics*. Cambridge: Cambridge University Press.

Zolo, D. 2000. *Cosmópolis*. Barcelona: Paidos.

# 11

# Mediations between Personal and "Global" Topics

Michel Wieviorka
*Maison des Sciences de l'Homme*

## Two powerful trends

For the past 30 years, two powerful and apparently unrelated trends have been dramatically changing the world itself as well as ways of approaching it. On the one hand, individualism includes important aspects referring to the idea of the "Subject," laden with the processes of subjectivation and desubjectivation. On the other hand, globalization has become a much more massive reality than during the Cold War.

First of all, these two phenomena deserve to be explained, even if sociological, legal, and political literatures deal with them abundantly. They also ought to be conceived in their articulation, so as to reduce the gap rejected by those who do not want to dissociate one from the other, the subject in its most personal, private sense, and the "global," in its most worldwide or general sense.

At first approximation, individualism presents two distinct facets. On the one hand, we have consumption: personal access to the fruits of modernity, money, work, health, education for one's children, etc. Here, individualism cannot be very distant from hedonism, egotism; it is made of more or less successful calculations of individual strategy and mobilization of resources to manage to satisfy the hunger of consumption, having money, etc. In a word, it is instrumental. The other facet is the Subject, the capability of acting, mastering one's existence, exercising one's freedom, making choices and building oneself up and achieving goals. This second aspect is itself more complex than what is too often said by those who resort to the notion of Subject, and who only see in it this capacity, this virtuality, which leads to accomplishment and self-discovery: the Subject may also at first be fragile, vulnerable, and sick, for example. It can then be barred from action, not being able to take place, for instance, due to racism, discrimination, or social exclusion. It may also take the appearance of the anti-subject, which is constructed only in the negation of the Other, in cruelty, in violence for violence's sake, or in sadism, for example.

Globalization is a vague category. On the one hand, it makes us aware of the state of the world and is used to formulate a historical diagnosis. The world is becoming globalized, meaning that financial and commercial fluctuations (markets) dismiss states and the borders between them. Globalization was first described as an economic phenomenon, but it is being increasingly presented as a total phenomenon, concerning every field of collective life. Arjun Appadurai was one of the first to show that culture is becoming globalized: religion is a global phenomenon, deserving a more precise analysis in this respect; Islamic terrorism, especially since the attacks on September 11, 2001, is certainly a global issue; international migrations do not come down to the classic image of a departure and an arrival in a country where the immigrant is responsible for integrating into society, but is more and more a question of transnationalism, of the logic of diaspora, of transit and circulation, etc. On the other hand, globalization may become a concept for understanding reality, a category which is not (or not merely) historical and concrete, but analytical, a tool for dealing with a problem or situation and highlighting it. This is a case of "thinking globally," which is a way of distancing ourselves from traditional ways used generally by social, legal, and political science, which traditionally operate within the double framework of the nation-state and its counterpart, so-called international relations. Thinking globally means keeping a distance from the "methodological nationalism" criticized for many years by the German sociologist Ulrich Beck in order to adopt another perspective: as for Beck, he suggests adopting "methodological cosmopolitism," an expression going back to the great philosophical tradition (especially Kantian philosophy) yet which, in France at least, has been disqualified because of its use by anti-Semites in the period between the World Wars, denouncing Jews as cosmopolites without land or roots.

Global thinking obviously does not keep us from imagining levels of analysis beyond the planetary. The key is to articulate these levels, for instance from the largest worldwide level down to the local level, passing through the indispensable nation-state, but without granting it any monopoly whatsoever. This is why in the 1990s, Roland Robertson suggested the neologism "glocalization," with the idea that the global and the local should be thought of as the same movement.

Global thinking also means integrating scientists and other professional actors into the same logic of coproduction of knowledge in order to deal with the great problems of the contemporary world, whether they are so-called natural disasters or those which are only partially natural, for example disasters concerning water, ecology, climate change, health, and epidemics.

## Is there a link between contemporary individualism and globalization?

At first glance, the two phenomena seem distinct and very far from each other. But in fact, they feed upon each other. Globalization, and more particularly the formidable double compression of time and space that it implies according to the famous expression of the geographer David Harvey, puts the whole world in immediate contact with each other, and particularly with the spectacle of consumption put on by the Internet, television, and the cinema, which can only increase the desire for reaching it. Dominated by the power of money and finance, it tends to dissolve and weaken the mediations which separate us from the universe of consumption and from the most direct and immediate access possible not only to goods and services, but also to culture or faith. Classical institutions are challenged by these processes, just like, in many respects, states and their borders, and also political systems, including whenever they are democratic. It is true that globalization also creates, in turn, phenomena of fragmentation and a closing of identity, but they must also be understood as linked to the push of individualism and, more precisely, the personal subjectivity of individuals: each person today chooses his or her individual identity or identities, or at least they do so much more than in the past when identities were reproduced much more than they were produced. For example, today we can choose to be Muslim, whereas in other times if we were Muslim, it was because our parents, grandparents, etc. were also. Moreover, there are more and more conversions to Islam in Western countries such as France; the phenomena is not only brought in from the outside by immigrants. And migrations themselves are carried by a logic which quickly turns global, while they simultaneously owe much to the subjectivity of immigrants wanting to construct their existence and who do not speak only of economic success: more and more educated and with more and more women among their numbers, contemporary immigrants are "connected," linked with one another across global networks, all while being individual actors of their existence.

The more mediations, institutions, states, classical political systems are weakened, the more each one of us is likely to lean on our own personal subjectivity, even if it means trying to belong to networks or communities not only to deal with norms, needs, hopes, and desires caused by globalization, but also to deal with the harm it may cause (growing inequalities, exclusion, financial instability). Such an evolution holds major implications for democracy either in its capability of ensuring internal treatment of social and political issues within a country, or in global life, which can no longer be reduced to mere international relations.

## The challenges of democracy

In the 1960s and 1970s, democracy was considered the opposite of all types of systems, aspirations, or political models. It was defined, with more dedication to controversy than a desire to delve more deeply into the concept, as the opposite of communism, of dictatorship, or revolution. There was no need to give it a more precise definition, and oftentimes, it was enough to fall back on the famous quip by Winston Churchill: "Democracy is the worst form of government, except for all the others."

Then, authoritarian governments crumbled, the Cold War ended with the defeat of the Soviet Union, Revolution became synonymous with terrorism in certain countries or with radical Islam (in Iran), which weakened its ideologies all over the democratic world. The general triumph of democracy was proclaimed, and when the Berlin Wall fell, Francis Fukuyama announced the End of History, that is the triumph of the market and of democracy. There was no longer any opposition to democracy, such was our political future, and the market was the only realistic prospect for the economy. Reason and law, which are universal values, would continue to break down cultural and religious idiosyncrasies. A certain concept of modernity was then at its peak, scarcely taking globalization into account, and even less the rise in power of individualism and the personal subjectivity of individuals.

A half century later, we have moved very far from this peak. Democracy is no longer the opposite of communism or of revolutionary ideology; it now confronts itself instead. But rather than appearing stronger than ever, alive, and self-confident, it often seems weak, hesitant, uncertain, all while remaining incapable of dealing with new risks. And everywhere in democratic societies, we hear about the crisis of democracy, decline, and difficulties.

## The crisis of democracy

For a long time, democracy was either direct or representative.

Direct democracy does without mediations between citizens and the moment where political decisions are made, it functions through referendums, through petitions of popular initiative, through plebiscite. It rallies the whole of the electoral body to make decisions without worrying about Parliament or political parties, which is hard to do in large territories, especially if this is to be the main way to make political decisions. Direct democracy criticizes and rejects the idea of having intermediaries between the people and power. It is constantly being heralded by opponents of parliamentarianism or political parties, and it may thus assume the appearance of populism. Populism denounces the "big" in favor of the "little." It believes that political actors are an elite and that they are easily corrupted regardless of the political positions of its members. It prefers elementary choices and simple formulations rather than debates about complex cases where politics must, however, often intervene. By pandering to the tendency of withdrawing community or identity, globalization quickly becomes an encouragement toward populism and procedures of direct democracy. We have numerous examples of this with the rise of the extreme Right in Europe, and even the growing trend of xenophobia and racism, expressed in the Swiss "vote" against the construction of mosques on November 29, 2009.

Representative democracy, however, has long been the predominant form of democracy, and if there is such a large crisis of democracy, it is in fact a crisis of representation itself. In representation, the will of citizens is expressed through the mediation of elected representatives. They incarnate the general will. They vote for laws, choose and sometimes control the executive.

Representative democracy depends upon a system of political parties and institutions, namely a Parliament. It is never stronger than when the political system is organized around a conflict opposing two main social positions that it represents. This was the case in European industrial national societies, the Left presenting the workers' demands and the Right incarnating order and the bourgeoisie. Representative democracy has always been weaker in countries where this conflicting structure was not so pronounced, and where political life was not largely informed by the social demands arising from two classes in conflict.

The less the political system is capable of representing social demands, the more democracy relies on the state, and on purely political games. Parliament and parties still exist in that case, but representation is cut off from civil society, at least it is not structured by it. The defining characteristic of the current situation, in many countries, is that the demands which stem from civil society seldom give rise to a Right–Left conflict. This aspect of the crisis of political representation is even more acute when the state itself is weakened, when it cannot impose the rules of a state of law, when it is corrupt, incapable of bringing conditions conducive to the smooth functioning of a democratic political system, weak to the point of entrusting certain sovereign functions to private operators. We can see this more and more often with the privatization of security, putting into question the famous statement by Max Weber (from a 1919 conference published under the name of "Politics as a Vocation"), wherein the state possesses the legitimate monopoly of force. Political representation needs a solid state and smoothly running institutions.

The demands by civil society are no longer the same as 20 or 30 years ago. These demands include more and more claims which destabilize classical political representation.

First of all, they are dominated by globalization, which, as previously mentioned, makes it so that all the great contemporary problems present global, worldwide aspects, which are often decisive. This phenomenon is obviously reinforced by modern technologies of communication, that is the Internet. This phenomenon is also exacerbated by the awareness of the fact that environment, climate, water, for instance, are nowadays global questions which call upon political responses which are not limited by the nation-state framework. However, political representation is traditionally organized within the framework of the nation-state and it has no hold on global logic, or a weak one at the very most. Today, social and cultural demands are also subject to the sway of individualism. The more citizens live as individuals, the more the vast systems on which political representation is built lose their importance. Social classes become diluted, great unifying ideologies lose their influence, and collective life becomes fragmented. Politics is then tossed around by the personal motivations and emotions of individuals, which are more and more orchestrated by modern media, and which invade the public space—political representation is yet again destabilized.

In economic matters, democracy is otherwise powerless, or at least uneasy, whenever it comes to no longer fairly doling out resources, that is developing the providence state, but dealing with social exclusion, job loss, slowing growth, business closures—all these phenomena exacerbated by globalization.

The same goes for cultural matters. On the one hand, collective identities make demands; they want to be recognized, gain particular rights; they want the historical drama they were victim to in the past—genocide, mass murders, slavery, etc.—to be taken into consideration. In certain cases, they demand political independence or at least a greater autonomy. Such demands may question the integrity of the nation, or even the principle of individual equality in the eyes of the law, which is at the heart of democracy. But if they are not heard and dealt with politically, those who make the demands feel an intense sense of injustice and may be tempted to retreat, or to resort to radical measures, even violence. Faced with these cultural demands, political parties split, languish in vagueness, and become disoriented. The same goes for religious matters. In the 1960s and even the 1970s, we could believe in the "disenchantment with the world" under the effect of reason, secularization, and the decline of religions. But since then, we must admit that religion is a part of modernity, rather than its opposite. So what role should we grant it? Here as well, political representation is uneasy. Let us be reminded that we must not pit the sway of individualism against that of collective identity. On the contrary: the former feeds the latter, since individual, highly subjective choices, and not the logic of reproduction, increasingly reinforce identities.

### New perspectives: Democracy renewed

In such a situation, a constructive response would consist of attempting to enrich democracy by supplementing representative democracy with other formulas, and even, in the most radical points of view, replacing it.

A first step would be that of participative democracy. This means allowing citizens to participate in decision-making, at the moment when decisions are being made, and especially prior to that moment, when the decision is being prepared through demanding and constructive debate. Various countries have tried this since the 1960s; the most famous of these experiments was in Porto Alegre, Brazil: after 1989, the political authorities entrusted decisions concerning a part of the municipal budget to relevant residents. They gathered in their neighborhoods to determine the projects that should be financed, and their delegates then negotiated with the municipal administration. This led notably, under various conditions and designations (consensus conferences, citizens' juries, etc.), to meetings between citizens, experts, and political (or other) actors meant to bring political decision to light through rigorous debate in which, on any given risk, citizens would question those who possess knowledge and skills, all to the point where possible choices, their advantages and disadvantages, and areas of uncertainty are laid out plainly. In this respect, participation is not the opposite of representation; it supplements and enlightens it, more or less according to the philosophy of Jürgen Habermas. Here, the Internet may comprise an important instrument, as Barack Obama understood quite well. This was apparent in his presidential election campaign, notably in the orchestration of concrete action in both field and on-line mobilization.

A second step, whose inspiration is actually very close at hand, is that of deliberative democracy, wherein citizens play a constructive role in formulating the terms of public debate, all while constructing themselves through the debate, learning from each other, shaping their values and their understanding of the world and their convictions. They use and sharpen their critical mind through the course of interactions with other participants in public discussion, in a direct line from a philosophical tradition that contemporary authors trace back to John Dewey.

Just as much as participative democracy, deliberative democracy requires certain conditions to be fulfilled in order to work: equal access areas of participation and discussion, transparency of procedures and debate, the opportunity for anyone to express him- or herself without running the risk of repercussion, the capacity for people to not only participate in discussion, but also to make themselves heard. Both types of democracy are firmly rooted in a profound renewal of democracy, giving much importance to local life while distrusting central authorities and the state, which all too often attempt to impose its rules, norms, and concepts of fairness or what is good. It is no coincidence that both are sometimes carried out by NGOs, which make them the central tenet of their internal policy and are simultaneously a decisive factor for a revival of the democratic spirit.

Was this renewal an extension of the very democratic idea invented by the ancient Greeks and developed in the so-called Western world before being spread across the planet? This view is debatable. It ignores the often ancient practices which characterize areas such as Africa, India, or the Arab world and which Amartya Sen echoed (2005). Moreover, according to Sen, the ancient Greeks were interested in Egyptian, Indian and Persian thought. For the Nobel laureate in Economics in 1998, democracy is not limited to political representation and the respect for majority rule, but also implies protecting individual rights and liberties, anyone's access to social benefits, and the right to access information and to participate actively in public deliberation.

This goes back to a point that deserves emphasis: participative democracy and deliberative democracy favor a bottom-to-top logic. They require individuals who are subjects of their existence, capable of producing something through their debates and participation, including rules for collective life or concepts of justice. This contradicts other viewpoints that favor the idea of representative democracy, which grants the state, its rules and its institutions a much greater importance and favors a top-to-bottom logic, that is from the state to individuals. In practice, there may be tension between both great families of democracy, but they may also be complementary. The renaissance of democracy in the world is not a one-dimensional phenomenon, owing everything only to states, or contrarily, only to the set of actors at the bottom. It comes sometimes from some people, and at other times from others, and there are times when it comes from a dialectic between the two.

## Post-democracy

The hypothesis of renewed democracy is a seductive one, and one which must be defended. But should we not be more realistic and examine the future in light of other, much darker trends? These trends cause us to speak, like the Russian political scientist Youri Levada, about a "contemplative democracy," or using a less vivid but more worrying expression, used, for example, by the British sociologist Colin Crouch, "post-democracy" (2004). From this point of view, democracy, which is especially a victim of globalization, instead of being renewed and widened, would lose its qualities, becoming less and less capable of organizing collective life. Democracy would decline, void of any substance, and lacking interest for individuals who would then turn away from it. In this point of view, politics would be confiscated by experts, with the argument that today's issues are much too complicated to be discussed in the public arena. The media, increasingly subjected to power and to interest groups, would shape opinion by playing on emotions rather than on reason, and would then themselves be incapable of offering any precise, diversified, and well-documented information. With deliberation and participation barely working, attributions of Parliament and, more widely, the system of parties and political representation, would become artificial, and citizens would become passive spectators, easily manipulated, and would abstain from voting. In a post-democracy, politics would be confiscated by a more and more powerful authority or it would actually be surrendered to the obscure game of lobbies, with no separation of powers, with no legislative control over the executive, and with no autonomy of the judiciary. Even political decision would be subordinate to outside forces, to logic such as economic globalization, and laws and important decisions would come from somewhere else, the United Nations, the International Monetary Fund, the World Bank, or from the European Union, for example. The Parliament would merely endorse them; governance would become global and undemocratic.

So in a world where the forces of globalization are at work on the one hand, and an individual logic of subjectivation and desubjectivation is at work on the other, there is not one single possible future for democracy, something desired by the arrogant thought of those who proclaimed the End of History when the Berlin Wall fell; nor is there a Western monopoly of the idea or spirit of democracy. The possible paths are numerous, varied, and they can go from the bottom to the top, or from the top to the bottom. They can also be lost in the sands of post-democracy: as the French sociologist Alain Touraine wrote (1994), democracy must imperatively reside in a new idea.

## Conclusion: Supranational spaces

The renewal of democracy concerns the local and national territorial level much more than strictly worldwide levels. However, the stakes here are considerable: how can we make it so that the democratic spirit, the meaning of justice, the respect for the universal values of right and reason play a role in these areas characterized, for now, especially with the forces of globalization?

A first response is given by social and cultural agents who design a global civil society. NGOs are in the first line, especially when they act upon global, or "glocal," risks. They indeed impose debates, they open conflicts which may eventually contribute to new forms of rules and institutions organizing this supranational space. They are important factors in creating conflict and politics at this level. This is why the anti-globalists, by ceasing pure opposition to globalization, and by affirming that "another world is possible" are an important movement, not only politicizing action at a supranational level, but because they oblige their adversaries (multinational companies, international institutions) to be established in such a field of conflicts and consequently contribute to the creation of a political space in which they must fight it out.

A second response is given by official international organizations, so long as they are capable of having a renewed legitimacy (I am thinking in particular of the United Nations, whose Security Council could be broadened, and whose General Assembly seems to have very insufficient power) and developing truly international legal institutions (the Penal Court of the Hague, created in 2002, still needs to be consolidated). Authorities who regulate international economics seem also to be quite insufficient when they are not suspected of operating in the most neoliberal form of capitalism—this was the criticism in the 1990s of the "Consensus of Washington." Reinforcing institutions of the United Nations, or something similar, could be a significant contribution faced with the difficulties in regulating globalization.

Individuals, as subjects who become agents, such as anti-globalists, and states, by accepting the fact of constructing supranational spaces of law and politics over themselves, and possibly in combination with themselves, can thus contribute to transforming these spaces, which are still largely devoid of rules, of forms of regulation or justice, and of institutions. Here as well, one can think that between the most vigorous forces of globalization and singular personal subjects, new or renewed forms of democratic life may see the day. It may also be extremely urgent to do so.

## Bibliography

Crouch, C. 2004. *Post-Democracy. Themes for the 21st Century*. Cambridge: Polity Press.
Sen, A. 2005. *La démocratie des autres. Pourquoi la liberté n'est pas une invention de l'Occident*. Paris: Payot.
Touraine, A. 1994. *Qu'est-ce que la démocratie?* Paris: Fayard.

# 12

# Europe as a Risk Averse Power

Zaki Laïdi

*Institut d'Études Politiques*

Is it possible to define the identity and strategy of an actor in the international system by referring to its aversion to risk? Can one speak of a Risk Averse Power? These are the questions we will set out to answer here in suggesting that the European Union is a political actor whose identity and strategy in the international field are based on a strong aversion toward risk. In order to make this hypothesis, we will (1) define the meaning of a Risk Averse Power, (2) propose criteria for measuring this risk aversion, (3) attempt to explain why Europe is risk averse, and (4) determine the implications of risk aversion for Europe as a global actor.

## What is a risk averse power?

A Risk Averse Power (RAP) can be defined as an international actor that defines and responds to the political stakes of a given identified risk in terms of a will to reduce its uncertainties and uncontrollable effects (Borraz 2008). Indeed, each international actor might be considered a Risk Averse Power since, when faced with a decision, it assesses its costs and benefits before acting. Even North Korea weighs the costs and benefits of launching missile strikes on Japan. But risk aversion is not a simple matter of rationality; it is also a matter of identity. This being said, we can say that an actor evinces strong risk aversion in the following cases:

1. The RAP tends, more than others, to steer clear of using force when faced with conflicts within the international system. The actor will reject the use of force outright and propose a cooperative alternative. Therefore, the actor generally accords greater import to civilian systemic risks than military risks. In ranking their eight major perceived risks, Europeans place armed conflict and nuclear

proliferation in the sixth and eighth spots respectively, while global poverty and climate change rank first and second (Eurobarometer 2009).

2. The RAP insists, more than others, on the indivisibility of systemic risks between actors. In doing so, the actor encourages joint, cooperative practices rather than emphasizing those tending toward confrontation and unilateralism. The actor is particularly interested in protecting "global public goods" and limiting the hardships of "global public bads" through civilian and normative procedures.

3. The RAP tends, more than others, to call for the actualization of global norms already legitimized by international institutions. Such an actualization would, in the view of the actor, reduce the most significant global risks.

Risk Averse Powers appear to resemble what is usually referred to as a Soft Power. However, the definitional field of the RAP is at once much wider and more precise than that of a Soft Power. Much wider, because an RAP deals not only with internal concerns (the aversion to genetically modified organisms (GMOs), for example) but also with external ones (risk of armed conflict). A Risk Averse Power considers dimensions that a Soft Power generally does not. Europe's aversion to biotechnological risks or to financial instability tells us much about the European Union's relation to risk. Such risk aversion allows us to make hypotheses and to draw conclusions about Europe's behavior on the international stage. In contrast, the Soft Power model takes into account only risks related to war and peace.

A Risk Averse Power, then, can be characterized by its determination to reduce the "risky behaviors" of state actors. In this perspective, it aims to integrate their actions within a normative framework tending at constraining their actions and making them more predictable. It should be noted that an RAP can only truly exist in a democratic political system where public deliberation plays a crucial role in evaluating risks. Naturally, the extent of public opinion involvement varies according to the subject at hand. Yet public opinion remains essential insofar as risk aversion illustrates marked social preferences. Aversion to the risk of war shows a strong preference for peaceful conflict settlements; aversion to food safety risks is related to a strong preference for the precautionary principle, etc.

Assuming the existence of three major systemic risks in the world system—environmental risks (climate- and biotechnology-based), market risks (financial or job loss), and war-related risks (war, weapons of mass destruction)—we posit that the European Union and/or the European member states manifest, generally speaking, a stronger aversion toward these risks than the United States, China, and Russia. European risk aversion is manifested in the following ways: (1) Strong aversion toward environmental risks, demonstrated by a demand for more stringent and more numerous international norms than those of other political actors. (2) Proposals for stricter market finance regulation than those of other nations (United States, emerging countries). (3) Marked reluctance as regards the use of military force (Europe never speaks of war or enemies) in spite of strong national differences on the issue.

## How can risk aversion be measured?

There is no composite index that would allow us to compare risk aversion between different actors (Europe vs the United States, for example). However, there are a certain number of relevant indices that allow us to measure aversion to risk. For the European Union, we can identify five such indices: job loss risk, biotechnology risks, climate change risk, financial risks, and the risk of war.

### Job loss risk

Intensified market globalization has, paradoxically, made it easier to discern national and regional differences. In effect, each actor within the international sphere is forced either to protect its singularity or adapt itself to the whole in the least adverse manner. In this new context, Europeans appear to the rest of the world as representative of societies that accord specific importance to social norms and, notably, to job protection. European job protection norms are probably the highest in the world. European employment protection legislation (EPL) is much more restrictive than in other advanced economies. Within Europe, of course, there are significant variations among nations. Yet all European employment protection legislation has a key index of commonality: it attempts, generally speaking, to protect salaried workers against the risk of layoffs. On the basis of an index ranging from 0 (weakest protection) to 6 (strongest protection) the results are as follows:

| | |
|---|---|
| European Union -19* | 2.3 |
| Canada | 1.2 |
| United States | 0.2 |

*The number indicates the number of European states taken into account in the study.

Source: OECD, "OECD indicators on job protection" 2008.

As far as these numbers are concerned, we can say that the European aversion to job loss risk is stronger than in the other, major Western countries. This does not, however, lead to the conclusion that Europe is better suited than other world regions to face the job market. More suitable is the proposition that, as a general rule, Europeans tend to arbitrate between losing one's job and finding a new one. The lower the risk of job loss, the lower the chances are of finding a new one in case of a layoff. Evidently, the reverse is also true. We can say that on average, job loss risk in Europe is better covered than in the rest of the world. However, we are not in a position to judge the efficiency of this disposition in terms of job creation. We should also note that this job loss risk aversion has not led to the creation of any specific European political strategy. There are several reasons for this. First, job-related issues are not addressed at the community level Second, the European member states are extremely protective of their individual jurisdictional prerogatives. Third, individual European states contain heterogeneous—and often divergent—social practices. Fourth and finally, we must highlight the *defensive* position of Europe vis-à-vis job protection: Europe looks to increase job protection measures, while other nations are currently attempting to reduce them. This is true even if certain (notably Scandinavian) states have shown that a reduction in job protection is perfectly compatible with other forms of social protection: high unemployment compensation and work activation politics aimed at protecting people rather than jobs. Nevertheless, there is hardly a European consensus on this issue.

There is, on the other hand, a wide European consensus concerning the fact that social norms (social protection) in Europe are relatively high, and that as a result the European Union must protect itself against social dumping. This is especially relevant for low-wage countries, and it is precisely for this reason that the European Union has always advocated respect and conformity to basic International Labor Organization (ILO) conventions. It was the European Union that pushed, unsuccessfully, for the WTO to recognize such issues. During the 2001 Doha summit, the European Union faced hostility from emerging countries. It also dealt with the indifference of the United States, which prefers to include social conditionality within bilateral trade agreements. Recently, the debate has shifted from social conditionality to environmental conditionality in the context of climate change struggles. Those EU member states that already have strong standards (carbon taxes, emissions trading systems) fear that the internalization of their environmental costs will harm their competitiveness in the global market, and, as a result, threaten jobs in the European market. We cannot effectively say that the European member states are more sensitive to climate change than the United States, even if the latter nation has not yet taken stringent measures to combat climate change. But because the European Union is more exposed to international trade than the United States, the competitive disadvantage for the European Union is higher. This is especially true given the fact that the European Union is not a hard power capable of putting pressure on reluctant partners. Climate change, therefore, ends up amplifying job loss risk for the Europeans, while equally serving to raise the risk of job loss to the level of a systemic risk within the international system.

## Biotechnology risks

In terms of biotechnology as a whole, Europeans do not manifest a specific or stronger aversion to risk than other world regions. For issues of gene therapy, nanotechnology, and genetic pharmacology, potential risk aversion is significantly discounted by the perceived social utility of the particular biotechnology. Risk aversion is also discounted by the moral acceptability of the technology, and by the confidence that a European population might have in the capacities for regulating it (Eurobarometer 2007). European optimism regarding biotechnology has markedly increased since 2002, after an obvious decrease during the 1990s. Even so, European risk aversion toward GMOs remains strong and persistent. In a 2007 Eurobarometer study, 58 percent of Europeans expressed a negative attitude toward GMO products. This figure (Figure 12.1) has been relatively stable throughout the years, whereas the general confidence in biotechnologies has significantly increased. Indeed, there are still national differences

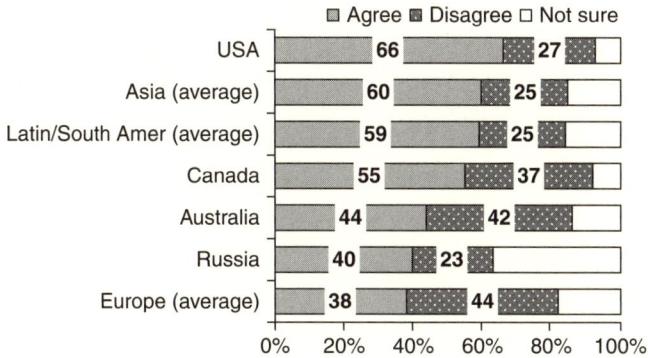

**Figure 12.1** Proportion of people agreeing or disagreeing with the statement "The benefits of biotechnology to create food crops that do not require chemical pesticides are greater than the risks."

*Source: The Environics International Poll of 2000. International Environmental Monitor 2000. Toronto, Canada, 2000.*

that prove considerable. But none of these differences act according to any principle of predictability. From an overall standpoint, for example, the new member states do not manifest more tolerance to GMOs than the other states. The strongest hostilities toward GMOs can be found among new member states as different as Slovenia and Cyprus. By the same token, the least hostility is also discernible in new member states such as Malta. The national differences in conceptions of GMOs are therefore neither political nor historical. They are also not, for that matter, geographical. Risk aversion to GMOs is much stronger in Cyprus and in Greece than in Germany or Denmark. But international comparative studies clearly indicate that Europeans, taken as a whole, are far from being the most hostile toward GMO products.

For certain authors inclined toward comparative studies of Europe and the United States, it is not possible to conclude that Europeans are more risk-averse than Americans, because areas exist in which the latter population is more risk-averse than the former (air pollution). European risk aversion is stronger in all areas linked to food production (Wiener and Rogers 2002). This being so, the aversion to GMOs has certain implications for international trade that are clearly absent in the case of air pollution. This explains the dissimilarity between European and US political behavior in the past several years each time risk regulation comes to the fore in international discussions. Europeans continue to lobby for recognition of the precautionary principle by the WTO. The United States, on the contrary, remains strongly hostile to the same principle. These particular divergences were articulated at the Convention on Biological Diversity as well as within WTO forums. They originate in each nation's approach to risk evaluation. The United States relies on risk evaluation that can be scientifically measured (sound science), whereas Europeans insist on risks resulting from the *uncertainty* of scientific results. The United States tends to base its decisions on what is already known—or what can ultimately be known—where Europeans prefer to approach decision-making processes which favor precisely what is *not* known (Tiberghien 2009). Americans are interested in final products; Europeans insist on considering production processes. As a result, the United States tends to consider that GMO-altered products are not substantially different from the original products, whereas Europeans consider such products to be fundamentally altered by GMO introduction (Pollack and Schaffer 2009). At the signing of the Carthagena Convention on biodiversity in 1998, the Europeans seem to have scored a point in winning recognition for the precautionary principle as an international principle (Faulkner 2000). But within the WTO, progress has been much slower. The United States deems the SPS (Sanitary and Phytosanitary) legislation sufficient to regulate risks, whereas Europeans want to go much further in ultimately securing formal recognition of the precautionary principle. There are no indications for European progress on this project. On the contrary, in fact. There are several reasons for this. First, the global trade agenda has become so weighty that it is now more and more difficult to add items to it. This is especially true given that the new WTO actors— emerging countries—are fiercely opposed to all propositions that appear to want to limit trade. For the second reason, we must recognize that these questions should be approached on regulated, case-by-case bases. We cannot answer such questions on the basis of a constraining international agreement, but rather by jurisprudent means such as the WTO dispute settlement procedures.

Over time, the WTO has evolved, ultimately becoming exceedingly sensitive to general shifts and developments. In the past, WTO jurisprudence tended toward a restrictive interpretation of GATT Article XX, which serves to define exceptions to international trade regulation. More recently, the WTO has stepped beyond a purely clinical interpretation of Article XX; now it takes other parameters, like environmental defense, into consideration. For the first time, a WTO panel recognized the right of a member state to invoke climate change risk as its justification for limiting particular imports into the country. The irony of history has it that the case in question was presented against the European Union (Brazil vs the European Union). Indeed, the evolution of WTO jurisprudence has not been linear. Perhaps, though, it shows that international trade regulation can progress without the need for additional norms.

## Climate change risk

Climate change risk aversion can be measured in at least three fashions: (1) By comparing the relative importance Europeans assign climate change risks as compared to other risks. (2) By examining the agreements, notably in terms of economic growth, that Europeans are willing to make in order to combat climate change. (3) By examining the concrete actions Europeans have taken on the international stage in order to fight climate change, even in light of potential economic costs should no international agreement be reached.

Europeans' particular evaluation of climate change risk becomes clear when one examines the measure of importance accorded to it. Such an evaluation is rendered clearer when climate change risk is compared with other possible risks. When Europeans were asked to identify the most serious among seven major risks, climate change appeared in second place:

| European opinion-based evaluation of systemic risks (in descending order) | |
|---|---|
| 1) Poverty and lack of drinking water | 69% |
| 2) Climate change risk | 47% |
| 3) Economic crisis | 39% |
| 4) International terrorism | 35% |
| 5) Spread of infectious disease | 32% |
| 6) Armed conflicts | 29% |
| 7) Increasing world population | 24% |
| 8) Proliferation of nuclear weapons | 15% |

*Source: Eurobarometer, special Eurobarometer 313; Europeans' attitudes towards climate change; January–February 2009.*

Obviously, climate change risk aversion is perceived differently among the EU member states. But we can effectively point out that it is stronger in Scandinavian countries than in new member states or in southern Europe. There are, as always, exceptions to this observation. Of all the European states, Slovenia is the most concerned by climate change issues. Unlike other southern European countries such as Portugal, Greece also demonstrates a significant degree of concern. This kind of heterogeneity renders difficult the construction of a unified European political position for international negotiations. Despite having presented a common political offer regarding greenhouse gas reductions, Europeans still have trouble deciding how to apportion reductions among member states such that the common goal might be reached. There is also difficulty reaching consensus on how to finance efforts to combat climate change in developing countries. The reluctance to reduce emissions as well as the reluctance to offer support for developing countries comes largely from new member states whose economies are more carbon-intensive than those of older states. As a result, new member states do not deem the problem as sufficiently serious. Often, these same states also lack the resources necessary to finance reductions.

There are no international comparative studies that would allow for a term-by-term comparison of climate change risk evaluation in relation to other risks in other world regions. However, we can reference opinion-based studies indicating the kind of balances that particular societies are willing to accept between economic growth and climate change.

In response to the affirmation, "We should maximize economic growth even if it would hurt efforts to combat climate change," the following figures result:

| | |
|---|---|
| European Union -12* | 21% |
| United States | 40% |

*The number indicates the number of European states taken into account in the study
*Source: German Marshall Fund of the United States (GMF), Chicago. Transatlantic Trends (2009 Topline data).*

Clearly, Americans are twice as ready as Europeans to accept climate change in favor of economic growth. This figure is a significant indication of Europe's and the United States's relationship to climate change. There is a third way of approaching the question of climate change risk aversion as regards the European population: we can compare the European Union's official commitments to reducing greenhouse gas emissions with their economic costs. Logically, a country or group of countries for which a failed international agreement would lead to a dramatic drop in Gross Domestic Product would be most likely to propose ambitious goals as regards climate change. Inversely, a country or group of countries for which failure to reach an international agreement would not significantly harm that country's economy would be most likely to propose a more modest engagement. We can say of a country or a group of countries, then, that an actor manifests strong climate change risk aversion when its international commitments outweigh the economic costs (relative to other countries) that global warming potentially presents.

**Climate change: Economic costs and unilateral commitments**

| Economic impact on GDP [1] | Copenhagen commitments |
| --- | --- |
| United States: -0.1% | -4%* |
| China: -0.9% | +79%** |
| Europe: -1% | -20%*** |
| India: -3% | Uncommitted |
| Africa: -4% | Uncommitted |

[1] Impact in the context of a hypothetical respect for the 2°/2.5° C temperature target. The figures are average numbers, and thus do not take into consideration the discrepancies between the strongest and weakest estimations. The discrepancies are especially marked for developing countries: because of the uncertainty in assessment, risk is always higher for these countries.
* The United States officially committed to a 17 percent greenhouse gas reduction by 2020 from 2005 levels. If we compare this figure with Europe's base year (1990), however, this 17 percent represents only a 4 percent reduction.
** China has not officially committed to reducing its greenhouse gas emissions. Rather, it has committed to a strong reduction in energy intensity. According to certain OECD estimates, such a reduction would lead to a 79 percent emissions increase between 2005 and 2020. This major increase would nevertheless ultimately decelerate the growth of greenhouse gas effects. At the same time, it is important to remember that, *per capita*, Chinese emissions remain relatively low.
*** The base year for Europe's measurements is 1990.
*Source: OECD,* The Economics of Climate Change Mitigation. Policies and Options for Global Action Beyond 2012. *2009 and interviews.*

Undoubtedly, these figures evince a very strong aversion to climate change risk on the part of Europeans. The unilateral commitments they are willing to make are not only in absolute value the highest in the world, but, moreover, they are proportionally much higher than those of other countries or world regions. This is true if one compares Europe's commitments with the risks it would run presuming that an agreement is met. In other words, Europe appears to be strongly committed to fighting climate change even in light of its modest vulnerability to climate change effects, compared to other world regions. That being so, we should hesitate before drawing hasty conclusions. If

Europe's Copenhagen commitments seem ambitious—more ambitious, it is true, than those of the United States—it is also because it is less expensive to reduce greenhouse gas emissions in Europe than in other world regions. In the United States, a 4 percent emissions reduction for 2020 would cost just as much as a 20 percent reduction for Europe for 2020. It is therefore only possible to compare emissions reduction commitments on the basis of the economic costs faced by each nation. If Europe proclaims to be governing by example on this subject, we must understand that it can afford to do so because its adaptation costs are the lowest. Therefore, environmental risk aversion on the part of Europeans is especially strong, since their economic risk remains relatively low. The reasoning given here for the United States can also be applied to emerging countries. If countries like India have shown reluctance to commit to emissions reductions despite their considerable economic risks, we might conclude that risk aversion is stronger on the part of Indians than on the part of Europeans. But this interpretation would have to be qualified by another interpretation: for Indians, it is the Western nations that should make significant reductions efforts since it is they who have, historically, been responsible for causing global warming.

## Financial risk

Like all other risks, there are several ways to gauge financial-based risk. One of these ways consists in an evaluation of the soundness of prudential bank regulation rules. These rules have proved immensely faulty during the economic crisis.

According to the World Bank, there are eight indicators which allow one to measure prudential regulation:

1. *Capital requirements* include minimum capital to asset ratios, variations of capital to asset ratios according to individual banks' credit.
2. *Liquidity and diversification requirements* include limits on exposures to single or related borrowers, limits on sectorial concentration of lending and liquidity reserves.
3. *Accounting and provisioning requirements* include information on accounting standards, definitions of nonperforming loans, disclosure of off-balance sheet items.
4. *External auditing and information disclosure requirements* include information on external auditing requirements and their disclosure to supervisors, the scope of legal action against auditors in the case of negligence and against directors in the case of erroneous or misleading information.
5. *Entry rules and ownership structures* includes information on the granting procedure and requirements for entry licenses, disclosure of and limitations on the source of funds, limits to engagement in securities, insurance, and real estate activities, foreign lending and ownership of nonfinancial voting shares.
6. *Exit rules and disciplining devices* include measures relating to the forced exit of banks, bankruptcy procedures for banks, and the powers of supervisors to override management decisions if the solvency of a bank is under threat.

7. *Depositor protection* includes information on the existence and limits of explicit deposit insurance protection systems, the collection of premia to such schemes, whether fees depend on banks' risk profiles and co-insurance provisions.

8. *Strength of the supervisory authority* includes the budget and number of professional supervisors relative to the size of the sector, the number and frequency of onsite inspections, the ability of supervisors to change banks' internal organization structures, the protection of the supervisory agency from political interference, and the protection of individual agency staff from law suits by banks.

*Source: World Bank, Bank Regulation and Supervision (updated June 2008).*

Using these indicators, a recent OECD study (Ahrend et al. 2009) attempted to determine if there exists a link between the quality of prudential regulation and financial stability. The study made use of three of the eight indicators in order to establish a correlation between prudential regulation and financial stability. It is important to note that "correlation" in this case does not necessarily imply causality. The three indicators are the following: *Entry rules and ownership structures, Exit rules and disciplining devices,* and *Strength of the supervisory authority.* Countries with the strictest of these indicators seem to have suffered less damage from the financial crisis than others. We can provisionally say, then, that these nations have more or less implicitly manifested a higher aversion to financial risk. The strength of this aversion is determined by the existence of strong regulatory principles. Then the question is: does this particular methodology allow us to determine whether Europe collectively managed superior resistance to the financial crisis *because* it adopted stricter prudential rules?

The indicators we have access to do not offer a clear response. However, we can compare the stringency of these three indicators (*Entry rules and ownership structures, Exit rules and disciplining devices, Strength of the supervisory authority*) among OECD countries. The United States, where the financial crisis began, reaches the OECD average for two of the three indicators (*Entry rules* and *Strength of the supervisory authority*). The United States is, however, highly above average for *Exit rules.* Great Britain, on the other hand, is far below average for *Exit rules.* The same is true for France, a nation considered particularly inclined toward regulation. Germany, in contrast, is within the OECD average for every indicator. However helpful these indicators may be, they fail to take into account the discrepancy between these formal indicators and their implementation. Theoretically, American regulative laxity does not seem glaring. In practice, the situation looks different. By refining the indicators and by comparing them with the true practices of various states, it would be easier to draw conclusions about the intensity of European financial risk aversion.

There are other, more reliable indices for measuring financial risk aversion: household financial assets are one of them. Indeed, the more households that take on risky assets, the weaker their aversion to risk. The inverse is naturally true. We can generally distinguish four classes of savings risks that range from (1) the weakest to (4) the strongest. Low-risk savings generally include bank investments and life insurance contracts, whereas high-risk savings essentially deal with stock market shares. The fewer stock market shares held by a given actor, the higher that actor's aversion to financial risk. The contrast between the United States and Europe is indisputable in this sphere.

**Stock market shares as a percentage of total net household assets:**

| | |
|---|---|
| France | 3.4% |
| Germany | 6.7% |
| United Kingdom | 8.8% |
| Spain | 10.7% |
| United States | 17.9% |

Source: *Autorité des marchés financiers;* Lettre Economique et Financière Printemps 2009; *DRAI, Département des études.*

These figures are confirmed by other indicators such as the net household savings ratio, which stands at 9.6 percent compared to 2.4 percent for the United States (OECD 2004). These two ratios illustrate the vast contrast in precaution and risk aversion on either side of the Atlantic. Since the 2008 financial crisis, the United States's net household savings ratio has increased to 4 percent, whereas for EU countries it has remained at 9.8 percent. The discrepancy between the European Union and United States rates remains considerable. The discrepancy is even more significant than the figures suggest, because retirement and health plans are generally public in Europe, but private in the United Kingdom and the United States. Logically speaking, since risks of old age and health are socialized in Europe, Europeans should tend to save less than Americans. The reality is, however, precisely the opposite. Given these facts, we understand that by and large, Europe claims stricter market finance regulation, even given the British exception.

## Risk of war

First, there are several means of expressing aversion to the risk of war. First, an actor might increase its military efforts in order to deter potential adversaries. Conversely, an actor might limit its defense efforts in the hope of encouraging other actors to do the same ("disarmament race"). The second approach has clearly been the favorite of most Europeans. Currently, the European member states allocate no more than 1.69 percent of their gross national product for military expenses, where the United States spends 4.5 percent (EDA). This European figure is in constant decline. It is less than the world average, which falls at 2.4 percent of GDP (Sipri 2010). Throughout the first decade of the twenty-first century, Europe was the region with the lowest growth in military spending. Europe's spending fell at 5 percent, compared with 87 percent for Russia, 66 percent for the United States, 56 percent for East Asia, 94 percent for North Africa, and 56 percent for the Middle East (Sipri 2010). Europe shows no inclination toward using military force, and its structural powers provide it with no such predisposition. Even if Europe's national armies possess abundant reserves, their operational capacities remain limited, especially for overseas operations. European land forces are quantitatively larger than those of the United States, but the number of deployed European forces cannot exceed 4 percent. In contrast, the maximum percentage of deployed forces for the United States is 14 percent. Despite certain political decisions intended to facilitate Europe's overseas intervention capabilities, the European Union continually has difficulty conducting operations overseas. The European Union pledged to create a joint rapid reaction force of 60,000 troops by the year 2003, but the project has hardly begun. The European armies, it is clear, are too poorly organized to deal with major shared risks, even if they proved capable in the recent fight against piracy in Somalia. The apparent efficacy of the European effort in this case was most likely due to the fact that the project was viewed as a maritime police operation rather than a strictly military endeavor. These structural difficulties point to three series of factors. First, the European states are prepared to share their military sovereignty, but only sparingly. This is an especially troubling issue given the fact that Great Britain, militarily the strongest European nation, is also the most hostile to the idea of a European military headquarters. The second series of factors is based largely on the decision, made by most European states, to outsource their security to NATO, and thus to the United States. The third series of factors comes from the way Europeans conceive of their purpose within the international system. Though the European Union boasts about its 22 ESDP missions, only 6 of them have been military operations:

> most European governments have proved highly risk averse, a criticism often leveled, with some justice, at the United States in the 1990s. The nature of EU decision-making is likely to sustain this risk-averse behavior. In NATO, military commitments are driven by the Alliance's dominant member, the United States. In the United Nations, such decisions are taken by governments that, for the most part, do not intend to hazard their own soldiers in the resultant operations. As a result, NATO is prepared to accept risks at which the European Union would balk, while the United Nations regularly takes chances which neither the European Union nor NATO would countenance. (Dobbins 2005–2006)

Secondly, this aversion to the risk of war has a markedly strong social basis, which we can confirm by examining numerous opinion studies on the European relation to war and to conflict in general. It is especially useful to compare European perceptions regarding war with those of other political actors, notably the United States.

*On the moral justification for war:*[1]

**For the affirmation "Under some conditions war is necessary to obtain justice," the following responses were received:**

| | |
|---|---|
| European Union – 12 | 25% |
| United States | 71% |

---

[1]　All of these study results come from the following source: German Marshall Fund of the United States (GMF), Chicago. Transatlantic Trends (2009 Topline data).

*On the importance of military compared to economic power:*

**For the question "Is economic power more important than military power?" the following responses were received:**

| | |
|---|---|
| European Union – 12 | 78% |
| United States | 61% |

This general attitude toward war and conflict proves all the more perceptible when one examines American and European public opinion concerning specific armed conflicts, notably those in Iran or Afghanistan.

*Attitudes regarding Iran:*

**In support of the option to "increase diplomatic pressure on Iran but rule out the use of military force," the following responses were received:**

| | |
|---|---|
| European Union – 12 | 48% |
| United States | 29% |

**In support of the option to "maintain the option of using military forces" the following responses were received:**

| | |
|---|---|
| European Union – 12 | 18% |
| United States | 47% |

From the point of view of the study, we observe that European opinions regarding the Iranian conflict are much more withdrawn compared to the political positions taken by certain European member states (France). It would be interesting to study how French opinion might evolve in the event of a conflict with Iran (nuclear bombardments). It would be equally interesting to observe how the French political position itself might evolve if faced with strong public opposition to war with Iran.

*On the conflict in Afghanistan*
Opinion studies taken on the subject of the Afghanistan conflict have similar results. A total of 77 percent of Europeans disapprove of sending European combat forces to Afghanistan; only 19 percent approve of such a maneuver. This condemnation is shared by almost all the European member states, including new member states such as Poland (80 percent) and Romania (84 percent).

The third possibility for qualifying European risk aversion toward war involves an examination of current European discourse on the subject. For the purposes of such an examination, there are several relevant documents that deal with the European relation to war. Here, we will cite just one.

The document in question is a rarely cited EDA (European Defense Agency) report. More than most academic research, which unfortunately either insists on institutional choices or takes European discourse for granted (Menon), this report perfectly summarizes the European philosophy vis-à-vis the use of force:

"Indeed interventions will not necessarily involve fighting battles. The presence of multinational forces (. . .) may well prevent hostilities from breaking out (. . .) or may help to stabilize a country or region after a political accord. The objective is not "victory" as traditionally understood, but moderation, balance of interests and peaceful resolution of conflicts—in short, stability" (EDA 2006, 36).

We are indeed at the heart of the European aversion to the risk of war. Military invention without war, without designating an enemy, and without aiming toward victory—these aspects completely reject the Schmittian notion which subordinates politics to the existence of an enemy. Europe's potential military operations are aimed not at fighting wars but rather at avoiding them. In the Petersburg missions, which define the European doctrine regarding recourse to force, three levels of action are laid out: humanitarian missions or citizen evacuation, peacekeeping missions, and combat missions for managing crises, including peace reestablishment missions. It is clear that the majority of past European interventions fall under the first two categories. No interventions to date have explicitly fallen under the third category, which would entail risks of exposition that would hold more significant implications for the risk of war.

## Why are Europeans risk averse?

In a general sense, we can approach the question of risk in three ways: cultural explanations, institutional explanations, and contingent explanations. Cultural explanations must be considered together with the history and structure of a society's social preferences. Institutional explanations are tied to the organizational modes of a society. Contingent explanations rely on situational factors that have the potential to influence societal attitudes and behaviors in relation to risk. Obviously, these three approaches are often complementary. But the weight of each varies according to the issue at hand. Aversion to the risk of war originates largely in post-World War II European history, whereas aversion to food safety risks is based on much more contingent factors. With time, contingent factors can take root and become structural factors. There is not, as far as we can tell, a global explanation for European risk aversion. However, there are several complementary factors that contribute to it: Europe's nonstate construction, the existence of deliberative European political spaces, Europe's long-held social model that aims at market risk minimization, and finally, the end of the need for Empire.

The European Union is not a state. Therefore, it cannot independently fulfill the traditional security functions generally assigned to states. At the same time, European citizens cannot think themselves out of Europe, despite their political disaffection for it. On the one hand, they cannot address all their demands to their respective states (as the Americans, Chinese, Indians, and Brazilians are tempted to do), nor can they redirect them toward Europe. European risk aversion results primarily from this ambivalence. This is all the more true given that Europe's competitors are large nation-states which aim to increase the traditional attributes of their sovereignty. At the end of the Cold War, the European model based on shared sovereignty seemed to prevail. But today, the situation is quite different. The rise of Russia, China, India, and Brazil led to the return to a political power structure with which Europe does not feel comfortable.

Even if European public space is far from having the coherence, force, or relative homogeneity of national public spaces, we cannot doubt its existence. The European Union is the only world region with a powerful system for transnational democratic representation (European Parliament). Ideas and representations circulate in the Parliament space. Without a dense European space to take risk management out of the control of individual governments, the growth of food safety, health, and environmental risk aversion over the past ten years would be unthinkable. We cannot emphasize enough the extent to which the Single Market also contributes to the creation of public space: free circulation of goods necessarily leads to free circulation of risks. The precautionary principle, for example, comes from the convergence of a German-born European philosophy from the 1960s and the loss of citizen confidence in risk regulation organs during the 1980s. This convergence explains why the principle evolved from an environmental principle to a broader crisis management and political governance principle (Ewald 2010). The same kind of reasoning can also be used when dealing with climate change. Europe's vigorous Copenhagen commitments were strongly supported by public opinion—indeed, the European Union's strategy was to publicly post its positions before negotiations even began. But if the European Union boasts about "governance by example," other actors are barely impressed. China, for example, went so far as to refuse the inclusion of unilateral European commitments in the Copenhagen Declaration. Still, we would have difficulty imagining the European Union refusing to make commitments as long as its negotiating partners had not made similar commitments. But is European public opinion ready to accept such a form of political bargaining? The question remains: is it really wise to show all of one's cards before negotiating?

Beyond its apparent diversity, the European Union's social model has always tried to minimize market risks by socializing them. One way to comprehend this is to measure the state's redistributive power. Before taxes and social transfers, the poverty rate indicator is as high for the United States as for the European Union: 13 percent of the population. After taxes and social transfers, the figure falls to 4 percent for the European Union, but only to 10 percent for the United States (OECD). Another way to comprehend this risk socialization is to examine public social expenses for old age health and unemployment risks. These expenses account on average for 24.6 percent of the EU countries' GDP, but only 15.9 percent of the United States's. From this point of view, even the United Kingdom is closer to the EU average than the United States (21.3 percent). The European Union–United States difference here is not so much the fact that risk aversion is stronger in Europe than in the United States, but that risk in Europe is strongly socialized, whereas in the United States it tends to be extremely privatized. Indeed, private social expenses in the US stand at 10.1 percent of the GDP. The figure is at 2.5 percent for Germany, 3.2 percent for France, and even less for Scandinavian countries. Only the Netherlands (6.6 percent) and Great Britain (6.7 percent) break with this tendency (Adema and Ladaique 2009). Even so, we can conclude that market risk aversion is a collective European concern. Though often judged obsolete and incompatible with rapid globalization, we find that models favoring this risk aversion are more appealing than expected. Proof of this lies in the Obama administration's recent efforts for providing the United States with stronger social security. Europe shows no particular genius in this sense: there is a universal aspiration for linking economic and social progress. Of course, the European Union may suffer from having high social standards, but this does not mean that its model is devalued. In fact, the 2008 financial crisis modified perceptions of the economic-social nexus.

Europeans have very clearly exhausted the need for Empire. After having spent centuries fighting one another, they have concluded that the safest way to pacify their relations is to reject the use of force. Constructed from its foundations against war and the use of force, it is appropriate that Europe should plead opposition to these notions. For this reason precisely, the typical French aspiration for Europe as a global power ("l'Europe puissance") is not shared by a good number of European nations. However, the aversion to the risk of war must be qualified by the fact that certain European nation-states have major military capabilities which give them protection, at least in part. In addition, when European nation-states perceive a common risk, they turn to coercion and pressure methods which are generally effective. The relative success of the Europeans in fighting Islamic terrorism (compared to the dismaying performance of the United States) bears witness to this fact.

## The political consequences of risk aversion

When speaking in terms of European political identity, risk aversion must be taken seriously. But as always, we must be careful: there are two traps into which we should not fall. The first consists of an idealization of the European political identity which places Europe at the avant-garde of a forthcoming, pacified world. The second, inversely, considers European political identity at a distance. The interest in this identity is distracted, tinged with a certain contempt. When the majority of Europeans refused to use the concept of a "war on terror," it was probably because the mere term "war" made them uneasy. At the same time, though, the term was absolutely inappropriate for facing a protean reality having nothing to do with the traditional forms of war. Indeed, European performance in the war against Islamic terrorism was by and large superior to the United States's. Being risk averse is in itself therefore neither an asset nor a weakness. It is, rather, a manner of being in the world. Europe's question is not to find out whether or not it should repudiate this identity, but to find out *how* it might put it to use and how it might accord value to it in the context of the current international system. In order to do this, the European Union must act in several ways. I will only discuss the first of these in this chapter.

The first will require a harmonization of European positions at a time when Europe's already multiple preferences are growing in various sectors. Europe's underachievement at Copenhagen can be partly explained by lukewarm mobilization in regard to the European Union's proposals. If, by some means or another, the Single Negotiator model was not extended to other strategic domains like climate change, the European position might weaken. Herein lays the elemental limit of Europe's normative power: it tends to stop precisely where it should begin. The production of norms means nothing if they are not given value, especially in areas where force relations between major actors prove decisive. When considering Afghanistan, the vast majority of Europeans weigh the dead ends of a military solution. As such, they are incapable of developing a shared strategy, one they could at least discuss with the United States while the latter nation is open to discussion. Here again, the question is not risk aversion in itself, but the possibility of shared strategic action. What is at stake then is less risk aversion as such than the inhibition to make choices as if making choices in Europe is becoming a risk in and of itself.

# Bibliography

Adema, W. and M. Ladaique. 2009. "How Expensive is the Welfare State? Gross and Net Indicators in the OECD Social Expenditure Database (SOCX)." *OECD Social, Employment and Migration Working Papers* 92. OECD Publishing.

Ahrend, R., J. Arnold, and F. Murtin. 2009. "Prudential Regulation and Competition in Financial Markets." *Economics Department Working Paper 735*. OECD.

AMF (Autorité des marchés financiers). 2009. *Lettre économique et financière Printemps 2009*. DRAI, Département des études. www.amf-france.org/documents/ general/9070_1.pdf.

Borraz, O. 2008. *Les politiques du risque*. Paris: Presses de Sciences Po.

Dobbins, J. 2005–6. "New Directions for Transatlantic Security Cooperation." *Survival*. Winter 2005–6, 47(4): 39–54.

EDA (European Defense Agency). 2006. *An Initial Long-Term Vision for European Defence Capability and Capacity Needs*. Endorsed by the Steering Board on October 3, 2006.

Eurobaromèter. Special Eurobarometer 313. 2009. *Europeans' Attitudes towards Climate Change*. Fieldwork January–February 2009, publication July 2009. http://ec.europa.eu/ public_opinion/archives/ebs/ebs_313_en.pdf.

Ewald, F. 2010. "Le principe de précaution oblige à exagérer la menace." *Le Monde* 10/01/2010.

Faulkner, R. 2000. "Regulating Biotech Trade: The Cartagena Protocol on Biosafety." *International Affairs/RIIA*. April 2000, 76(2): 299–313.

GMF (German Marshall Fund of the United States). 2009. *Transatlantic Trends (2009 Topline Data)*. www.gmfus.org/trends/2009/docs/2009_English_Top.pdf

Menon, A. 2009. "Empowering Paradise? Europe at Ten." *International Affairs* 85(2): 227–46.

OECD. 2008. "Les indicateurs de l'OCDE sur la protection de l'emploi." Paris. www.oecd.
    org/document/12/0,3343,fr_2649_33927_42764428_1_1_1_1,00.html
— 2009a. *The Economics of Climate Change Mitigation. Policies and Option for Global
    Action beyond 2012.* Paris. www.oecd.org/document/56/0,3343,en_2649_34361_43705
    336_1_1_1_1,00.html.
— 2009b. *Economic Outlook* 2009/2,86, November.
Pollack, M. and G. Schaffer. 2009. *When Cooperation Fails: The International Law and
    Politics of Genetically Modified Foods.* Oxford: Oxford University Press.
Sipri. January 2010. Recent Trends in Military Expenditures.
The Environics International Poll. 2000. *International Environmental Monitor 2000.*
    Toronto.
Tiberghien, Y. 2009. "Transitional Competitive Governance and Agenda-Setting in the
    EU: The Battle over the Regulation of GMOs since the mid-1990s." *Journal of European
    Integration.*
Wiener, J. B. and M. D. Rogers. 2002. "Comparing Precaution in the United States and
    Europe." *Journal of Risk Research* 5(4): 317–49.
World Bank, Bank Regulation and Supervision (updated 2008), http://econ.worldbank.
    org/WBSITE/EXTERNAL/EXTDEC/EXTRESEARCH/0,,contentMDK:20345037~
    pagePK:64214825~piPK:64214943~theSitePK:469382,00.html#Survey_III

# Conclusion: How to Manage a Changing World

Javier Solana

*Centro de Economía y de Geopolítica Global*

Western countries are experiencing a time of crisis, a time of challenges, whose outcome is extremely uncertain. What does seem clear, however, is that whenever we manage to get out of this deep economic rut, the structure and the organization of the world will be very different from what we know today.

Today's world is more multipolar that it was a few years ago, but this does not mean that it is better. Everything will depend on its ability to build institutions of global governance (a feat that we Europeans know well). Certainly, a Bismarckian world was no better. It too was a multipolar world, but one that did not have enough collective power structures; this led to conflict, thus the supreme importance of a debate on the construction of global institutions today.

Many authors have tried to explain and to sketch out this changing structure in which we are living in order to understand it globally and, particularly, efficiently. Joseph Nye, for his part, imagines three levels to explain our current situation and to show that the distribution of power depends on the context.

On the top level, there is military power, which is largely unipolar. At our current stage, it is likely that the United States will continue to act as a superpower for some time.

On the middle level, that of economic power, multipolarity has been the norm for more than a decade now, with the United States, the European Union, Japan, and China acting as major players, with others gradually gaining more importance (Brazil, India, South Africa).

On the lower level, cross-border transactions take place beyond governments' control. Here we find several nonstate actors. Nye also places new challenges such as pandemics and global warming at this level. Here, power is more dispersed, and there is no sense speaking about a unipolar or multipolar world—but rather a nonpolar world.

Organizing a world that unfolds on these three levels is a very complex task, and even more so if we consider the causes that have led to this new reality: the transfer of power.

History has experienced several periods of power transfer, resulting from wars or technological progress. The twentieth century is a good example. But today these transfers are more profound, for example from the Western or Atlantic World, toward the Eastern or Pacific World. For example, recall that in 2004, the United States and Europe made up 65 percent of global GDP. In 2050, it is estimated that they will only represent 32 percent. This means a loss of 33 percent of the global GDP, and a transfer of power toward the Pacific zones, to emerging powers.

Meanwhile, there are important transfers of power within states themselves. New actors have appeared in their territory, ones who hold enormous power. Some of them are positive and constructive, NGOs for example. But others contribute nothing to global stability: terrorist groups, organized crime, drug smugglers, etc. These new protagonists play an increasingly important role in our collective lives, and decrease the action capacity of state institutions.

It is obvious that if we want to build a better world, we must take into account this new reality, one that counteracts the traditional function of the state, that is solving problems. In a crisis of the magnitude of this one, we must be honest with ourselves and recognize that our political systems fail whenever they address this reality. Governments, businesses, and opinion leaders still act in such a short perspective that if we do not change our strategy, those who reason in the longer term will eventually win the battle.

This battle is taking place in a globalized and interdependent world, whose problems we will never solve if we are incapable of looking at them head on. From poverty to global warming to the proliferation of nuclear weapons, these are global challenges and, as such, they require global solutions.

Development, with all that it entails—poverty, rapid population growth, urban concentration, or population displacement—is a problem to be addressed in all its dimensions. In the case of population growth, the problems and threats attached to it are not as quantitative as they are qualitative, not so much the growth itself but rather the way in which it is happening. Our world is characterized by an explosion of the urban demographic. In 1950, only 29 percent of the population lived in cities, whereas in 2009, this figure climbed to 50.2 percent, and predictions show that it will go up to 70 percent by 2050, with a total of more than five billion people in the least developed areas, and slightly more than one billion in the most developed areas, according to the World Bank. If this rapidly growing population does not build on a solid structure, this growth will lead to unemployment, marginalization, the lack of basic services—everything needed to ignite violence within a society.

As for the proliferation of nuclear weapons, it is now a fundamental problem needing an urgent solution, not only because of its destructive potential, or the use that some states may make of these weapons, but also because they may fall into the hands of terrorist groups. Here, I am not only alluding to Iran, but also to such complex countries as India and Pakistan, two states possessing nuclear weapons that are situated in an unstable area.

As for safety, another problem is that of global warming. This constitutes one of the most dangerous threats. It is not difficult to see that the current model of resource management cannot last, and that it will seriously threaten our safety. Moreover, the imbalance between decreasing supply and increasing demand is greater than ever, and it is putting extraordinary pressure on our resources. If we fail to manage it correctly, very significant tensions will arise, not only regarding energy, but also concerning food and water prices.

All of these problems can be reduced to practically nothing as easily as they can explode in our hands in a relatively short period of time. Everything will depend on the way in which we handle everything and whether we manage to establish the political strategies necessary to solve these problems and the leadership that is required.

So what instruments do we have to manage such a world? Essentially, global institutions of an economic nature like the World Bank, the International Monetary Fund (IMF), the World Trade Organization (WTO), or even worldwide institutions like the World Health Organization (WHO) or the International Labor Organization (ILO). And, of course and especially, the United Nations.

The current global crisis shows that these institutions, unfortunately, have flaws and weaknesses which must be remedied.

Let us start with economic institutions, receiving the most attention at the moment. The two main institutions according to Bretton Woods, the IMF, and the World Bank, have been unable to predict global economic problems, and especially, the seriousness of the financial crisis. They have started to react, and we can see some signs giving hope that they can better cope with future crises. They must, however, solve many internal problems before being able to function properly.

Here is one example to give us an idea of these problems: China's voting rights within the World Bank or the IMF are equivalent to those of Belgium. Such fundamental institutions cannot function with voting rights that were defined in an era so different from our own.

As for the WTO, it is the most global organization. Yet, for lack of political will, it has not achieved its own goals. Trade is essential to overcome the economic crisis. If we take a step back toward protectionism, we will never get out of this crisis.

At each G20 summit, declarations have been adopted highlighting the importance of the Doha Round, all without the emergence of the political will necessary for its financing. The trend of bilateral agreements of free trade will not solve the problem. To me, the multilateral nature of commercial agreements is paramount.

Finally, a few words about the most important organization, the United Nations. We know that it experienced a strong impetus toward reform during the last mandate, that of Kofi Annan, which unfortunately has not been fruitful. The United Nations failed to adapt its Security Council to current realities. In truth, the only positive outcome was the introduction and the acceptance of the concept of "the responsibility to protect," that is responsibility on the part of the international community to act when a state does not fulfill its responsibility toward its citizens. But even though the General Assembly approved this concept, there has never been agreement on the very cases to which it could have applied.[1]

A major criticism of the United Nations is its weak ability to anticipate and confront problems. It is important to remember that the structure of the Security Council relies on the concept of a victorious nation, that is, reflecting the situation at the end of the Second World War. At that time, it was impossible to foresee the changes that the international community would go through. This is why it is necessary today to reinforce the role of the Organization in the international community, to grant it more effective tools and mechanisms which could foresee new threats and deal with them, from international terrorism to global warming.

The United Nations is an extremely important organization, the only one which legitimizes actions of the international community. We must be aware of its great responsibility, for in the field of global governance, nothing can take place, finally, without legitimacy.

An important step toward the management of multilateralism is the G20, which has replaced the G7, which was evidently insufficient. The pragmatic and responsible actions of the first two Summits of Heads of State have led to avoiding a global recession, overcoming protectionism and achieving tangible results. The G20 is now approaching a second step, that of strategy, where it must proceed with caution. The 20 countries have paved the way for growth at variable speeds, and the G20 is in danger of giving preference to national perspectives to address problems which are nonetheless global.

It is clear that in the near future, the economy will be decisive. This is why we must continue to bet on the G20 as a pillar for the construction of global governance, an instrument to make effective decisions. However, the G20 will have a harder time appearing legitimate once it addresses more political- or security-related problems. In these areas, we are condemned to live a while with structures having a variable geometry, before finding a definitive and legitimate solution that will lead us toward the fundamental reform needed by the United Nations.

An analysis of the current international landscape, with its threats, its institutions, and their weaknesses, will allow us to identify four possible ways to handle this situation: cooperation, competition, confrontation, and hesitation. The question we are facing is: what to do?

It is not whether global institutions should cooperate or compete (obviously they must cooperate), but whether *the institutions of civil society* should cooperate or compete. What should we do with China, for example? Which of the four ways should we adopt?

Hesitation would not be possible, or desirable, even if the future might prove otherwise . . .

Confrontation, of course, does not necessarily mean military confrontation. Rather it is a confrontation whose goal is to enforce the norms and rules respected by everyone.

---

[1]   At the time of this writing, this concept is at the center of debates in the Security Council on the possibility of applying it for the first time in Libya.

With regards to the WTO, for example, we want China to be a crucial stakeholder in international institutions, one that meets its obligations.

Competition, yes, of course. And to do this, we must double our efforts in the fields of scientific research and technological innovation. We will enter into a relationship of competition with China in regard to products with a high added value. This necessarily requires improvement in the quality of our educational systems at every level.

We must recognize that we misuse our human capital. Many are those, among the best and brightest, who choose to become stock traders for financial reasons instead of making the choice of developing science and technology by becoming researchers or engineers.

But I would like to emphasize that cooperation is the most appropriate formula to inspire confidence and to find favorable solutions for everyone in this interdependent and global world.

Keeping in mind these four ways of managing the world, and considering the realities taking shape on the international scene, it is essential to get back to building a concept as fundamental as sovereignty. No state, no matter how strong it may be, can solve the problems of our era, all of which are global problems. In the same way, borders are becoming more permeable every day, and it no longer makes much sense to think of the concept of sovereignty in the same way.

The postmodern state must adopt the concept of responsible sovereignty and prove its ability and its political will to forge the instruments enabling it to build an effective multilateralism, without which we will never live in a peaceful world. Global warming is an eloquent example of this: "your pollution does not stop at your borders; the whole atmosphere is affected." The only solution is the responsibility of everyone.

That said, it is clear that such goals are not easy to reach. Every state does not share the same analyses, the same values, the same goals, or the same instruments. The existence of common interests does not automatically mean common actions or tactics, as is clearly visible on the international scene.

In this process of reconciliation and building the architecture of "world government," the European Union can play a very constructive role in the world today. By voluntarily giving up a part of their sovereignty, Europeans have constructed a model of supranational governance better equipped to face the challenges of globalization. Problems are solved today through dialog and consensus, and no longer by confrontation and violence. Fortunately, there is also the trend toward regional integration, in Asia (Association of Southeast Asian Nations) or in Latin America.

However, Europeans, who have a stable regional system, must not let their strategic vision—with assets such as the single currency, an area of freedom, and common values and defense—be put into question. Short-term perspectives, electioneering, and demagogy pose a serious threat to a model that represented a great innovation at its beginning and that is now fundamental to the management of our changing world.

To sum up, today's world is very different from the world of yesterday. I believe that we are not yet aware of the extent to which this is true or the changes the world will face or the speed at which changes are occurring. It would be best if we started thinking quickly and seriously about all of this and found both solutions and the leadership needed to implement them. We have not yet secured long-term leadership or ways of thinking about these issues. There are others who are already at work on them. If we do not begin to tackle them ourselves, we will surely lose out.

# Index